P9-EEH-210

LUIS CERNUDA

A Study of the Poetry

Derek Harris

LUIS CERNUDA

A Study of the Poetry

❁

TAMESIS BOOKS LIMITED
LONDON

Colección Támesis
SERIE A – MONOGRAFIAS, XXXIII

ISBN 0 900411 70 8

Designed and Printed by
The Compton Press Ltd.,
Compton Chamberlayne, Salisbury, Wilts.
for
TAMESIS BOOKS LIMITED
LONDON

Contents

Acknowledgements

This book is based on the material contained in two theses, "The conflict between aspiration and reality in the poetry of Luis Cernuda: A study of the first five books of La Realidad y el Deseo*", M. A. Nottingham,* 1962, *and "The poetry of Luis Cernuda", Ph. D. Hull,* 1968. *I wish to thank the supervisors of these two theses, respectively Dr. G. W. Connell and Mr. C. B. Morris, for their teaching, advice and helpful criticism from which I continue to draw benefit. I am also very grateful to the many people whose interest in my work on Cernuda has been a great encouragement to me, and I should like to thank especially Mrs. Helen Grant, don Jorge Guillén, Professor Arthur Terry, Professor Edward M. Wilson, and, last but not least, Janet Chapman, for her extremely valuable comments on the typescript of this book. I also acknowledge the great kindness of Luis Cernuda's literary heir, don Angel Mª. Yanguas Cernuda, who has allowed me to consult the private papers of Luis Cernuda now in his possession, and who has given his permission to quote from Luis Cernuda's works. Above all, I must express my profound gratitude to Professor Brian Tate, who, during the five years I was a student at Nottingham University, taught me more than I shall perhaps ever consciously realise.*

D.R.H.

I
THE MAN AND HIS POETRY

El testimonio más auténtico respecto a un hombre es sin duda su obra.

(Luis Cernuda, 'Bécquer y el romanticismo español', *Cruz y Raya,* no. 26 (1935), 62.)

Luis Cernuda was a member of that brilliant group of Spanish poets commonly known as the Generation of 1927, but the critical acclaim accorded to his contemporaries, Lorca, Alberti, Guillén, Salinas and Aleixandre, came more slowly to him. Almost up to the time of his death in 1963 Cernuda remained a poet's poet, admired and respected by his fellows yet ignored or even scorned by the Spanish literary establishment. The comment that his poetry had attracted most frequently was unsympathetic and on occasions hostile, the product of what seems to be an uneasy mixture of the critics' regard for his literary ability and their distaste for the sensibility it expressed. Twenty years ago a casual reader discovering Cernuda's name in an anthology or literary history would be likely to find a comment such as this:

> Luis Cernuda, poeta si los hay, frío y ajeno, desligado de la vida, displicente, que quisiera olvidarse de sí, que vive porque no hay más remedio . . .[1]

Yet ten years later another critic could make an assessment of Cernuda that might appear to refer to a completely different poet:

> La obra de Cernuda es un camino hacia nosotros mismos. En esto radica su valor moral. Pues aparte de ser un alto poeta – o, más bien: por serlo – Cernuda es uno de los poquísimos moralistas que ha dado España . . .[2]

Both critics agree on the high quality of Cernuda's poetry, but in 1954 he was presented as an acerbic, pessimistic personality, aloof from life and disdainful of it, while in 1964 he is made to appear as a moralist whose work has a profound universal significance. Paradoxically, both views of Cernuda are true; his work does express a deep sense of alienation and an evasive attitude to life, while at the same time it contains a firmly ethical viewpoint. This, however, is not a contradiction but an indication of conflict.

Cernuda's literary activity encompassed poetic prose, short stories, criticism

[1] Max Aub, *La poesía española contemporánea* (Mexico, 1954), 175.
[2] Octavio Paz, *Cuadrivio* (Mexico, 1965), 169.

and translation, but he was the author of only a single volume of verse spanning the years from 1924 to 1962 and made up of eleven separate collections of poems. The title he gave to this collective volume, *La Realidad y el Deseo*, holds the key to a tragic view of life where personal aspiration is engaged in an unequal conflict with objective reality. This conflict is presented in the terms of his own life, making of *La Realidad y el Deseo* a poetic autobiography, and here in the poetry's personal dimension can be found some of the reasons for the critics' unease with Cernuda. He had a complex, difficult character and exhibited pronounced symptoms of a neurotic personality. He was pathologically shy and hypersensitive, with a reputation for waspish vindictiveness. He was also an active homosexual, overtly defiant of the heterosexual society around him. The image of a homosexual neurotic is reflected in the assessment of Cernuda as an embittered, alienated poet, but the critics who see him in this way have failed to separate the personality of the man from the *persona* he created in his poetry. In his poems, in the literary record of his life, Cernuda transcended the unsympathetic, unconventional aspects of his character by illuminating his personal experience with an ethical insight that turned his work into a critique of human existence.

La Realidad y el Deseo is the account of a persistent search for an ideal existence of perfect unity between self and world, between the conflicting subjective and objective dimensions of life. Since Cernuda experienced a profound sense of alienation in the society in which he lived, the longing to end the separation between himself and the world frequently became a desire to seek refuge from the world in a private haven. But these attempts at evasion met with inevitable failure and with each successive disillusionment he was able to learn from his experience until he came to see that the ideal he had pursued was the reflection of a desire for self-affirmation and a wish to validate himself. Cernuda's poetry recounts his emotional and spiritual evolution from adolescence to the approach of old age in a prolonged exercise in self-analysis. It is the journal of a voyage of experience whose purpose is to give coherence and meaning to that experience. The search for meaning in the multifarious experience of life turns Cernuda's biography into poetry and distills from the circumstantial events of his existence an accumulation of self-knowledge. What Cernuda sought was the truth of himself, distinguishing between that hidden truth and the illusory appearance surrounding it. This search, pursued with passion and integrity, made him into an exemplary poet, the recorder of one man's struggle to affirm his individuality in an indifferent, hostile world with only his strength of will to aid him.

As far as Cernuda's poetry is concerned, the strange, unsympathetic, evasive personality he seems to express in his work is an illusory appearance and the hidden truth is the exemplary, ethical intention with which he pursues the critical analysis of his experience. It is my aim in this study to follow Cernuda in his search for the truth of himself, tracing in a thematic examination of his poetry the way in which his self-knowledge expands and deepens. I shall examine the contradiction between the apparently evasive personality that continually strives to withdraw from the world into the haven of the hidden garden, an image that recurs throughout the poetry, and the figure of the moralist engaged in a struggle to come to terms with himself and the world in which he lives. I do not claim to provide a complete study of Cernuda's poetry, but seek to understand this contradiction and to put the contradictory elements into perspective *vis-à-vis* each other. I only wish to present a reading of the poetry which may help to balance the distortions in the portrait of Cernuda that have been produced by even some of his most well-meaning critics.

To set the circumstance in which Cernuda undertook his search for himself I shall, in this introductory chapter, survey the development of *La Realidad y el Deseo*, examine some aspects of critical opinion on his poetry, and contrast the critics' views with Cernuda's own well-developed poetic theory.

"La Realidad y el Deseo"

Such is the richness and variety of the poetry produced by the Generation of 1927 that it is not easy to distinguish common denominators that group these poets together as a generation. An event that symbolises their unity is the celebration of the tercentenary of Góngora's death in 1927, for which they organised several acts of homage. In Góngora they found not an influence but a kindred spirit, a poet for whom poetry was an exercise in linguistic artifice, a poet who, in the terminology of the period, was a *poeta puro*. Valéry's theory of 'pure' poetry aroused considerable interest in Spain during the 1920s and the term *poesía pura* may be considered one of the hallmarks of that decade, although it was more of a fashionable idea than a properly assimilated theory. From a practical point of view *poesía pura* meant an attempt at disengagement in the poem from what one member of the Generation of 1927 called "fines sentimentales, ideológicos, morales".[3] Few, if any, of the poets achieved this ideal, but such an attitude did result in the creation of imagistic poetry based on a cult of ingenious, daring metaphor, a cult exemplified by the homage paid to Góngora, the master of baroque conceit. The post-symbolist theory of 'pure' poetry is linked with a basic symbolist inheritance these poets receive from Juan Ramón Jiménez, who is the master presiding over the early poetry of the Generation of 1927. Against this symbolist background is set a great interest in the whole tradition of Spanish poetry, particularly popular verse and the poetry of the Golden Age, which is in turn given added colour by a complex of *avant-garde* ideas, deriving from Futurism and Cubism, introduced into Spain after the Great War by the *ultraísta* and *creacionista* movements. The character of the period is essentially one of synthesis as new ideas are absorbed into a revitalised awareness of the Spanish poetic tradition.

In each member of the Generation of 1927 the ingredients in their literary background are mixed in different proportions but it is possible to distinguish certain common attitudes to life. In their early poems most of these poets express a deep sense of confidence and optimism, a feeling that they are in control of their destiny, summarised in the well-known statement by Jorge Guillén: "el mundo está bien hecho."[4] Although they were not indifferent to

[3] Jorge Guillén, 'Carta a Fernando Vela sobre la poesía pura', *Verso y prosa*, no. 2 (February 1927).

[4] "Tornasol", *Cántico* (Buenos Aires, 1950). This poem was first published in *Revista de Occidente*, no. XV (September 1924).

the difficult social and political circumstances of Spain in the 1920s, little of their concern finds its way into their poetry where it might have adulterated the ideal 'purity' then in fashion. The title of Ortega y Gasset's essay *La deshumanización del arte* (1924) becomes another modish phrase of the 1920s, reflecting the attitudes of that period. In his analysis of the ideas of post-Cubist literature Ortega saw a tendency to eliminate *impure* human elements in order to emphasise *pure* aesthetic elements, and carrying this idea to its logical conclusion, he declares that such an art, lacking transcendent pretensions, must therefore become merely a game. The rather unhappy term *deshumanizado* has been used in recent years as a stick with which to beat the poets of the 1920s, but, even though their work is not dehumanised, Ortega's speculations do reflect something of the Generation of 1927's system of values in their early poetry, where 'pure' literary considerations tend to take priority over a concern with the problems of the human condition. Even a poet as tormented as Lorca took part in his early work in the cultivation of brilliant imagery and ingenious metaphor.

However, towards the end of the decade of the 1920s some of the younger members of the group experienced a profound conflict of values and crisis of confidence. To express their disillusionment they turned to surrealism which provided them with a means of giving voice to feelings of intense anguish, frustration and rage. The surrealist phase in the work of the younger poets ended their dalliance with the concept of *poesía pura* and the idea that art is a game. Aesthetic concerns were overwhelmed by existential anguish, producing a growing involvement in human problems that led on in the following decade to a direct political commitment on the part of several of these poets.

Most of those members of the Generation of 1927 who survived the Civil War went into exile after 1939. Bitterness at the outcome of the war and the exile's nostalgia for his native land naturally became common themes with them. For some, like Alberti, exile also brought a diminution of their poetic ability and their work tended to lose its urgency. The poets in exile continued the process of humanisation in their work that had begun in the late 1920s, a move that is paralleled by the development of a more colloquial expression. Exile effectively broke the tenuous unity of the group, which had already begun to waver in the years before the war.

Luis Cernuda was one of the younger poets of the Generation of 1927, born in Seville in 1902, a younger brother to two sisters in a middle-class family.[5] He seems to have had a secure, uneventful childhood, and despite some caustic comments in his poems, he always maintained a bond of affection with his family. The first important event in his literary career occurred while he was a student at Seville University where he studied Law from 1919 to 1925. When he was about twenty years old he records that he had the experience of seeing things as though for the first time and as a result wrote a series of poems of which none has survived. His earliest extant poems date from 1924, some two

[5] Unless stated otherwise all biographical data is derived from Cernuda's autobiographical essay 'Historial de un libro', *Poesía y literatura* (Barcelona, 1960), 233-80. All page references to this source will, where convenient, be embodied in the text with the abbreviation *PL*.

years later. Towards the end of his student days his literary activities were brought to the attention of Pedro Salinas, then a lecturer at the university. Salinas gave the young poet every encouragement, urging him to broaden his reading, especially of French literature. His first published poems appeared in the *Revista de Occidente* in December 1925, followed by a number of contributions in prose and verse to other literary magazines and in 1927 by the publication of his first book of verse, *Perfil del aire*.

Many of these early publications have not been collected by Cernuda, and *Perfil del aire* itself is outside the canon of *La Realidad y el Deseo*, since it was extensively revised before being incorporated, with the new title of *Primeras poesías*, into the first edition of Cernuda's collected poems in 1936.[6] The revision of this first book involves changes of style and tone but the thematic content remains substantially unaltered. *Perfil del aire* is an impressive first book of poems by a young poet, a delicate and assured evocation of the nebulous, ambivalent emotions of adolescence. The basic technique is an impressionistic symbolism learnt from Juan Ramón Jiménez with a little direct assistance from Mallarmé, while echoes of Jorge Guillén and Pedro Salinas indicate Cernuda's youthful position amongst his generation. These are influences to be expected in a young poet in 1927, but the additional influence of Pierre Reverdy, whose work Cernuda discovered by chance, adds an individual note. The dominant tone of these poems is a quiet melancholy, although there is also an underlying vein of optimism that is greatly reduced when the poems are revised. The traditional verse forms used in the book, mainly assonanted heptasyllabic quatrains and *décimas*, are often a vehicle for the ingenious metaphors that are characteristic of poetry at this time, and this imagistic element is also subdued in the revised *Primeras poesías*. The elegance and artifice of *Perfil del aire*'s expression point to a link with the modish concern for 'pure' poetry, and the reviewers in 1927 certainly all acknowledged this aspect of the book. Cernuda himself, however, has commented on what he describes as an instinctive tendency towards a colloquial expression in his early poems, and some of the compositions of *Perfil del aire* do have a direct, unrhetorical diction. This may be partly due to the influence of Salinas, but is more likely to be the result of his reading of Pierre Reverdy whose simple, reticent style he found attractive and from whom he learnt a quality he calls "ascetismo poético". It is in fact this quality of rhetorical leanness that remains with Cernuda's early poems when they reappear in 1936, shorn of the self-conscious metaphors that were the young poet's genuflection to fashion in 1927.

Although Cernuda sought to bury *Perfil del aire* beneath the revised *Primeras poesías*, his first book of poems remained to haunt him like a shadow throughout his life. In 1927 it had been given a mixed reception by the critics, several of whom found it rather old-fashioned and lacking in emotional vitality while condescendingly accepting it as a work of promise if not of actual achievement. His disappointment at this grudging reception of his poems was sharpened into an intense pain by the charge, which was subsequently to become widely

[6] For a detailed examination of the problems surrounding *Perfil del aire* see *Luis Cernuda: "Perfil del aire". Edición y estudio de Derek Harris*, (Colección Támesis, London, 1971).

accepted, that he was an imitator of Jorge Guillén. The presence of Guillén in these early poems is undeniable but it is not an important influence and the emphasis given by critics to this superficial likeness was, for Cernuda, proof of a basic misunderstanding of his poetry. He was left with a legacy of bitterness that stayed with him until his death.

After *Perfil del aire* Cernuda engaged upon a series of more ambitious poems in which he attempted to give a more expansive treatment to the adolescent thematic material of his first book. Four of these poems were later gathered together in 1936 to form *Egloga, elegía, oda*, the second section of *La Realidad y el Deseo.* These extensive poems in classical metres, *estancias* and rhymed hendecasyllable quatrains, have been defended by Cernuda with the maxim: "aquello que te censuren, cultívalo, porque eso eres tú" (*PL*, 240).[6bis] They are in part intended as a defiance of the criticism that *Perfil del aire* was old-fashioned and as an affirmation of the authenticity of that first collection. While still maintaining a symbolist manner, these poems are distinctly classical in tone as well as form. The *estancias* of the "Egloga" and the "Oda" are modelled on those of Garcilaso, and the flowing, elegant melody of the verse shows a close affinity with the sixteenth-century Toledan poet. But there is also a strong presence of Mallarmé, particularly in the "Egloga", which is partly a gloss on "L'Après-midi d'un Faune".[7] The presence of Mallarmé underlines a thematic continuity with *Perfil del aire*; the additional influence of Garcilaso, however, is remarkable since these poems date from the time of the celebration of Góngora's tercentenary. Cernuda did take part in the homage to Góngora, but the choice, at this time, of Garcilaso as a model is a striking example of his individuality and of a willingness to disregard literary fashion if it does not conform to his personal requirements.[8] The exuberant metaphor of Góngora is not suited to the adolescent melancholy of Cernuda's early poems, whereas Garcilaso's restrained elegance can accord with such a mood.

Cernuda's father had died in 1920, and when his mother died in July 1928 he collected his small inheritance and in the following September left his native Seville. After brief stays in Málaga and Madrid he spent the first half of 1929 as a teaching assistant in Spanish at the Ecole Normale in Toulouse, returning to Madrid in the summer of that year and finding employment in the bookshop of León Sánchez Cuesta. Even before his departure from Seville he had begun to take an interest in the poetry of the French surrealists in whose spirit of rebellion he found a deep sympathy. It was at this time that Cernuda seems to have

[6] bis Guillermo de Torre, 'Ultra-manifiestos', *Cosmópolis,* no. 29 (1921), quotes the phrase "Ce qui le public te reproche, cultive-le, c'est toi", which he attributes to Jean Cocteau in *Le Coq et l'Arlequin*. See P. Ilie, *Documents of the Spanish Vanguard* (Chapel Hill, 1969), 131.

[7] Stanzas five and six of Cernuda's poem are a paraphrase of Mallarmé's *églogue,* lines 14-22.

[8] Some of Cernuda's poems were read by one of the speakers at the meeting in homage to Góngora held in the Ateneo in Seville in December 1927. See Dámaso Alonso, *Poetas españoles contemporáneos* (Madrid, 1952), 169-70. Cernuda also contributed the uncollected poem "Sólo escollos de sombra, débilmente" to *Litoral,* nos. 5-7 (1927), the special number of this magazine dedicated to Góngora. For the text of this poem see *Luis Cernuda: "Perfil del aire"* (London, 1971), 157.

become fully aware of his homosexuality. The influence of surrealism dominates his next two collections of poems, *Un río, un amor*, written in Toulouse and Madrid in 1929, and *Los placeres prohibidos*, which dates from 1931. In these books he abandons the fixed metres of his early poems for free verse in order to express wilder emotions of frustration and anger. They are the record of a violent disillusionment that finds an uninhibited release in the surrealist disregard for logic, although Cernuda, like other poets of his generation also influenced by surrealism, does not use the technique of automatic writing.

In 1933 the spirit of rebellion that had found expression in his surrealist poems was translated into a declaration of support for Communism.[9] Cernuda thus followed the same path towards political commitment as many of his companions in the Generation of 1927, but this Marxist faith was short lived and never intruded upon his poetry. His next collection of poems, *Donde habite el olvido*, published in 1934, returns in fact to a traditional mold. By that time the influence of surrealism had exhausted its usefulness, having released his violent feelings, and *Donde habite el olvido* is a delicate work of evocation and suggestion, plainly influenced by Bécquer. There was a revival of interest in Bécquer in the early 1930s but it was a deep emotional affinity between himself and Bécquer that influenced Cernuda at this time rather than a literary fashion. *Donde habite el olvido* is the account of a disastrous love affair that finds a close parallel with the desolate experience expressed in many of the *Rimas*. These poems were well-received by the critics, although the emphasis given by reviewers to the book's mood of emotional lassitude adds to Cernuda's reputation for indolence already established by the critics' attitude to *Perfil del aire*.[10]

Donde habite el olvido brings to an end a stylistic and thematic cycle that embraces Cernuda's first five collections of poems in which he presents an impressionistic record of his emotional reaction to events and circumstances. These five books are Cernuda's "Songs of Experience", the account of his attempts to seek the dreams of desire in a hostile reality. But within *Donde habite el olvido* there occurs the beginning of a radical change in the aim of his poetry; the final poem, "Los fantasmas del deseo", is in a different style, a style of statement rather than of suggestion, that reflects an intention to analyse his experience instead of simply recording it. This change of attitude marks the moment of his transition towards maturity as a poet. His next book, *Invocaciones a las gracias del mundo* (1934-1935), a title later shortened to *Invocaciones*, develops this new attitude as part of a reappraisal of the values on which he had tried to base his life. These invocations are extensive poems with an ample discursive diction, which, Cernuda has observed, reflect a dissatisfaction with the short song-poems favoured by 'pure' poetry (*PL*, 252). The movement away from the style of his early poems is also revealed by attempts to use symbolic personages as a means of giving an objective dimension to his ideas

[9] Cernuda's statement of support for Communism appeared under the title 'Los que se incorporan' in *Octubre*, nos. 4-5 (1933), 37. It has been republished, in a censored form, in Luis Cernuda, *Crítica, ensayos y evocaciones* (Barcelona, 1970), 91.

[10] Cf. the following comment on the Cernuda of *Donde habite el olvido*: "Tranquilamente reclinado . . . en las playas sin calma y sin anhelo de una indolencia que quiere desesperarse y no puede . . ." Enrique Azcoaga, 'Sereno llanto', *Ardor* (March 1936), s.p.

and emotions. This capacity for self-detachment is another indication of Cernuda's approaching maturity. It is also in these invocations that the influence of Hölderlin appears in his poetry, an influence that has a greater effect on his ideas than on his style, but which begins his involvement with a wider European literary tradition.

In April 1936 the first edition of *La Realidad y el Deseo* was published, gathering together the six collections of poems so far mentioned, and was given a warm reception.[11] However, the outbreak of the Civil War in the following July swept aside the critical recognition Cernuda had received. The war also had a more lasting consequence for him. In February 1938 he left Spain to go on a lecture tour in England on behalf of the Spanish Republic; he was never to return. On his way back he was halted in Paris by the news of the way the war was going, and in September he returned to England, first to a post as Spanish Assistant at Cranleigh School in Surrey and then in January 1939 to a position as *lector* at Glasgow University. The experience of war and the shock of exile tended to push Cernuda's personal preoccupations into the background, and his next collection of poems, *Las nubes* (1937-1940), is the product of his reaction to these traumatic events. Cernuda avoided any partisan political attitude and created a series of Spanish elegies where he laments the war and meditates on the sad existence of exile. Separation from Spain awakened in him, at least initially, the same nostalgia for his native land as it did in other exiled poets, but in his case it also had more fertile effects. The transplantation into a completely alien environment forced Cernuda to deepen his analysis of himself in order to find a faith to sustain him in such a difficult situation, and the fact that he went into exile in England encouraged him to broaden his knowledge of English literature. The progressive discovery and assimilation of English poetry is the last major influence Cernuda received. He found in the work of English poets like Browning and Eliot the lack of rhetoric he had always admired, as well as a meditative manner that aroused a deep sympathy with his own approach to poetry. No English writer, however, can be said to have had a determining influence on Cernuda; rather than an influence, English poetry was for him a tradition that he was able to use to validate his own literary preferences.

The Baudelairian *douleur fertilisante* of exile and the example of meditative poetry offered by the English tradition combine to produce the great poems of Cernuda's next book, *Como quien espera el alba*, completed in 1944 in Cambridge to where he had moved the year before to take up another position as *lector* at the university. In these poems the sad meditations on exile give way to a concentrated attempt at self-analysis expressed with consummate technical ease and confidence. He was now able to seek to come to terms with himself, in the knowledge that he had discovered his personal truth. Henceforth his primary concern would be to maintain that truth. *Como quien espera el alba*

[11] See Juan Ramón Jiménez, 'Con la inmensa minoría. Crítica', *El Sol,* 26-IV-36; Pedro Salinas, 'Luis Cernuda, poeta', in *Literatura española siglo XX* (Mexico, 1949); and Arturo Serrano Plaja, 'Notas a la poesía de Luis Cernuda', *El Sol,* 17-V-36 and 4-VI-36. A banquet was given in Cernuda's honour at which Federico García Lorca delivered the eulogy; see Lorca, *Obras completas* (Madrid, 1957), 89-91.

contains many of his finest poems and also some of the best Spanish poetry written since the Civil War; subsequent collections perhaps lack the intensity given to these poems by the partial resolution they offer to Cernuda's existential problems. His next two books continue the examination of life in the alien environment of exile, which, as Cernuda enters his middle age, is set against a sharp awareness of time. Both these preoccupations are reflected in the titles of these books, *Vivir sin estar viviendo* and *Con las horas contadas*. The former was begun in Cambridge in 1944, continued in London from 1945 to 1947 when Cernuda was a lecturer at the Instituto Español, and completed in 1949 in America where he went in 1947 to take up a teaching post at Mount Holyoke College, Massachussetts; the latter collection was begun in the United States in 1950 and completed in Mexico in 1956 after his move to that country in 1952. After the years of exile in Anglo-Saxon countries Mexico became for him a spiritual home, all the more so because it was the setting for a love affair that formed the climax to his life. This love affair is the subject of a separate series of poems, "Poemas para un cuerpo", contained in *Con las horas contadas*. In Mexico his life-long erotic ideal was fulfilled, and momentarily reality and desire became one.

Cernuda's final collection, *Desolación de la Quimera*, contains poems written between 1956 and 1962, although the majority were composed from 1960 to 1962 as the result of a new change of environment; during these years he was a Visiting Professor in the University of California at Los Angeles and at San Francisco State College.[12] After the climactic experience of "Poemas para un cuerpo" these poems are an epilogue to the whole of *La Realidad y el Deseo*, reflecting a preoccupation with the approaching end of his life and a consequent attempt to summarise and make a last affirmation of his beliefs. The presentiment that his death was near was fulfilled in Mexico City in November 1963 when he died of a sudden heart attack.

In 1958 Cernuda had published the third edition of *La Realidad y el Deseo*, which brings together all of his poems he wished to preserve written up to 1956. Since 1950 there had been a gradual increase in critical interest towards him and the appearance of his collected poems gave added impetus to this interest. In the few years before his death he finally gained the recognition that had eluded him for thirty years, and in particular he began to win esteem from the younger generation of Spanish poets and critics, who are not in the main well-disposed towards their elders. Cernuda's poetry is today beginning to exercise an influence on the young poets who have succeeded him.[13]

This brief survey of the evolution of *La Realidad y el Deseo* shows that Cernuda followed much the same pattern of development as his contemporaries, although the directly autobiographical frame of reference in his poems tends to limit his involvement in literary fashion. Yet he underwent a variety of influences far wider than those which affect many other members of the Genera-

[12] For details see C.P. Otero, 'Cernuda in California', in *Letras I* (Colección Támesis, London, 1966), 190-97.

[13] For the opinion of some of the young Spanish poets on Cernuda see the contributions by Francisco Brines, Jaime Gil de Biedma and José Angel Valente to the *Homenaje a Luis Cernuda* produced by *La caña gris*, nos. 6-8 (1962).

tion of 1927, and associated himself with literary traditions foreign to that of Spain. It is, moreover, the wealth of his knowledge of European literature that helped him reach the peak of his achievement as a poet in the years after the Civil War when the inspiration of some of his fellow poets seemed to wane. His poetry, in fact, develops through a series of influences, but they are homogeneous influences carefully selected to further Cernuda's intentions, the result of his recognition of himself in the work of others. The control he exercised over the influences that affected him predicates a deep integrity of purpose and reveals the commitment he had to his poetry as a means of self-expression.

The Creation of a Legend

Cernuda's shy, withdrawn character had attracted attention even before he had published his first book of poems.[14] His diffidence and incapacity to establish satisfactory human relationships have been described by many of his acquaintances. Concha Méndez, who knew him well in Madrid before the Civil War and during his last years in Mexico, asserts that he was a "hombre hermético, retraído, incapaz de revelar en su trato un rasgo sentimental de clase alguna".[15] Cernuda himself, who in his later years did not shrink from vehement, and sometimes venomous, attacks on critics and writers who displeased him, has provided substantiation for this reputation of astringent aloofness.[16] He was, however, well-aware of this public image as a complicated, tortured personality and this became a matter of deep concern for him in his last collection of poems, *Desolación de la Quimera.* "A sus paisanos", the final poem of this book, is an *envoi* to his countrymen who form the audience for his work, in which he trenchantly criticises their acceptance of the image he had acquired. He calls this image his *leyenda*, and makes clear that he regards it as a gross distortion of the truth about himself :

¿Mi leyenda dije? Tristes cuentos
Inventados de mí por cuatro amigos
(¿Amigos?), que jamás quisisteis
Ni ocasión buscasteis de ver si acomodaban
A la persona misma así traspuesta.
Mas vuestra mala fe los ha aceptado.
Hecha está la leyenda, y vosotros, de mí desconocidos,
Respecto al ser que encubre mintiendo doblemente,
Sin otro escrúpulo, a vuestra vez la propaláis.[17]

[14] "¡Figúrate que dicho señor dice de mí, a escondidas, desde luego, que soy muy raro y que sólo me gusta estar escondido en casa . . . !" Letter of 2-XII-26 from Cernuda to Higinio Capote, in F. López Estrada, 'Estudios y cartas de Cernuda', *Insula,* no. 207 (1964), 16. It would appear that Cernuda is referring to Juan Guerrero.

[15] Concha Méndez, 'Luis Cernuda', *Insula,* no. 207 (1964), 13.

[16] Cernuda's critical essays in his *Estudios sobre poesía española contemporánea* (Madrid, 1957) have added to this reputation. Cf. "Ante este libro [*Estudios sobre poesía española contemporánea*] sentimos no se sabe qué extraño escalofrío . . . Cuando nosotros hemos creído que se podía hacer un hogar nos hallamos en el frío y las tinieblas de fuera. Sopla un viento inmisericorde." A. Tovar, 'El paso del tiempo y un libro sobre la poesía española', *Papeles de Son Armadans,* no. XXIV (1958), 319.

[17] *La Realidad y el Deseo,* fourth edition (Mexico, 1964), 366.

I believe it is possible to identify the four friends mentioned in this poem as Juan Ramón Jiménez, Pedro Salinas, Vicente Aleixandre and José Moreno Villa. The first three of these friends have all produced well-known pen portraits of Cernuda;[18] Jiménez's portrait in particular has achieved a wide circulation, and Cernuda has commented unfavourably on the way he has been described by Salinas and Aleixandre.[19] He has also taken exception to some of the comments about him in Moreno Villa's autobiography.[20] The picture of Cernuda presented by these four fellow poets is a strange one; he appears as an anguished neurasthenic, a delicate, fragile person who sought to live in the rarefied atmosphere of a solitary private world. He emerges from Jiménez's highly mannered portrait as aloof and effete to the point of sickliness :

> Bajó, ledo confesor oriental, de su pétreo pie de la puerta grande ¡inconmovible catedral sevillana! atravesó gradas por el aire estrecho, en superpuestos perfiles, y vestido de actual modo negro su moreno amarillo, llegó al tren de la tarde con un ramito de clavellinas blancas en la cuidadosa mano. ¡Adiós! ¿Cómo se perdía luego y sin madre, en el crepuscular laberinto de Santa Cruz, este delgado solitario, erecto desdeñoso? ¿Qué fina y fuerte aguja interior, qué eje sutil lo sostenía bajo el grana sorbo asfixiante, azucena de hierro giraldina para todos los vientos de la poesía, quieta, triste por falta atmosférica.[21]

Aleixandre emphasises Cernuda's solitariness and detachment from the world :

> Dominaban allí unos ojos oscuros y un poco retrasados, tan pronto fijos, tan pronto vagos y renunciadores. Le vi con ellos recorrer las cosas, como si las estuviese viendo pasar en una corriente . . .[22]

[18] J. R. Jiménez, 'Héroe español: Luis Cernuda', *Héroe*, no. 4 (1934). Reprinted with the title 'Luis Cernuda (1927)' in Jiménez, *Españoles de tres mundos* (Buenos Aires, 1942), 163-4, *ibid.*, second edition (Madrid, 1960), 263-5. Also published in *Cuadernos de Juan Ramón Jiménez* (Madrid, 1960), 190-1.

P. Salinas, 'Nueve o diez poetas', in E. L. Turnbull, *Contemporary Spanish Poetry* (Baltimore, 1945), 14-16. Reprinted in *El hijo pródigo,* no. VIII (1945), 78-9, and in Salinas, *Ensayos de literatura hispánica* (Madrid, 1958), 372-3.

V. Aleixandre, 'Luis Cernuda deja Sevilla', *Cántico,* nos. 9-10 (1955), s.p. Reprinted in *Mito,* no. 7 (1956). Republished with considerable variants in Aleixandre *Los encuentros* (Madrid, 1958), 139-43. See also Aleixandre, 'Luis Cernuda en la ciudad', *La caña gris,* nos. 6-8 (1962), 11-12.

[19] See the poem "Malentendu", *La Realidad y el Deseo* (1964), 348, for Cernuda's attitude to Salinas in his later years. Cernuda was displeased by Aleixandre's contribution to *La caña gris* (see note 18 above): "Excepto un trabajo (el del señor Gil-Albert), aunque mejor diría dos trabajos (incluyendo el de Vicente Aleixandre), todo el número es en extremo halagueño de ser leído por el objeto del mismo: mi persona." Letter of 29-IX-62 from Cernuda to the present writer.

[20] J. Moreno Villa, *Vida en claro* (Mexico, 1944), 144-50 *passim.* "Ya otros se encargarán de referir a su manera, deformando o inventando, tal o cual detalle de mi vida, como recientemente ha hecho Moreno Villa al aludir a mí en su *Vida en claro.*" *Apud* J. Tello, 'Hablando a Luis Cernuda', *El Tiempo* (Bogotá), 7-X-45.

[21] *Españoles de tres mundos* (Madrid, 1960), 263.

[22] *Los encuentros,* 139.

Moreno Villa concentrates on the tortured aspect of his character and on his effeminacy :

> Era entonces un jovencillo fino y tímido, muy atildado y muy triste. Sufría con las cosas materiales y con las de la relación humana. Dicen que lloraba delante de los escaparates de prendas de vestir porque no podía comprarse unas camisas de seda; pero, desde luego, yo lo he visto casi llorar por no tener amigos ni nadie que le quisiese.[23]

It is Salinas, however, who must take the prize for presenting Cernuda as a delicate, timid, solitary creature :

> Delicado, pudorísimo, guardándose su intimidad para él solo, y para las abejas de su poesía que van y vienen, trajinando allí dentro – sin querer más jardín – haciendo su miel. . . . Por dentro, cristal. Porque es el más *licenciado Vidriera* de todos, el que más aparta a la gente de sí, por temor de que le rompan algo, el más extraño.[24]

It is noticeable that each of these four descriptions refers to the young Cernuda in his middle or late twenties, but they were written some years later and no attempt is made to see if the description still fits the mature man. It would seem that in the minds of his friends he was indelibly marked with the first impression he made on them. Even more dubious is the attempt by Jiménez and Salinas to evoke the character of Cernuda's poetry through the brittle, languid, exquisite personality they found in the young man. The autobiographical nature of his poetry makes it all the easier to succumb to a dangerous confusion between his private personality and his poetic *persona*, and this can lead to some curious critical commentaries when the image of Cernuda described above is projected by critics onto his poems.

Indolence is one of the basic characteristics of what Cernuda calls his *leyenda* and indolence is a quality that has frequently been ascribed to his poetry. It is true that an indolent atmosphere does characterise sections of his work, particularly his early poems, but it is unreasonable to see indolence as a dominant feature in all his poetry. Undue emphasis on this aspect can lead even a well-meaning critic to make such an extraordinary comment as this :

> Su palabra poética es naturalmente y hasta corporalmente triste, indolente, pesimista, y, desde luego, más desengañada y desdeñosa que francamente desesperada . . . una palabra fría y anti-creadora, quiero decir : palabra de poeta al que no le interesa demasiado crear nada.[25]

The shy, solitary personality Cernuda presented to his friends finds an echo amongst many critics who see him as a poet of solitude; indeed, solitude has often been regarded as an essential attribute of his existence, the optimum circumstance of his life.[26] Again it is true that in his poetry he frequently seeks

[23] *Vida en claro,* 148.

[24] *Ensayos de literatura hispánica,* 373.

[25] Luis Felipe Vivanco, *Introducción a la poesía española contemporánea* (Madrid, 1957), 296.

[26] See Eugenio Florit, 'Como quien espera el alba', *Revista hispánica moderna,* nos. 1-4 (1950), 141-2. Also Anon. 'Libros recientes', *La Nación,* 21-VI-59, sección tercera, 6.

a protective isolation, and this has been seen by critics as a sign of his effeteness. One critic, noting the unhealthy aspects of such a withdrawn existence, has even suggested that he was incapable of living outside this introverted condition:

> . . . el poeta probablemente más huraño de todos, Luis Cernuda, quien toda su vida ha buscado un aislamiento de indiferencia, de orgullo, o surgido de su incapacidad de adaptación . . . / . . . Está ya tan acostumbrado a vivir rodeado sólo de las creaciones de su propia mente – las cuales le obedecen siempre y se dejan regir mucho más fácilmente que los hombres –, que la verdadera compañía le molesta.[27]

Here is a clear echo of Salinas's view of Cernuda as a *licenciado Vidriera*, the brittle personality that evades any involvement in life. This is one of the most persistent elements of the *leyenda*. Ricardo Gullón defines Cernuda as "un ausente", a quality which he describes as ". . . la distancia desde la cual crecen sus sueños y su obra. Distancia que no depende de circunstancias exteriores, pues está suscitada, como en Bécquer, por la inclusión del poeta en un ámbito aparte, aunque no independiente del nuestro".[28] The mention of Bécquer is symptomatic of the idea of Cernuda as a "Romantic" poet, which is also a recurring theme amongst critics, based on this supposed detachment from the world about him.

One aspect of Cernuda's private personality that could interfere with critics' judgement of his poetry is his homosexuality. However, this aspect of his character has rarely been mentioned, despite the overt homosexual eroticism that appears in his poems. It is tempting to believe that the way in which so many critics studiously avoid this topic is a sign of unease and that their emphasis on the neurotic elements of his personality is the result of a suppressed moral judgement of his unnatural passion. This may well explain the comments of some critics who suggest that as a man and a poet Cernuda suffered from diminished responsibility:

> . . . Cernuda podrá ser un día uno de los ejemplos más fehacientes de la decadente *impureza* a que puede llegar la poesía que se pretende *pura* y persigue su inefabilidad esencial en la dimisión de su condición humana de poeta.[29]
>
> ¿Podría decirse que la pregunta por la autenticidad del ser no se le ha presentado con todo su rigor? ¿Y que por eso echamos de menos en su última obra un lirismo humano?[30]

The comments I have quoted to illustrate the *leyenda* that has grown around Cernuda are necessarily one-sided, but they do suggest a relationship between the personality Cernuda presented as a man and the critics' view of his poetry. The man and the poet have been confused. The distorted view of Cernuda's

[27] Birute Ciplijauskaite, *La soledad en la poesía española contemporánea* (Madrid, 1962), 197 and 213.

[28] Ricardo Gullón, 'La poesía de Luis Cernuda', *Asomante*, no. 2 (1950), 35.

[29] Juan Chabás, *Literatura española contemporánea 1898-1950* (Havana, 1952), 349.

[30] Ciplijauskaite, *La soledad*, 213.

poetry established by such a confusion has become part of the general consensus of critical opinion about him and even seems to have cast its shadow over the only two complete studies of Cernuda's poetry produced to date. Moreover, both these monographs are by non-Spanish critics who do certainly not approach the poetry via the personality of Cernuda the man.[31] Elisabeth Müller finds in her study that Cernuda's major preoccupation is time. She believes that he is continually seeking to escape temporality and that he finally achieves this, in a quasi-mystical fashion, when he discovers in Mexico a paradigm of the Andalusia of his childhood. Philip Silver's monograph closely parallels the ideas expressed by Dr. Müller; he also believes that Cernuda is striving to regain the timeless world of his childhood and that this ideal is finally attained through the *via mystica* of love by which the poet enters into symbiotic union with the natural world. Cernuda, in fact, emerges from these two highly sympathetic academic studies with an evasive personality of a kind that is not dissimilar to the view of him I have described as the *leyenda*.

Only in the last decade have a few critics presented a view of Cernuda's poetry that conflicts with the *leyenda*. These are the critics who see in him an ethical poet, seeking his personal truth and concerned to affirm it with integrity and dignity. Many of the critics who see Cernuda's work in this way are fellow poets, like Octavio Paz who has produced some of the most perceptive comments that Cernuda has yet received.[32] Paz's view of Cernuda as a moralist, quoted at the beginning of this chapter, is shared by several of the young Spanish poets of today who are beginning to look upon Cernuda as a guide. The two following comments can serve as examples of the attitude of the new generation :

> Fidelidad a un destino, el cual es conocido por una vigilancia y desvelamiento personal implacables : el resultado de esto es la formulación de una verdad, la suya, a la que se debe; de aquí su sentido de la dignidad.[33]
>
> Por su triple contextura intelectual, estética y moral ha de considerarse esa obra como una de las piezas capitales en el desarrollo contemporáneo de nuestra poesía.[34]

The view of Cernuda I wish to present in this study is very much in accord with opinions such as these, and, in fact, owes much to the acute critical insight of Octavio Paz. The reality of Cernuda the poet is not the brittle man of glass found in the *leyenda* but this seeker after truth, who can also be distinguished clearly in Cernuda's own theory of poetry.

Poetry as Truth

Cernuda was deeply concerned with the nature of poetry and of the poetic

[31] Elisabeth Müller, *Die Dichtung Luis Cernudas* (Geneva, 1962). Philip Silver, *"Et in Arcadia ego": A Study of the Poetry of Luis Cernuda* (Colección Támesis, London, 1965). Alexander Coleman, *Other voices: A Study of the Late Poetry of Luis Cernuda* (University of North Carolina, 1969), totally accepts Silver's approach to the poetry.

[32] Octavio Paz, 'La palabra edificante', in *Cuadrivio* (Mexico, 1965).

[33] Francisco Brines, 'Ante unas poesías completas', *La caña gris*, nos. 6-8 (1962), 137.

[34] J. A. Valente, 'Luis Cernuda y la poesía de la meditación', *ibid.*, 38. See also J. M. Castellet, *Veinte años de poesía española 1939-1959* (Barcelona, 1962), 97-100.

experience, a concern that is clearly visible in his own poems as well as in his literary criticism. But he has made only one attempt to state his personal view of poetry in purely theoretical terms, in the essay 'Palabras antes de una lectura' (1935), which could well serve as an introduction to *La Realidad y el Deseo*. In this essay he describes the birth of his poetic vision :

> El instinto poético se despertó en mí gracias a la percepción más aguda de la realidad, experimentando, con un eco más hondo, la hermosura y la atracción del mundo circundante. Su efecto era, como en cierto modo ocurre con el deseo que provoca el amor, la exigencia, dolorosa a fuerza de intensidad, de salir de mí mismo, anegándome en aquel vasto cuerpo de la creación. Y lo que hacía aún más agónico aquel deseo era el reconocimiento tácito de su imposible satisfacción.[35]

For Cernuda, then, poetry is concerned with the relationship between himself and the world towards which he feels an overwhelming desire for union, but this desire is itself an indication that he is living a separate, incomplete existence. This provokes an ambivalent attitude towards the external world; on the one hand he is attracted to it, "como si sólo con su posesión pudiera alcanzar certeza de mi propia vida", and on the other hand he feels hostility towards its "irónico atractivo" and concludes "que la realidad exterior es un espejismo y lo único cierto mi propio deseo de poseerla".[36] The separation between self and world is the conflict between *realidad* and *deseo*, terms which Cernuda first uses as antonyms in this essay, and this conflict is for him the principal concern of poetry :

> La esencia del problema poético . . . la constituye el conflicto entre realidad y deseo, entre apariencia y verdad, permitiéndonos alcanzar alguna vislumbre de la imagen completa del mundo que ignoramos, de la 'idea divina del mundo que yace al fondo de la apariencia', según la frase de Fichte.[37]

The purpose of poetry, as set out in this theoretical statement, is to gain contact with a transcendent reality where the separation of self and world is ended. It is from such ideas as these that support can be found for the view of Cernuda as a poet of evasion, seeking to live in a private world superior to and set apart from the world of other men. Yet, while the tragic feeling of separation and the longing to overcome it are fundamental to Cernuda's poetic vision, the concept of two distinct levels of reality also has other implications. The statement that he felt only the possession of the world could assure him of his own existence indicates that the perception of the dichotomy between himself and the world is, in fact, the discovery of self-consciousness. Underlying the idea that poetry is an expression of the conflict between the subjective and objective dimensions of life is a concern with self-affirmation. The use of the terms *apariencia* and

[35] *Poesía y literatura* (Barcelona, 1960), 196. Amongst Cernuda's papers in Seville is a rough draft of this essay bearing the inscription: "Palabras en el Lyceum Club antes de la lectura de algunos de mis poemas. 19 enero 1935."

[36] *Poesía y literatura*, 196.

[37] *Ibid.*, 196-7.

verdad as synonyms for *realidad* and *deseo* also point to a similar underlying concern. What Cernuda seeks in his poetry is the truth hidden behind appearance, the truth of his own aspirations set against an objective world that denies them.

Cernuda's own practice as a critic gives support to the ethical and existential preoccupations which I have suggested lie behind his theory of poetry as a vehicle for communion with a quasi-mystical transcendent reality. He has vehemently castigated Juan Ramón Jiménez, for example, because he felt Jiménez had turned his back on the world in order to live in a private microcosm of his own creation.[38] For Cernuda the poet is not someone who dwells on a separate level of existence from other men, but someone who is in even closer contact than normal with reality, tangible reality.[39] He is, moreover, adamant that a poet's personal experience, his own included, has no particular value other than that of being a reflection of common human experience, and that it can only acquire a special value if it is transmuted into poetry where the personal quality of the experience is lost.[40] This is not to say that he regards personal experience as unimportant, on the contrary, he requires that a poem should have a basis of personal experience to give it authenticity :

> Siempre traté de componer mis poemas a partir de un germen inicial de experiencia, enseñándome pronto la práctica que sin aquel, el poema no parecería inevitable ni adquiriría contorno exacto y expresión precisa (*PL*, 271)

In addition, he requires that the poet should give the greatest possible objectivity to the expression of his personal experience. He quotes to support this attitude T. S. Eliot's dictum : "mientras más perfecto el artista, más completa será en él la separación entre el hombre que sufre y la mente que crea."[41] The distinction between individual experience and its expression as literature can be easily related to the division between "truth" and "appearance" in the theory of *realidad* and *deseo*, and leads to the conclusion that Cernuda sees the aim of poetry as the discovery of the general, universal dimension lying beneath the circumstancial elements of individual existence. The purpose of such a search is clarified in a most revealing passage in his autobiographical essay, 'Historial de un libro', where he equates the intention of his poetry with that of a teacher :

> . . . el trabajo de las clases me hizo comprender como necesario que mis explicaciones llevaran a los estudiantes a ver por sí mismos aquello de que yo iba a hablarles : que mi tarea consistía en encaminarles y situarles ante la realidad de una obra literaria española. De ahí sólo había un paso a comprender que también el trabajo poético creador exigía algo equivalente, no

[38] *Estudios sobre poesía española contemporánea* (Madrid, 1957), 121-35.

[39] "El poeta no es, como generalmente se cree, criatura inefable que vive en las nubes (el nefelibata de que hablaba Darío), sino todo lo contrario; el hombre que acaso esté en contacto más íntimo con la realidad circundante." *Ibid.*, 18-19.

[40] ". . . en cuanto tal dolor o angustia individual del poeta, no valen más ni menos que el dolor y la angustia de otro hombre cualquiera; cuando pueden cobrar algún valor singular es cuando quedan transformados en poesía, que es cuando desaparecen como tal dolor o angustia personal del poeta." *Ibid.*, 146.

[41] *Ibid.*, 146-7.

> tratando de dar sólo al lector el efecto de mi experiencia, sino conduciéndole por el mismo camino que yo había recorrido, por los mismos estados que había experimentado y, al fin, dejarle solo frente al resultado. (*PL*, 260)

Here is a clear statement that Cernuda is not concerned with his experience itself, but with the effect it has had on him, with what he has learnt from it. His purpose in writing poetry is to understand himself and to communicate this understanding to the reader. If the parallel with the teacher is continued, the aim of his poetry can be seen to be the presentation to the reader of the reality of Luis Cernuda.

The idea that his poetry is a vehicle for understanding himself introduces the ethical considerations that are a most important and fundamental element of Cernuda's poetics. The critical analysis of experience implicit in such an attitude predicates a system of values and a judgement of an essentially ethical nature. It is, indeed, Cernuda's view that poetry is, in essence, an ethical exercise and not an aesthetic occupation, a point he makes in the course of a penetrating commentary on the poetry of San Juan de la Cruz:

> . . . en San Juan de la Cruz la belleza y pureza literaria son resultado de la belleza y pureza de su espíritu; es decir, resultado de una actitud ética y de una disciplina moral. No es quizá fácil apreciar esto hoy, cuando todavía circula por ahí como cosa válida ese mezquino argumento favoreciendo la pureza en los elementos retóricos del poema, como si la obra poética no fuera resultado de una experiencia espiritual, externamente estética, pero internamente ética.[42]

Even taking into account the distance and the difference between the Saint and Cernuda, this statement expresses a fundamental tenet of Cernuda's concept of poetry: beneath the aesthetic appearance of the poem lies hidden an ethical truth. This is the type of poetry he admires and this is the type of poetry he seeks to produce himself. He has also referred to the mixture of aesthetic and ethical elements in poetry in relation to the "Epístola moral a Fabio":

> Su realidad sólo puede hallarla el hombre, relativamente, en la aprobación y satisfacción de la conciencia; aprobación y satisfacción nacidas del equilibrio entre esa porción espiritual y esa material que componen la existencia, guiadas por el distante estímulo de una virtud en parte ética y en parte estética. Así acompasará y medirá el hombre su naturaleza propia y las acciones "que han de ser compañeras de la vida".[43]

Cernuda's own poetry is such a quest to measure and give meaning to himself, he too seeks to come to an acceptance of himself on a moral and spiritual level according to the dictates of his conscience. In his comments on the anonymous seventeenth-century author of the "Epístola moral", Cernuda, as is frequently the case in his criticism, is reflecting the aims of his own poetry. *La Realidad y el Deseo* is the record of his search for his personal reality.

Even a brief and schematic examination of Cernuda's views on poetry illus-

[42] 'Tres poetas clásicos', *Poesía y literatura* (Barcelona, 1960), 53.
[43] 'Tres poetas metafísicos', *ibid.*, 71.

trates that he held a number of beliefs that seem quite alien to the poetics one might normally associate with the kind of poet he is presented as in the *leyenda.* The image of the effete *licenciado Vidriera* is hardly compatible with a poet concerned to turn his personal experience into objective truth in accordance with a deep sense of ethical responsibility. Yet the *leyenda* has a basis of truth, even though it is not the whole truth; Cernuda presents in his poetry an even more complex character than that seen by his critics. Something of this complexity is expressed in the long poem of religious scepticism, "La adoración de los Magos", included in *Las nubes,* where the Magi are given three distinct personalities which correspond to three major facets of Cernuda's character. Melchior is world-weary but determined to follow the star in the hope it will lead him to a truth that will give purpose and meaning to his life; Balthazar is a cynical empiricist who believes in the rule of force and has no interest in abstract truths; Gaspar is a hedonist who prefers the pleasures of the flesh to any vague concept of truth. Melchior dominates the other two kings and forces them to set off with him after the star. He corresponds to Cernuda the seeker after truth, while Balthazar and Gaspar represent the cynical and the indolent Cernuda of the *leyenda.* Just as the seeker after truth dominates the Magi's journey of experience, so the larger journey of experience described in Cernuda's poetry as a whole is dominated by the search for truth.

Cernuda's belief that the poet's aim is to seek the truth hidden beneath appearance has important implications for the way in which he treats the autobiographical material that forms the basis for his poetry. An idea that does much to illuminate his attitude towards his poetic autobiography is the concept of a *mito personal* to which he refers in a commentary on the poetry of Unamuno:

> . . . en Unamuno esa lucha por Dios era paralela a la de crearse a sí mismo y no tenía otra causa que la de crearse a sí mismo y creer en sí mismo . . . Vivo y afanándose lejos de lo que sólo era actualidad, momento que pasa y no queda, Unamuno esperaba crearse a sí mismo, o al menos crear su mito personal, y ser lo que pasó quedando.[44]

Leaving aside the religious reference specifically relating to Unamuno, this is again a statement where it is possible to see Cernuda's own view of poetry reflected in his comments on another's work. He too is concerned to create and to perpetuate himself in his poetry, translating his circumstancial personal experience into myth, which can be taken as another term for truth. Both Octavio Paz and Philip Silver have seen the concept of the *mito personal* as central to Cernuda's poetry, although they have different opinions about its nature. Silver has made the important comparison with Cernuda's comments on Francisco de Aldana's *hombre interior* :

> Nada encierra de groseramente personal su concepto del hombre interior: es el ser que nos habita, como distinto de nuestra figura exterior, a cuya dualidad representativa parece responder la otra dualidad que halla Aldana entre realidad visible e invisible. El excesivo contacto exterior, si no traiciona,

[44] *Estudios sobre poesía española contemporánea,* 101.

> daña a este amigo incomparable, que sentimos diferente e idéntico a nosotros, que nos dicta nuestros gestos más puros, brotados de la naturaleza y del espíritu íntimamente individuales, no por presión de los acontecimientos en torno, los cuales tantas veces al individuo acorralan y oponen.[45]

Reflected here are Cernuda's own distaste for excessively personal poetry and his division of reality into two distinct levels, while the idea of an inner man, separate from the "figura exterior", recalls his distinction between hidden truth and superficial appearance. I suggest that Cernuda's own inner man is what he calls the *mito personal,* the truth of himself that is distilled from the circumstantial experiences of his "figura exterior", or *leyenda.*

The conflict between *realidad* and *deseo*, the struggle to end his sense of alienation in the world is the central experience that provides Cernuda with the material whose analysis leads him to the discovery and progressive understanding of his inner man. I shall now trace that process of discovery and understanding, using first a chronological approach to examine the early experiences of conflict presented in his first five books of poems, then turning to an examination of the major themes in his mature poetry: the search for a private world, the poet and poetry, and love and desire. A final chapter will examine the mature poems from the point of view of Cernuda's concern with his personal truth.

[45] Tres poetas metafísicos', *loc. cit.,* 64. See Octavio Paz, *Cuadrivio,* 170, and Silver, *"Et in Arcadia ego",* 47-8 and note 24.

II

THE LOSS OF INNOCENCE

Esperé un dios en mis días
Para crear mi vida a su imagen,
Mas el amor, como un agua,
Arrastra afanes al paso.
(Poem III, *Donde habite el olvido*)

Adolescence – the Dreams of Desire

The recreation of adolescent experience in *Primeras poesías* and *Egloga, elegía, oda,* with which Cernuda begins his poetic autobiography, is the point of departure for his journey of self-discovery, the seminal experience to which, in later years, he is drawn back again and again in his memory as he seeks to come to an understanding of himself. The sexual awakening of adolescence creates the erotic ideal that provides the dynamic for so much of his poetry, and the new emotional receptivity of that age gives him his first awareness of the world's equivocal attraction. In "Belleza oculta", a prose poem of his maturity, Cernuda describes an experience which he had in his early adolescence as he gazed at the countryside from the window of his room :

> Como en una intuición, más que en una percepción, por primera vez en su vida adivinó la hermosura de todo aquello que sus ojos contemplaban. Y con la visión de esa hermosura oculta se deslizaba agudamente en su alma, clavándose en ella, un sentimiento de soledad hasta entonces para él desconocido.[1]

This adolescent experience of a heightened perception of the world occurring simultaneously with a sense of separation from it bears a striking resemblance to the statement in 'Palabras antes de una lectura' of how Cernuda's poetic instinct was awakened by an acute perception of the world's beauty, which provoked a desire to become united with the world together with a simultaneous awareness of such a desire's impossibility. It is, in fact, in adolescence that Cernuda acquires the sense of separation between self and world which he later develops into the theory of the conflict between *realidad* and *deseo.*

Primeras poesías and *Egloga, elegía, oda* attempt to evoke the awakening of sexual desire and the new perception of the world as the adolescent Cernuda

[1] *Ocnos,* third edition (Mexico, 1963), 47-8. All subsequent references to *Ocnos* will be to this edition, unless stated otherwise.

would have experienced them, that is, intuitively and without being aware of the nature and import of such experience. The possible danger of a disturbing intrusion of hindsight into an attempt to recreate adolescent emotional states is accentuated by Cernuda's subsequent revision of his first book of poems, but even so he manages in the main to preserve the innocent gaze of the adolescent beset by emotions not yet fully understood. Thus, Cernuda's comments on *Perfil del aire* can also serve as a description of *Primeras poesías* :

> . . . es el libro de un adolescente, aún más adolescente de lo que era mi edad al componerlo, lleno de afanes no del todo conscientes, melancólico, precisamente por la impotencia en que me hallaba para satisfacer esos afanes ('la melancolía no es sino fervor caído', leí yo entonces en alguna página de Gide). (*PL*, 240)

The dominant mood of this book is, indeed, a melancholic frustration created by the adolescent protagonist's inability to fulfill his half-conscious desires. This adolescent leads a solitary, enclosed existence in the limited environment of his room, so that his world consists only of the objects in the room, the view from his window and his dreams. The only element in this restricted world that provides his vague, unorientated longings with any stimulus is the view from his window, which does create a sense of potential fulfillment, a sense of fervour, but when the scene outside the window disappears, as it often does, in the darkness of night, this becomes the impotent *fervor caído*. The contrast between urgent, new emotions and the inability to give them satisfaction is well described in an article Cernuda wrote in 1931 :

> Tengo veinte años, una familia y ninguna libertad. Ya usted sabe . . . De un lado, impulsos, fervores, deseos ardientes como sólo la juventud conoce; de otro, limitaciones ignorantes, vacía terquedad. Estudio vagamente unas cosas que no me importan.[2]

He claims this to be an extract from a letter to him from a young man, but this fictional correspondent is clearly a mask for Cernuda himself, and these sentiments fit exactly the mood of *Primeras poesías*, which has the same complex mixture of aspiration and frustration.

Unlike most of Cernuda's poetry, his first collection is not in chronological order, being arranged to produce an alternation of the *décimas* with the poems in heptasyllable *coplas* and also a general progression of mood from optimism to melancholy.[3] The opening poem is a landscape description that expresses feelings of confidence and security, although these optimistic sentiments are tempered with the indolence present in almost all these early poems. The experience evoked here is strongly reminiscent of the adolescent sensation of seeing things as though for the first time, recorded in the prose poem "Belleza oculta". This first poem of *Primeras poesías* is a statement of the emotional state, which

[2] 'La escuela de los adolescentes', *Heraldo de Madrid*, 5-XI-31, 12.

[3] For the chronology of Cernuda's early poems and for a more detailed study of Cernuda's poetry from the period 1924-1928 the reader is referred to *Luis Cernuda: "Perfil del aire". Edición y estudio de Derek Harris* (London, 1971).

Cernuda calls *fervor*, that is provoked by his heightened perception of the world. The adolescent lists a series of good omens for the future as he gazes from the window of his room at the twilight landscape outside; it is Spring, the trees are in leaf, the birds are singing, the first swallows wheel overhead, and the air is vibrant with a near wondrous sense of newness :

Va la brisa reciente
Por el espacio esbelta,
Y en las hojas cantando
Abre una primavera.

Sobre el límpido abismo
Del cielo se divisan,
Como dichas primeras,
Primeras golondrinas.

Tan sólo un árbol turba
La distancia que duerme,
Así el fervor alerta
La indolencia presente.

Verdes están las hojas,
El crepúsculo huye,
Anegándose en sombra
Las fugitivas luces.

En su paz la ventana
Restituye a diario
Las estrellas, el aire
Y el que estaba soñando.[4]

This poem is a good example of Cernuda's use of the symbolist technique of the *paysage d'âme* learnt from Juan Ramón Jiménez. The landscape described here is both a stimulus for the adolescent's emotions and a reflection of the emotions thus stimulated, although the precision of the elements in the scene make of it a view of the specific reality the young Cernuda could have seen from the window of his room, and not the formalised, abstract setting that often appears in Jiménez's poetry. Cernuda's landscape is, however, subjected to a restrained process of personification and anthropomorphic activation, which is designed to contrast with the adolescent's inactivity and thus highlight in the poem the opposition of fervour and indolence. The world outside the window is full of movement and action, while the adolescent is reduced to just a vague presence in the pronoun "el que". The poem's expression matches the simple, direct description, containing only one contrived image, the conceit of the first quatrain where bird-song is confused with budding leaves. In the simplicity of the diction used to portray the equally simple elements of the poem can be seen

[4] *La Realidad y el Deseo,* fourth edition (Mexico, 1964), 11. All subsequent references to the poems of *La Realidad y el Deseo* will be made by the page numbers of this edition.

something of the influence of Pierre Reverdy from whom Cernuda learnt a calculated reticence of expression, which he defines as "desnudez ascética".[5]

The vision of the world presented in "Va la brisa reciente" reflects a mood of tranquil optimism as the adolescent gazes in rapture at a smiling landscape where, despite the presence of the cycle of day and night, there is no sense of time's flux and the world seems to be reborn afresh with each new day. This combined feeling of wonder and reassurance is also to be found in a number of poems which express delight in simple objects or phenomena; for example, the ingenious, playful description of dawn, presented in the terms of a revolutionary conspiracy, in the *décima* "La luz, dudosa, despierta", and the wonder inspired by a mechanical ventilator in another *décima,* "Urbano y dulce revuelo". The feeling of confidence contained in such poems is the adolescent Cernuda's response to a world which he sees with eyes newly endowed with an awareness of its beauty. His new emotional receptivity provides him with an affirmation of his existence reflected in his vision of the world, an affirmation that is succinctly stated in the *cogito* :

> Existo, bien lo sé,
> Porque le transparenta
> El mundo a mis sentidos
> Su amorosa presencia. (p. 14)

In the optimistic emotional fervour created in the adolescent there is no sense of division between him and this welcoming, secure world, just as no distinction is made between him and the natural phenomena of the stars and the breeze in the final stanza of "Va la brisa reciente". An added note of exultation is brought to the feeling of oneness with the world in the poem "Ninguna nube inútil", where the common symbolist image of a clear sky represents a state of perfect harmony for which Cernuda proclaims an unconditional acceptance :

> Y el acorde total
> Da al universo calma :
> Arboles a la orilla
> Soñolienta del agua.
>
> Sobre la tierra estoy;
> Déjame estar. Sonrío
> A todo el orbe; extraño
> No le soy porque vivo. (pp. 13-14)

This joyful consonance with the world is a product of that awakening to the world which is related both in the prose poem "Belleza oculta" and the essay 'Palabras antes de una lectura', but in these optimistic poems it is presented without the accompanying sense of solitude. This is the perfect harmony between self and world, between *realidad* and *deseo,* that is Cernuda's ideal state of existence. His experience of this condition during his adolescence explains the importance this age assumes for him in later years.

[5] 'Recuerdo de Pierre Reverdy', *Poesía y literatura II* (Barcelona, 1964), 200-1.

Such poems as "Va la brisa reciente" and "Ninguna nube inútil" might lead an incautious reader to see a similarity with the bright, wonderful vision of the world presented by Jorge Guillén. The feeling of residence in a marvellous, secure universe, however, appears in only a few of the poems in *Primeras poesías* where the adolescent surveys the world through a rose-coloured glass of inexperience. This glass also has a concrete reality as the window of his room, mentioned in the final stanza of "Va la brisa reciente". The window is a recurring image and a most important symbol in these early poems, representing the adolescent's isolation and the consequent innocence of his gaze. The window enables him to see what is outside his room, but it is also a barrier which prevents him from gaining access to what he sees. The separation from the world, which the window symbolises, contradicts the experience of the *acorde total* with that simultaneous awareness of solitude described in the prose poem "Belleza oculta". The significance of the window is expressed clearly in the *décima* "No es el aire puntual", which is a description of the simple wonder provoked by the colours of the spectrum reflected in a window-pane. This reflection, however, makes visible the "imposible confín" of the glass, which, when completely transparent, had been perceptible only to the touch of the adolescent's lips. This concept at once conjures up a picture of the adolescent, alone in his room with his face pressed against the window, gazing longingly at the world outside. "No es el aire puntual" is, in effect, a statement of the circumstance of solitude that is a major element of Cernuda's adolescent experience.[6] The perception of the outside world through the barrier of the window also has an important effect on the idea of the *acorde total*, since this means that the landscapes of "Va la brisa reciente" and "Ninguna nube inútil" are visions of the world conceived in innocence, visions of the world as it ought to be if the promise of the adolescent's awakening emotions is to be satisfied. His view of the world outside his window is not *realidad*, but a projection of the subjective dimension of *deseo*.

The adolescent's isolation is responsible for introducing into his optimistic vision of the world an element of languor – the "indolencia presente" of poem I and the trees drowsily overhanging the water's edge in poem V. This indolence is an emotional as well as a physical inactivity in which the adolescent awaits the stimulus his still nebulous, untried desires need to give them form and life. His idealised view of the world about him does seem to offer him the prospect of a future fulfilment, but when he looks within himself he finds a near vacuum where nothing exists to activate his emotions, which are reduced to vague, formless longings. Sleep does not lead him to a realm of dreams but encloses him in a timeless limbo where he must await sadly the appearance of an object that will turn his undirected yearnings into desire. The third poem of *Primeras poesías*, one of the most perfect in the collection, evokes this leaden emotional state with paradoxical precision :

> Desengaño indolente
> Y una calma vacía,

[6] I am in complete disagreement with Andrew P. Debicki's interpretation of this poem, *Estudios sobre poesía española contemporánea* (Madrid, 1968), 287.

Como flor en la sombra,
El sueño fiel nos brinda.

Los sentidos tan jóvenes
Frente a un mundo se abren
Sin goces ni sonrisas,
Que no amanece nadie.

El afán, entre muros
Debatiéndose aislado,
Sin ayer ni mañana
Yace en un limbo extático.

La almohada no abre
Los espacios risueños;
Dice sólo, voz triste,
Que alientan allá lejos.

El tiempo en las estrellas.
Desterrada la historia.
El cuerpo se adormece
Aguardando su aurora. (p. 12)

Cernuda here employs a technique similar to that used in the landscape poems, the personification of inanimate objects to emphasise by contrast the adolescent's inactivity. He himself has little direct presence in the poem, appearing only in an allusive manner in the reference to "los sentidos" and "el cuerpo", which neatly draws attention to his lack of intellectual understanding of his experience which is contained within the limited area of sense perception. A similar reticent expression is employed in the personalised use of the verb "amanecer" to indicate the absence of a personal object for desire. The emptiness of dreams creates the melancholy condition of *fervor caído*, as desire is frustrated by its own as yet undeveloped and incoherent nature. This melancholic mood is felt particularly in the ironic tone of the first stanza where there is an almost sardonic interplay between noun and adjective, emphasised by the image of a flower in shadow, which affects even the verb "brindar" with a derisive air. The creation of an equivocal relationship between noun and adjective, as in "calma vacía", is a technique Cernuda frequently employs to express the emotional ambivalence of the adolescent. By such means he can convey a sense of dissatisfaction – the *emptiness* of the adjective – while retaining an underlying mood of confidence – the *tranquility* of the noun. The absence of an object for desire creates frustration and brings a sharp awareness of solitude, as the adolescent exists "frente a un mundo", but the symbolic dawn, the sense of future fulfilment still exists and all the poem laments is that it is yet to be achieved.

Although the inchoate yearnings of nascent desire may disconcert the adolescent, sleep can bring him a repose where he is able to relax in the confident expectation that the new day will come to reveal again a smiling universe and its reassuring sense of harmony. This is the theme of "La noche a la ventana", which ends on a note of untrammelled optimism :

Acreciente la noche
Sus sombras y su calma,
Que a su rosal la rosa
Volverá la mañana. (p. 20)

The conventional image of the rose here links with other natural images, such as the "aurora" and the "espacios risueños" of poem III, which are also used in the context of Cernuda's adolescent eroticism. Such images are an expression of the naiveté of his still undirected desire, the result of an inability to find human terms of reference for his elementary emotions. The use of the same images for desire as for the idealised vision of the world reveals the lack of differentiation between the general emotional awakening of adolescence and the specific emergence of desire. The deliberate confusion of these images is one of the ways these poems are able to evoke with such skill the amorphous sentimentalism of early adolescence.

In a moment of greater lucidity, however, the adolescent protagonist sees that the vague yearning which troubles him in the twilight hours before sleep is a desire for love, and with this realisation he rejects the only two dimensions his life knows, his room and the world seen from his window, in favour of this one dream :

Mas no quiero estos muros,
Aire infiel a sí mismo,
Ni esas ramas que cantan
En el aire dormido.

Quiero como horizonte
Para mi muda gloria
Tus brazos, que ciñendo
Mi vida la deshojan.

Vivo un solo deseo,
Un afán claro, unánime;
Afán de amor y olvido.
Yo no sé si alguien cae. (pp. 14-15)

Here is the emphatic proclamation of love's dream as the sole aim and purpose of his existence, a love so powerful that it will overwhelm him and in so doing abolish any sense of guilt, any shadow of the Fall. This is an overt identification of love with life, already implicit in images of rebirth, such as *aurora*, used for erotic dreams. But the dream of love remains only a "muda gloria", an equivocal state comparable to the *calma vacía*, except that the ambivalent relationship of noun and adjective has now become distinct paradox. The commitment to love expressed here is, nonetheless, of the greatest importance since Cernuda has totally identified himself with the dimension of *deseo* before he has had any experience of *realidad*.

Poems which express sentiments of optimism or confidence form only a small part of *Primeras poesías*, which is dominated by evocations of moments of depression, as symptomatic of adolescence as are moments of elation. The melancholic poems also employ the symbolist technique of the *paysage d'âme,* transforming the smiling Spring landscape into a dismal Autumn scene of cold, rain and falling leaves. The symbolic change of season reflects not only a different mood but is also indicative of a sharper consciousness of time and a greater awareness of being alone. When confidence wanes and the adolescent feels that the promise awakened within him seems to have moved away still further into the future, the world about him loses its attraction. The *acorde total* is broken, leaving him trapped in the claustrophobic atmosphere of his room, which is now filled with an intense emotional dissatisfaction :

Eras, instante, tan claro.
Perdidamente te alejas,
Dejando erguido al deseo
Con sus vagas ansias tercas.

Siento huir bajo el otoño
Pálidas aguas sin fuerza,
Mientras se olvidan los árboles
De las hojas que desertan.

La llama tuerce su hastío,
Sola su viva presencia,
Y la lámpara ya duerme
Sobre mis ojos en vela.

Cuán lejano todo. Muertas
Las rosas que ayer abrieran,
Aunque aliente su secreto
Por las verdes alamedas.

This is in some ways a unique poem in *Primeras poesías*; apart from being the only composition in eight-syllable *coplas*, it contains the only verb in a past tense in the book and also what appears to be the only allusion to the discovery of a personal object for desire. The disappearance of the fleeting presence that brought life to the dream of desire leaves the adolescent profoundly frustrated and overwhelmed by a feeling of impotence. This, as the image "hastío" indicates, is a more positive emotional condition than the indolent reverie of the *calma vacía,* although the adolescent still retains a passive rôle while the elements about him are made active by personification. But despite this discouragement the dream persists, hidden in the distant "verdes alamedas", which echo the "espacios risueños" of poem III.

The autumnal images – cold, clouds, rain –, which are the negative counterparts of the symbols of optimism, can on occasions acquire an air of menace, imprisoning the adolescent in the refuge of his room. In his mood of depression, the darkness of night, in particular, becomes an inimical element, a negation of the reassuring vision of the world seen from the window of his room, and the symbiosis between him and that world is broken. Trapped in this claustrophobic situation, hemmed in by the four walls of his room, he seeks to escape, but the only escape route open is a withdrawal into dreams – "la fuga hacia dentro" (p. 15). This is a retirement to those *verdes alamedas*, which have remained untouched by the autumnal images of depression, and the beginning of a characteristic reaction of evasion in the face of difficulties.

The withdrawal into dreams takes several forms. The writing of poetry itself becomes a means of giving expression and release to frustrated desire. In "El amor mueve al mundo" new life is given to a state of indolent calm, and sublimation brought to repressed desire, through the sonnet composed by the angel/poet who appears in the poem. But in moments of greater depression Cernuda sees that poetry is only a substitute for the realization of his desires, and thus the writing of poetry becomes a symptom of solitude and impotence. In the sonnet "Vidrio de agua en mano del hastío" the image, borrowed from Mallarmé, of the white sheet of paper lit by the circle of light from the lamp in the adolescent's room, symbolises the sterility of poetry, which can give only a shadow of life to the indolent dream. Poem XXII is an even clearer statement of the link between the writing of poetry and the frustrated attempts to give substance to the dreams provoked by the emotional awakening of adolescence. From the very beginning poetry was for Cernuda a means of self-expression; the last two lines of this *décima* can, in fact, provide a succinct description of all his early poems, both *Primeras poesías* and *Egloga, elegía, oda* :

Tu juventud nula, en pena
De un blanco papel vacío. (p. 23)

The withdrawal into self-contemplation, implicit in the poems on the theme of the writing of poetry, can become overt narcissism, which also proves to be a sterile occupation. For Cernuda narcissism is both the expression of self-consciousness, which it commonly is in symbolist poetry, and an image of solitude, since he becomes the object of his own dreams because of his isolation and impotence. The deeply unsatisfactory nature of the narcissistic dream is briefly exposed in the *décima* "Se goza en sueño encantado", where impotence congeals self-desire into an "inmóvil paroxismo", and in the sonnet "La desierta belleza sin oriente", which also reveals a sad awareness of the deception inherent in the adolescent's reflection in the mirror. The most extensive treatment of the Narcissus theme occurs not in *Primeras poesías* but in the "Elegía". This elegant poem in classical hendecasyllable quatrains is set in a languid, almost soporific atmosphere of indolent sensuality in the adolescent's room at dusk, where the single dim light, which shields the room from the growing darkness outside, reveals amongst the shadows the vague outline of a sleeping form. Evoked at first through the erotic image of the rose, this shadowy figure gradually emerges as an ideal of human beauty, and then vanishes to leave in solitude the adolescent of whom the figure was a narcissistic projection. The awakening from this self-centred dream provokes one of the most bitter statements of disillusion in these early poems :

¿Y qué esperar, amor? Sólo un hastío,
El amargor profundo, los despojos.

Llorando vanamente ven los ojos
Ese entreabierto lecho torpe y frío.

Tibio blancor, jardín fugaz, ardiente,
Donde el eterno fruto se tendía
Y el labio alegre, dócil lo mordía
En un vasto sopor indiferente.

De aquel sueño orgulloso en su fecundo,
Espléndido poder, una lejana
Forma dormida queda, ausente y vana
Entre la sorda soledad del mundo. (p. 33)[7]

The severity of this disenchantment at the end of the poem is alleviated by the coming of dawn and the reassuring appearance again of the world outside the adolescent's window, but the profound feeling of impotence expressed here serves to show that the retreat into dreams accentuates rather than resolves the problem of frustration.

On a few occasions also in *Primeras poesías* Cernuda can reveal a similar intensity of dissatisfaction at his solitude and the impotent dreams that are the only outlet for his stifled emotions. In poem XXI he is in his room at dusk, acutely aware of his loneliness as he shelters from a menacing, almost violent nightfall in the world outside. The discovery of his solitude is greeted with sardonic irony, and he derisively brushes aside, with a sarcastic reduplication, any possibility of consolation to be found in dreams :

Cuán vanamente atónita
Resucita de nuevo
La soledad. ¿Soñar?
Soñaremos que sueño.

Es la paz necesaria.
No se sabe; se olvida.
Otra noche acunando
Esta dicha vacía. (p. 23)

This is a concentrated statement of embittered deception, all the stronger for the self-mockery it contains; frustration has produced a mood of petulance in which the adolescent peevishly seeks the oblivion of sleep as an escape from empty, sterile dreams. The condition of "dicha vacía" is clearly related to the states of *calma vacía* and *muda gloria*, but the equivocation of noun and adjective has become a violent paradox reflecting a profound sense of impotence. Here there is no trace left of any emotional fervour or even of patient expectation for the future.

Such positive unhappiness is the third distinct mood of Cernuda's adolescence, taking its place alongside his sense of wonder and his vague, indolent

[7] The "Elegía" here strongly recalls Albanio's hallucinations in Garcilaso's "Egloga segunda", lines 895-7 and 910-15.

melancholy. This more intense feeling of frustration reaches a peak in poem XVIII, where the adolescent, alone in the claustrophobic atmosphere of his room, is overwhelmed by a desolate sense of the emotional deadlock created by his inability to realize his dreams. The direct, forceful expression of this poem produces an emphatic statement of unrelieved anguish :

> Los muros nada más.
> Yace la vida inerte,
> Sin vida, sin ruido,
> Sin palabras crueles.
>
> . . . .
>
> ¿He cerrado la puerta?
> El olvido me abre
> Sus desnudas estancias
> Grises, blancas, sin aire.
>
> Pero nadie suspira.
> Un llanto entre las manos
> Sólo. Silencio; nada.
> La oscuridad temblando. (p. 21)

The concept of "olvido" here is not consistent with that equated with love in poem VII; this is not now the abnegation of the self in desire but a prison of abortive dreams. The use of the same term as in poem VII can, however, be seen as another example of sarcasm prompted by disillusionment, although this is the anguish of a moment, a complement and not a contradiction of the adolescent's optimistic sentiments. What he is lamenting here is the frustration of that emotional potential to which he had awakened, and which has not been diminished, only repressed, by the difficulties it has encountered.

While for the most part the adolescent's retreat into dreams proves to be a sterile solution for the repression that weighs on his desires, there is one dream which does provide some solace. This is the vision of a hidden garden insulated against the outside world and free from the disturbing consciousness of time and solitude. The garden is a representation of the world as it ought to be if the promise of adolescence is to be sustained, a garden of delights where the adolescent can recapture the experience of the *acorde total.* A walled or hidden garden is a common symbolist topic, which also has a long heritage beginning with the Book of Genesis, but Cernuda's garden is not, at least initially, a lost paradise, nor a symbol of cloistered aestheticism. His garden is a private world created by him to protect his dreams against the incursions of reality. It makes its first appearance in the final poem of *Primeras poesías* and acquires a more extensive description in the "Egloga" and the "Oda".

In the "Egloga", with the aid of Garcilaso and Mallarmé, Cernuda creates an erotic landscape out of the traditional *locus amoenus* of the Renaissance eclogue. The elements of the classical idyll are all present, the place of peaceful solitude and shade, the flowers and the cool water, but, apart from the sound of a distant flute, there is no human presence. The dominant feature of this edenic scene is a rose, a "presencia pura" whose Spring-time blooms symbolise the emotional awakening of adolescence and turn the landscape into a representation of that rapturous fervour expressed in a poem like "Ninguna nube inútil". Time is foreshortened, seeming to stand still and an ecstatic indolence pervades the scene, while the pool, "gozando de sí misma en su hermosura", hints at a self-satisfied narcissism. As the title suggests, the "Egloga" is the vision of a perfect world, a dream from which all discordant elements have been excluded, and it remains as the ideal even when it is invaded by the consciousness of time, in the form of night-fall. The "Oda" is an erotic fantasy that peoples this solitary paradise with a young god, who is both a paragon of human beauty and a symbol of unfettered sensuality.[8] The fantasy is completed when the young god is absorbed by the natural world as he leaps after his reflection into a river, achieving here, most significantly, an *acorde total* through a symbolic enactment of sexual union, although there is also an element of auto-eroticism here. This is the most overtly sensual of Cernuda's early poems and one of the few that present a personalised object for desire, but it is only a dream created to match the bucolic landscape.

The *locus amoenus* of the "Egloga" brings to mind the deep attachment Cernuda showed throughout his life to a real place of peace and natural beauty – the gardens of the Alcázar in Seville. The memory of these gardens and the profound significance they had for him is clearly presented in one of the prose poems of *Ocnos*:

> Hay destinos humanos ligados con un lugar o con un paisaje. Allí en aquel jardín, sentado al borde de una fuente, soñaste un día la vida como embeleso inagotable. La amplitud del cielo te acuciaba a la acción; el alentar de las flores, las hojas y las aguas, a gozar sin remordimientos.[9]

The old Moorish gardens of the Alcázar were a real manifestation of his idealised vision of the world, a place where he could feel complete harmony between the world about him and the emotional fervour within him. The character of this garden, and of the dream it inspires, is explained in the final poem of *Primeras poesías*:

Escondido en los muros
Este jardín me brinda
Sus ramas y sus aguas
De secreta delicia.

Qué silencio. ¿Es así
El mundo? Cruza el cielo
Desfilando paisajes,
Risueño hacia lo lejos.

[8] The late José de Montes, a close friend of Cernuda during this period, has asserted that the "Oda" was inspired in part by a film starring George O'Brien. *Viva voce* to the present writer, Seville, April 1967.

[9] *Ocnos,* 54-5.

Tierra indolente. En vano
Resplandece el destino.
Junto a las aguas quietas
Sueño y pienso que vivo. (p. 24)

This secret garden is a refuge from the world outside; its walls are not like those of the adolescent's room, which enclose him in his frustration, but are there to protect the dream in the garden against the destructive contact with reality. He knows that the question "¿es así el mundo?" has a negative answer; outside the garden, it can be assumed, are the autumnal rain and cold which reflect his melancholic, repressed desires.

"Escondido en los muros" is reminiscent of a poem by Pierre Reverdy, which many years later Cernuda singled out for commentary :

> En él, un hombre que semeja buscar algún refugio, como tantas veces ocurre en los poemas de Reverdy, halla en el campo una puerta, una puerta sola, sin paredes a los lados ni habitación tras de ella; la abre, atraviesa su dintel, la cierra, cobijándose detrás, como al fin seguro. En ese personaje adivino al poeta, acosado por algo o en busca de algo, y creyéndose de momento protegido del mundo y contra el mundo, de su terror y de su atracción.[10]

The ambivalent attitude towards the world described here immediately recalls Cernuda's own experience referred to in 'Palabras antes de una lectura', giving these comments a particular significance that illuminates his personal haven from the world. His garden is a place where the duality of attraction and hostility to the world can be resolved, where the conflict of *realidad* and *deseo* can apparently be eliminated, but this is also in Cernuda's case the product of wishful thinking. The hidden garden is merely another paradigm of the world as it ought to be, a surrogate for the benign reality he has failed to discover, and in the melancholy irony of the *cogito* "sueño y pienso que vivo" he reveals his awareness that this is no substantive solution to his problem. However, the image of the hidden garden, the creation of a private world of dreams where the promise of adolescence can be sustained, does indicate Cernuda's commitment to the dimension of his life he was later to call *deseo*. This is an early sign of a refusal to compromise the dream with reality, should reality not prove to be equal to the ideal.

The adolescent vision of the world evoked with such skill and sensitivity in *Primeras poesías* and *Egloga, elegía, oda* is the basis for all subsequent developments in Cernuda's attitude towards life. It is in adolescence that he experiences the sense of harmony with the world which is his existential ideal, and it is also then that he acquires the awareness of solitude, which disturbs that harmony. The adolescent's indolent existence in the melancholic half-light of dreams establishes one of the most characteristic postures of the mature Cernuda. Perhaps the most important element in this adolescent experience is its innocence, the awakening to the dream of *deseo* in ignorance of the reality in which it must

[10] 'Recuerdo de Pierre Reverdy', *Poesía y literatura II,* 201-2. The poem to which Cernuda refers is "Belle étoile", *Les Epaves du Ciel* (Paris, 1924), 24.

be realized. In the world of Cernuda's adolescent poems the only objective reality is the environment of his room, since the world beyond his window, whether of promise or of menace, is a reflection of his emotions. The dream is thus nurtured in a restricted setting where there is little external stimulus and the dream must live off itself in the form of narcissistic self-desire or take refuge in a hidden garden. But the pressure of frustration makes this innocence difficult to sustain – Cernuda himself records that he felt unable in *Egloga, elegía, oda* to give adequate expression to "mucha parte viva y esencial" in his personality (*PL*, 241) – and the emotional constraint of the adolescent poems is soon swept aside by the flood of experience encountered in the real world beyond the window of the young Cernuda's room.

The Discovery of Reality

Cernuda leaves behind the dreamy, sheltered existence of his adolescence when he leaves Seville in 1928. This entry into the world gave him at first an exhilarating sense of freedom, but he also brought with him a growing feeling of alienation resulting from the need to make his way alone in the world where he felt that any occupation or profession would compromise what had by this time become a total commitment to poetry. He has also alluded to an unspecified deeper reason why he should feel alienated (*PL*, 242), and the course his poetry takes suggests that this was a conscious awareness of his homosexuality, an awareness fostered perhaps by his reading of Gide and brought into the open by the change of environment. Commenting much later on the transformation in Gide's attitude to life, as expressed in *Les Nourritures terrestres*, Cernuda emphasised the close relationship this had with Gide's changed circumstances :

> Semejante transformación tal vez exigía para realizarse la mudanza exterior de ambiente, ya que es éste quien a veces propone y hace inevitable algún gesto nuestro latente, que sin la modificación del contorno acaso nunca sugiera a luz, tanto más si es íntimo y profundo.[11]

Cernuda's new surroundings in Madrid and Toulouse may not have been as exotic as Gide's Algiers but their effect was much the same, the change of circumstance brought a clearer understanding of the nebulous desire of adolescence and released the inhibitions he had felt constrain him in *Egloga, elegía, oda*. However, this clarification of desire brought only deeper frustration, since the fulfillment of that desire still remained beyond his grasp. The depression provoked by this increase in self-awareness is clearly expressed in a letter written from Málaga shortly after Cernuda had left Seville :

> Vuelvo otra vez a la tristeza. Verdaderamente no puedo vivir sin tener al lado algo o alguien por quien sentir afecto. Y estoy solo . . . Pero no estoy en mi sitio; lo siento físicamente y espiritualmente. Lo mismo me ocurrirá en Madrid . . . Ya no puedo volver atrás. Esto no se lo diría a Salinas; ya sé lo que me diría; '¡Falta de vitalidad!'. No lo creo así. Sé lo que me falta; pero mejor sería que no lo supiera.[12]

[11] 'André Gide', *Poesía y literatura*, 126.

[12] Letter to Higinio Capote of 6-IX-28. F. López Estrada, 'Estudios y cartas de Cernuda', *Insula*, no. 207, 16.

Here is a definite statement that Cernuda's indolence is the result of frustration, and, in the final phrase, a tacit admission that he now recognises the nature of his desire. The loneliness of adolescence has developed into a feeling of spiritual exile.

Cernuda's two collections of poems influenced by surrealism, *Un río, un amor* and *Los placeres prohibidos*, give voice to this mood of intense frustration and record the painful experiences he encountered in the search to realize his adolescent dreams. For the first time he appears to have had the opportunity to translate his erotic aspirations into reality, but the result was a cruel deception of his innocent desire as he discovered that antagonistic dimension of *realidad*. Both these books are concerned in part with what seems to have been an experience of unrequited love, or at least of a failed dream of love. The title of *Un río, un amor* indicates an experience of love and the titles of poems like "No intentemos el amor nunca" and "Dejadme solo" suggest that this is an unhappy experience, perhaps the "amor menospreciado" referred to in one poem (p. 47).[13] This collection is the product of what in "La canción del oeste" is described as "Furia color de amor/Amor color de olvido" (p. 60). In *Los placeres prohibidos* there is a clear statement of a spurned love :

> Estaba tendido y tenía entre mis brazos un cuerpo como seda. Lo besé en los labios, porque el río pasaba por debajo. Entonces se burló de mi amor. (p. 70)

The fact that most, if not all, the poems of this latter book were written in the space of little more than a fortnight in April 1931 points firmly to the impact of a particular event or experience, and there is external evidence that Cernuda was, at about this time, "mortificado por culpa de un gran cariño".[14]

The disillusionment of the erotic dream he had so carefully nurtured bewildered Cernuda and provoked a violent response of anguish and impotent rage. In this disturbed, alienated state of mind he found a ready sympathy with the violent subversion of the French surrealists, who also offered him a mode of expression capable of containing the emotional convulsion that overtook him. Cernuda has been more explicit than many of his contemporaries about the nature and intention of his surrealist poetry, explaining that he sought a means of giving direct expression to his experience, even to experience of an apparently trivial kind :

> Quería yo hallar en poesía el "equivalente correlativo" para lo que experimentaba, por ejemplo, al ver a una criatura hermosa . . . o al oir un aire de *jazz* . . . Al lector que estime inadecuado a mi experiencia su resultado

[13] The title, *Un río, un amor,* evokes echoes of Eluard's *L'Amour la Poésie* (Paris, 1929). However, the poems, "Drama o puerta cerrada" and "Duerme muchacho" were published under the title, in English, "A Little River, a Little Love" in *Nueva Revista,* no. 6 (1930), 3. This English title would appear to be the echo of a popular song.

[14] C. Morla Lynch, *En España con Federico García Lorca* (Madrid, 1958), 232. See Appendix for the dates of composition of these poems. The prose poems of *Los placeres prohibidos* were not published until their inclusion in the third edition of *La Realidad y el Deseo* (Mexico, 1958). They were, however, written at the same time as the other poems of this collection, letter from Cernuda to the present writer of 26-II-62.

> emotivo, y frívolo éste además, al tratarse sólo, al menos en una de las instancias que mencioné, de una experiencia consistente en oir un aire de *jazz*, le recordaré aquellas palabras de Rimbaud, cuyo sentido creo posible comparar al de mi experiencia : "un título de *vaudeville* erguía espantos ante mí". (*PL*, 242)

This statement reveals that Cernuda found himself in a state of hypersensitivity in which trivial objects and phenomena could acquire extraordinary emotional significance. This condition of heightened emotional response can be seen in its most striking form in poems like "Nevada" which incorporate the titles of films or popular songs in a way that Cernuda relates to a painter's use of collages (*PL*, 246), although the technique is also reminiscent of surrealist *objets trouvés*. However, the nature of this hypersensitive condition is best explained by Cernuda himself with the quotation from Rimbaud, which comes from the section entitled "Délires" in *Une Saison en enfer*. The paragraph containing this phrase reads in full as follows :

> Je m'habituai à l'hallucination simple : je voyais très-franchement une mosquée à la place d'une usine, une école de tambours faite par des anges, des calèches sur les routes du ciel, un salon au fond d'un lac; les monstres, les mystères; un titre de vaudeville dressait des épouvantes devant moi.

Cernuda was experiencing his own delirious descent into a private hell, seeing a world inhabited by monsters and subjected to the distortions of a nightmare. I suggest that his emotional turmoil, and the consequent state of hypersensitivity, leads in him to a similar hallucinatory vision as that described by Rimbaud. I further suggest that Cernuda substitutes this principle of hallucination for the normal surrealist principle of automatic writing, although the hallucinatory principle may produce very similar results in the poetry. Cernuda's surrealist poems are closer in spirit to the example of Rimbaud "le voyant" than they are to any of the French surrealists with the possible exception of Eluard. The light thrown on Cernuda's surrealist influenced poetry by the example of Rimbaud could also perhaps be used to illuminate the nature of the similar poetry of Alberti and Lorca, although I would not suggest here any direct contact with the author of *Illuminations*.

In Cernuda's statement about his surrealist poetry quoted above the reference to the "equivalente correlativo" is a translation of T. S. Eliot's concept of the objective correlative, another idea which reveals much about the nature of this type of poetry.[15] The allusion to Eliot dates from some thirty years after *Un río, un amor* was written, by which time Cernuda had acquired a profound knowledge of English poetry, and it may be assumed that his reference to the objective correlative is the product of a mature understanding. T. S. Eliot defines the objective correlative as a device that gives immediate expression to an emotion,

[15] The allusion to Eliot has been confirmed by Cernuda in a letter to the present writer of 21-V-62.

producing a gain in intensity at the expense of clarity.[16] It is such qualities of immediacy and intensity which Cernuda needs to convey the violent emotional upheaval he has undergone, and which he finds in the poetry of the French surrealists.

The surrealist disregard of the logical associations of language would find a ready sympathy with Cernuda in his emotional turmoil, since his ability for rational response had been overwhelmed by violent feelings of anger and frustration. Unlike the French surrealists who had consciously sought to will themselves into a state where the controlling function of the intellect was relaxed, Cernuda's emotional disorder has created that condition of hypersensitivity which enables him to exploit the mental process of free association in the form of the objective correlative. I would term this use of non-rational techniques of expression "natural" or "necessary" surrealism, as opposed to the "forced" surrealism of so many French poets. What is more, within the appearance of irrationality in his poetry written in this manner, Cernuda, through the technique of the objective correlative, was able to retain a framework of emotional logic while rational control was thrust aside by the violence of his feelings. He was thus able to avoid the fragmented, incoherent emotionalism, which too often occurs as a result of the uncontrolled liberation of subconscious material in French surrealist poetry. Cernuda's poems influenced by surrealism require from the reader a suspension of belief in the normal conceptual links between words and in the rational development of ideas; they have their own emotional logic, which, if accepted, turns what may appear as a series of disjointed images into a specific expression of an emotional state, even though this may be no more than a scream of pain or a cry of anger.

This is a poetry of private and often seemingly arbitrary symbols, yet the images are rarely without a discernible emotive significance. The poems are complex but not hermetic, the result of an attempt to produce intensity at the expense of clarity, so that the poems may contain the violent emotional disturbance that has broken down the ordering process reason normally imposes on experience. The technique of free association, of the objective correlative, which Cernuda learnt from surrealism, is perhaps the only mode of expression which could give full voice to the bewildered welter of violent reactions provoked by the shattering of the adolescent illusions. Moreover, in the subversive spirit of surrealism he found the freedom publicly to declare his homosexuality, and the release he was thus able to give to this vital element of his character marks a decisive step in Cernuda's journey of self-discovery.

The clash of dream and reality is presented by Cernuda as an unexpected,

16 "The only way of expressing emotion in the form of art is by finding an 'objective correlative'; in other words, a set of objects, a situation, a chain of events which shall be the formula of that *particular* emotion; such that when the external facts, which must terminate in sensory experience, are given, the emotion is immediately evoked." T. S. Eliot, *Selected Essays,* second edition (London, 1953), 145. "In some minds certain memories, both from reading and from life, become charged with emotional significance. All these are used, so that intensity is gained at the expense of clarity." From an unpublished lecture by Eliot on Joyce's *Ulysses, apud* F. O. Matthiessen, *The Achievement of T. S. Eliot,* second edition (New York, 1947), 56.

violently destructive catastrophe, which is reflected in the frequent use in these poems of images of mutilation. The life-force of desire has been crushed, cut down like a flower at the moment of blooming :

Alguien cortó la piedra en flor,
Sin que pudiera el mundo
Incendiar la tristeza. (p. 50)

In this alogical compression of images learnt from surrealism is a striking statement of the experience of the dream's failure : the flower of desire that seemed to offer life to the inanimate poet/stone was destroyed with such suddenness by a mysterious personal agent that the event passed unnoticed in the world. The unforeseen quality of this tragedy is an indication of Cernuda's ingenuousness; he had approached the possibility of love blithely expecting that his adolescent dreams would be fulfilled only to find an unyielding reality that rebuffed his questing desire. The instinctive, innocent approach to love, and the painful vulnerability created by this innocence, is evoked with quiet sadness in the poem "No decía palabras" from *Los placeres prohibidos* :

No decía palabras,
Acercaba tan sólo un cuerpo interrogante,
Porque ignoraba que el deseo es una pregunta
Cuya respuesta no existe,
Una hoja cuya rama no existe,
Un mundo cuyo cielo no existe. (p. 69)

The expression of these lines deliberately harks back to *Primeras poesías*, using the same natural images for desire to give greater poignancy to the transition from hope to disillusionment. The inquiring body is the same as that of adolescence, still without a proper intellectual understanding of the desire motivating it, but the smiling landscape of youthful dreams has broken into meaningless fragments. There is a strong continuity of imagery with *Primeras poesías* in these poems but the adolescent symbols are negated or degraded to become bitter expressions of blighted hope. Thus the moon, which in *Primeras poesías* symbolised the promise of love, becomes now a travesty of the ideal beyond the reach of the poet's outstretched hands, while these, with a surrealist disregard for logic, dissolve into tears of anguish :

Lejos canta el oeste,
Aquel oeste que las manos antaño
Creyeron apresar como el aire a la luna;
Mas la luna es madera, las manos se liquidan
Gota a gota, idénticas a lágrimas. (p. 60)[17]

Cernuda's reaction to the failure of his dreams to live up to reality varies from a bemused emotional lassitude, such as that skilfully evoked in "Estoy cansado" and "El caso del pájaro asesinado", to wild and bitter iconoclasm, as

[17] Cf. the final stanza of poem XIV of *Primeras poesías*.

in the ironically entitled poem "¿Son todos felices?". Between these extremes of tranquility and violence is a stupefied mood in which his emotions have been numbed and bewildered by the shock of the dreams' collapse. This numbness is superficially similar to the condition of indolence in earlier poems, but it is due now to the crushing experience of reality, not to the lack of emotional stimuli. The commitment, made in adolescence, of his life to the dream of love, means that when the dream fails he is reduced to a state of lifelessness. His blood is frozen in his veins and he is turned into an empty body, the spiritually dead shell of a man whose soul has been destroyed, fleeing aimlessly through a nightmare world as his identity is lost.[18] A sense of being trapped appears in a number of poems; he is shut out in a city street or more often imprisoned within himself, cut off from communication with other people by the very failure of his dreams. In "Telarañas cuelgan de la razón" the image of walls associated with his adolescence acquires metaphysical proportions as he addresses the ambivalently attractive and implacable person who is the cause of his anguish:

Tú nada sabes de ello,
Tú estás allá, cruel como el día;
El día, esa luz que abraza estrechamente un triste muro,
Un muro, ¿no comprendes?,
Un muro frente al cual estoy solo. (p. 67)[19]

The stunned desolation produced by the collision of dreams with the wall of reality is treated in some detail in the poem "Cuerpo en pena", whose title is an image of thwarted desire. Cernuda here uses for himself the symbol of a drowned man, a body in torment swept away by the river of love in *Un río, un amor*. He becomes a living corpse shut away from the world in a silent, colourless limbo in which he is condemned to wander, like an automaton, in a perpetual night of bewildered desolation. This poem expresses forcefully the state of shock provoked by the disillusionment of those innocent dreams of youth:

Lentamente el ahogado recorre sus dominios
Donde el silencio quita su apariencia a la vida.
Transparentes llanuras inmóviles le ofrecen
Arboles sin colores y pájaros callados.

Las sombras indecisas alargándose tiemblan,
Mas el viento no mueve sus alas irisadas;
Si el ahogado sacude sus lívidos recuerdos,
Halla un golpe de luz, la memoria del aire.

Un vidrio denso tiembla delante de las cosas,
Un vidrio que despierta formas color de olvido;

[18] The image of the empty body is found in both Alberti's *Sobre los ángeles* and Lorca's *Poeta en Nueva York*; it also evokes a distinct parallel with Eliot's "The Hollow Men", although I do not suggest a direct influence of Eliot here.

[19] The image of the wall here brings a renewed echo of Reverdy, in particular of "Autres Jockeys Alcooliques": "La situation d'un homme devant un mur infini/Sans aucune affiche." *Les Epaves du Ciel*, 144.

Olvidos de tristeza, de un amor, de la vida,
Ahogados como un cuerpo sin luz, sin aire, muerto.

. . . . . .

Su insomnio maquinal el ahogado pasea.
El silencio impasible sonríe en sus oídos.
Inestable vacío sin alba ni crepúsculo,
Monótona tristeza, emoción en ruinas. (pp. 42-43)[20]

This poem takes the symbolist landscape that reflected the hopes of adolescence and subjects it to a cruel distortion; in particular, this dead world is a bitter parody of that hidden garden where the adolescent had formulated his dreams of the future.[21] This is the inscape of emotional torment, a torment made worse by Cernuda's acquisition, with his disillusioning experience, of a faculty of memory. The memories of the dream before it failed provide another meaning for the term "olvido" : the bitter memories of things dead. "Cuerpo en pena" is a description of the havoc created in Cernuda's inner world by the shattering of his hopes; he has been left bemused, incapable of coherent feeling. The phrase "emoción en ruinas" graphically summarises the disastrous effect of the first contact of his dreams with reality.

The external world, whose discovery is partly the reason for this violent crisis, makes only fleeting appearances in these poems, but it is nonetheless clear that Cernuda is now living in an environment different from the refuge of his room in adolescence. He is in an urban situation, alone in the crowd of a city, or wandering, lost and homeless, through the streets. There are other inhabitants of this desolate world, but they are subject to a similar fate, reduced to a state of living death like the "cortejo de fantasmas" in "No sé qué nombre darle en mis sueños" or the beggars in "Linterna roja". This is the world of a nightmare, as in the poem with the disorientating title "Decidme anoche" :

Sí, la tierra está sola, bien sola con sus muertos,
Al acecho quizá de inerte transeúnte
Que sin gestos arrostre su látigo nocturno;
Mas ningún cuerpo viene ciegamente soñando.

El dolor también busca, errante entre la noche,
Tras la sombra fugaz de algún gozo indefenso;
Y sus pálidos pasos callados se entrelazan,
Incesante fantasma con mirada de hastío.

[20] "Cuerpo en pena" is closely linked with Eluard's poem "Armure de proie le parfum noir rayonne" from *L'Amour la Poésie,* a book with which Cernuda was familiar since he translated some of the poems in *Litoral,* no. 9 (1929), 28-30. Cf. the last stanza quoted above and these phrases from Eluard's poem: "les mouvements machinaux de l'insomnie" and "son émotion est en morceaux", Eluard, *Choix de Poèmes* (Paris, 1964), 101.

[21] Cf. "Estoy instalado, al fin, en un barrio distante; barrio rodeado de jardines, de parques silenciosos. Hace frío; hay niebla y lluvia." Letter from Cernuda in Toulouse to Higinio Capote dated 17-XI-28. López Estrada, *Insula,* no. 207, 16.

Fantasma que desfila prisionero de nadie,
Falto de voz, de manos, apariencia sin vida,
Como llanto impotente por las ramas ahogado
O repentina fuga estrellada en un muro. (p. 46)

The hostile, violent world of basilisks which destroy the innocent and the defenceless is a horrific development of the symbolist *paysage d'âme* now seen through the distorting prism of disillusionment. The process of activating the landscape, used in *Primeras poesías* to indicate the adolescent's separation from the world, here creates monstruous forces, which are the projection of Cernuda's anguish and whose strength and power totally overwhelm him.

In such a nightmare world the dream of love could not survive and one by one the symbols of promise in adolescence are corrupted; the clear blue sky becomes a "cielo engañoso" (p. 48), or a "cielo de vergüenza" (p. 62), and the "futuras auroras" of which he had dreamed are now "remendadas como harapos de rey" (p. 56). The sense of deception in these poems is strong and bitter; an amputated plaster hand is sardonically labelled "la verdad del amor" (p. 82), while in the poem which has for a title that significant injunction "Dejadme solo", the truth of love is roundly declared to be a lie :

En cuanto a la mentira, basta decirle 'quiero'
Para que brote entre las piedras
Su flor, que en vez de hojas luce besos,
Espinas en lugar de espinas. (p. 58)

The flower of love blooming amongst the stones, which elsewhere was said to have been cut down by disillusionment, is here revealed to be itself an illusion. The innocent dream has been destroyed by reality, and the rose of the "Egloga" bristles with the thorns of frustration. These lines are a striking example of the multiple image created by the surrealistic suppression of the conceptual links between the various elements of the image. The basic idea is a simple image, the flower of love has grown thorns, but the associations which spring from this are combined with a disregard for logical relationships; love is a lie which becomes a flower growing on stony ground, here both the unyielding environment and the inanimate body given life by love, whose leaves, in accord with the central conceit, become kisses, but the thorns turn only into thorns, revealing a disillusioned awareness that they were there all the time and that the truth of love never did exist. By such processes of poetic logic, where emotional associations replace rational links, Cernuda creates that expression which gains intensity at the expense of clarity, as well as remarkable beauty.

In the state of shock at the deception and mutilation of his dreams Cernuda can see only one hope, the recapture of his lost innocence :

Si mis ojos se cierran es para hallarte en sueños,
Detrás de la cabeza,
Detrás del mundo esclavizado,
En ese país perdido
Que un día abandonamos sin saberlo. (p. 56)

One such attempt to rediscover the lost world where dreams are still possible is made by the drowned man in "Cuerpo en pena" who tries to flee from his prison of anguish to a distant paradise, which he can only describe as "la flor sin nombre" (p. 43).[22] In other poems this dreamland is fixed in exotic places culled from the cinema or from popular songs, places like Daytona and Nevada, or the Southern States of America in "Quisiera estar solo en el sur", inspired by a fox-trot of the time, and Tahiti in "Sombras blancas", occasioned by one of the earliest talking films (*PL*, 245-6).[23] Cernuda has recalled how his interest in America, fostered by his liking for the cinema, was linked with the idea that the United States at that time represented an "ideal juvenil, sonriente y atlético" (*PL*, 247). Also, he had been fascinated when a child by the names and pictures of foreign places he had found in the books of his father's library. This had awakened in him a desire to travel which, in his adolescence, had become a belief that fulfilment for his frustrated desires could be found in these distant places (*PL*, 278).[24] The exotic paradises which appear in some of the poems of *Un río, un amor* are thus linked with Cernuda's adolescent experience and are an attempt to find an environment where dreams can be re-established with the innocence they possessed prior to their disillusionment.

Because of their distance from the nightmare in which Cernuda now exists these far-off dreamlands are immunized against the effects of disillusion. In the American South of "Quisiera estar solo en el sur" the elements of rain, fog and darkness, which menace him in his desolate world of failure, are totally devoid of any hostility because they are part of an edenic situation still untouched by the emotional Fall. Such distant paradises are above all places where love is still possible. In "Sombras blancas" the Tahitian lovers on the beach are in a state of beatitude, unaware of "el ardiente color de la vida" (p. 42) and of the world outside their paradise, inhabited by the living dead who have lost love. In "Daytona" the light of love pervades everything, dispelling the clouds of sadness and banishing the threat of time. In "Nevada" the images of pain are reversed, tears become symptoms of happiness, and sadness, with a delicate surrealist sleight of logic, is made to melt away. The result is a joyous world where emotions are unoppressed and love flourishes exultantly :

[22] At this point "Cuerpo en pena" contains a further echo of Eluard's poem "Armure de proie le parfum noir rayonne" (see note 20 above). Cf. Cernuda's lines "En plena mar al fin, sin rumbo, a toda vela; / Hacia lo lejos, más, hacia la flor sin nombre," with Eluard: "En pleine mer dans des bras délicats / Aux beaux jours les vagues a toutes voiles", *Choix de Poèmes,* 101. The voyage to a dream world also awakens echoes of Mallarmé's "Brise Marine". Ricardo Gullón, *Asomante,* no. 2 (1950), 45, relates "Cuerpo en pena" to Rimbaud's "Bateau Ivre", but curiously interprets the "ahogado" as a symbol of the common man.

[23] See also for the source of "Quisiera estar solo en el sur" Cernuda's letter to Higinio Capote dated 2-VIII-29, López Estrada, *Insula,* no. 207, 17. This poem has been erroneously assumed to refer to Andalusia, Gullón, *Asomante,* no. 2 (1950), 44, and J. L. Cano, *Poesía española del siglo XX* (Madrid, 1960), 315.

The film which inspired "Sombras blancas" was "White Shadows in the South Seas", begun by Robert Flaherty but finished by W. S. Van Dyck. See Herman G. Weinberg, 'The Legion of Lost Films' *Sight and Sound* (Autumn 1962), 172. I am indebted to Dr. G. W. Connell for this last item of information.

[24] See also "El viaje", *Ocnos,* 75-8.

Las lágrimas sonríen,
La tristeza es de alas,
Y las alas, sabemos,
Dan amor inconstante.

Los árboles abrazan árboles,
Una canción besa otra canción;
Por los caminos de hierro
Pasa el dolor y la alegría.

Siempre hay nieve dormida
Sobre otra nieve, allá en Nevada. (pp. 44-5)[25]

The connection of such dream worlds with the cinema, in "Sombras blancas" and "Nevada", underlines the escapist element in these fantasies. The cinema is a refuge for the lonely man and provides him with ready made dreams when his own have failed. These distant paradises are, in effect, a variation on the theme of the hidden garden, a further example of retreat into a private world protected from the intrusions of reality.

The longing to escape to distant places untouched by disillusion is a piece of wishful-thinking that does little to relieve the despair provoked by the failure of the dream in Cernuda's present environment. Indeed, such is the depth of this despair that in a number of poems the far-off paradises lose their enchantment. Shock and despair breed the thought that the dreams of adolescence were incapable of fulfilment and that their pursuit must lead to inevitable disaster. The beggars who inhabit the doss-house in "Linterna roja" have been reduced to this state of degradation because they sought an impossible ideal, "la flor jamás abierta" (p. 53), which brings an immediate resonance of "la flor sin nombre" imagined by the drowned man in "Cuerpo en pena". This bitter disaffection with all dreams spills over into the exotic places where Cernuda had hoped love could still flourish. Virginia in "Carne de mar" is a place of violent emotional anguish and mutilated dreams, and in "Durango" the city is laid waste by hunger, fear and cold while its youthful defenders are reduced to a state of impotence.[26] The disillusionment of distant dream worlds is presented in "No intentemos el amor nunca" as a fable with the sea as protagonist. The sea is bored and suffering from insomnia, and so decides to go far away to find someone to comfort it. After passing through a world in torment, like that in "Decidme anoche", it reaches the exotic cities of "Cielo Sereno", "Colorado"

[25] I disagree with the interpretation of this poem in C. B. Morris, *A Generation of Spanish Poets 1920-1936* (Cambridge, 1969), 200. Morris has not appreciated the significance, in the second stanza quoted above, of the echo of Bécquer's *rima* IX:

la llama en derredor del tronco ardiente
por besar a otra llama se desliza,
y hasta el sauce inclinándose a su peso
al río que lo besa, vuelve un beso.

[26] "Durango" is another poem associated with the cinema, although Cernuda was unable to remember the title of the film with which it is related. Letter from Cernuda to the present writer dated 13-XII-61.

and "Glaciar del Infierno" where innocence still prevails, but discovers that these places can offer no fulfilment for love and so turns back to take refuge in complete oblivion.[27] This poem, with its astringent title and the bitterly ironic use of the tone of a children's story, is a parable of despair : the dream of love is impossible anywhere and the only solution is to withdraw from the possibility of emotional involvement. This prostration of all hope is expressed with more vehemence in "La canción del oeste", where, after an evocation of a nightmare world and the anguish of failed love, the poem ends with a rejection of all dreams and even of the possibility of a future love :

> Olvidemos pues todo, incluso al mismo oeste;
> Olvidemos que un día las miradas de ahora,
> Lucirán a la noche, como tantos amantes,
> Sobre el lejano oeste,
> Sobre amor más lejano. (p. 60)

This embittered despair introduces a cynical, iconoclastic element into Cernuda's reaction to his disastrous encounter with reality. In *Un río, un amor* he produces a macabre distortion of a lullaby, "Duerme, muchacho", where the traditional elements of a cradle song are replaced by images of violence and torment. In "De qué país", from *Los placeres prohibidos*, a new-born child is presented with gifts by the shades gathered around its cradle; these are mostly gifts of pain, among them desire, which will bring corruption and destroy the child's innocence. Cernuda's caustic advice to the child is to die before it is overtaken by the horrors of life. This is the crabbed comment of a man who feels himself condemned to live alone in an alien world, "aparte, como naipe cuya baraja se ha perdido" (p. 73). These acrimonious sentiments are vented with greatest violence in the poem with the sarcastic title "¿Son todos felices?". In impotent fury he seeks the total destruction of the world he now blames for having destroyed him :

> El honor de vivir con honor gloriosamente,
> El patriotismo hacia la patria sin nombre,
> El sacrificio, el deber de labios amarillos,
> No valen un hierro devorando
> Poco a poco algún cuerpo triste a causa de ellos mismos.
>
> Abajo pues la virtud, el orden, la miseria;
> Abajo todo, todo, excepto la derrota,
> Derrota hasta los dientes, hasta ese espacio helado
> De una cabeza abierta en dos a través de soledades,
> Sabiendo nada más que vivir es estar a solas con la muerte.
>
> (pp. 60-1)

The spleen here is directed against the values of "respectable" society – honour, patriotism, self-sacrifice, duty – which are seen as the cause of love's failure.

[27] "No intentemos el amor nunca" bears a striking resemblance to a poem by Vicente Risco, "O poema do mar", published in *Alfar*, no. 26 (1923), 11.

Here is a sign, albeit still confused as a result of the emotional mutilation Cernuda has suffered, of an awareness that social hostility was a reason for the catastrophe that has overtaken his adolescent dreams. A similar despair and a similar revulsion for the conventional values of society also inspire the calculated nihilism of the statement Cernuda contributed as a preface to his poems in Gerardo Diego's famous anthology of 1932 :

> No valía la pena de ir poco a poco olvidando la realidad para que ahora fuese a recordarla, y ante qué gentes. La detesto como detesto todo lo que a ella pertenece : mis amigos, mi familia, mi país.
>
> No sé nada, no quiero nada, no espero nada. Y si aún pudiera esperar algo, sólo sería morir allí donde no hubiese penetrado aún esta grotesca civilización que envanece a los hombres.[28]

The violence of such rebellious sentiments, and the general emotional violence of these surrealist poems, after the reticence of *Primeras poesías*, are an indication of the degree of shock Cernuda has experienced. The voice of rebellion is a new element in his poetry, but this does not represent, as has been suggested, the acquisition of a more distinctive personality.[29] The crisis of *Un río, un amor* and *Los placeres prohibidos* is a product of the naiveté of those adolescent dreams created in innocence of the reality he has now so painfully discovered. The conflict between *realidad* and *deseo* has begun in earnest, as Cernuda, in a bewildering turmoil of emotion, loses his innocence :

> Derriban gigantes de los bosques para hacer un durmiente,
> Derriban los instintos como flores,
> Deseos como estrellas,
> Para hacer sólo un hombre con su estigma de hombre. (p. 55)

The Restoration of the Dream

In *Los placeres prohibidos* the failure of the erotic dream is no longer the unforeseen catastrophe it had been in *Un río, un amor*, and, although Cernuda loses none of his embittered anguish, he is more able to view what has happened to him with some detachment. His second collection in the surrealist manner is in part an inquest on the failure of love, an inquiry into why it failed and an attempt to protect the dream of love from further failure. Also in this book the voice of rebellion gains in strength and clarity, as Cernuda, in deliberate defiance of social convention, exalts the forbidden pleasures of his homosexuality.

The mood of inquiry, and the conclusion reached by it, is the subject of the survey of life made in "He venido para ver", where an enumeration of strange or absurd elements is presented as a statement about the purpose of existence. This poem is imbued with feeling of complete unreality and a profound emotional lassitude prompted by a sense that life is futile and meaningless. Cernuda

[28] G. Diego, *Poesía española contemporánea (1901-1934)*, third edition (Madrid, 1966), 658.

[29] A. Serrano Plaja, 'Notas a la poesía de Luis Cernuda', *El Sol*, 17-V-36, 2. P. Salinas, *Literatura española siglo XX* (Mexico, 1949), 220.

recognises that the only thing which can give meaning to this impotent existence is love; love was the ultimate reason for his coming into the world and his failure to find it has reduced his life to a nugatory state. In "He venido para ver" Cernuda is still dazed, but he is in a condition that might be termed the calm after the storm where he is more capable of investigating what has happened to him.[30] In the vacuum left after the violent emotional disturbance has passed he can try to piece together the shattered fragments of his dream of love, but before he can succeed in this task he must try to discover what went wrong with the dream.

The poem "Veía sentado" is a fine example of this analytical mood where he looks back on his experience and in particular turns his gaze to the hidden garden of adolescence where he had dreamt beside the still waters and so unknowingly begun the conflict that has overwhelmed him. The garden, although still perfectly recognisable, is seen through a veil of disillusionment; it has been overrun by a listlessness which softens the violence of the surrealist images now describing it and creates a delicate atmosphere of sadness :

Veía sentado junto al agua
Con vago ademán de olvido,
Veía las hojas, los días, los semblantes,
El fondo siempre pálido del cielo,
Conversando indiferentes entre ellos mismos.

. . . . .

Veía reinos perdidos o quizá ganados,
Veía mi juventud ni ganada ni perdida,
Veía mi cuerpo distante, tan extraño
Como yo mismo, allá en extraña hora.

Veía los canosos muros disgustados
Murmurando entre dientes sus vagas blasfemias,
Veía más allá de los muros
El mundo como can satisfecho,
Veía al inclinarme sobre la verdad
Un cuerpo que no era el cuerpo mío.

Subiendo hasta mí mismo
Aquí vive desde entonces,
Mientras aguardo que tu propia presencia
Haga inútil ese triste trabajo
De ser yo solo el amor y su imagen. (pp. 82-3)

In this disenchanted return to the gardens of the Alcázar in Seville, the *hortus deliciarum* of youth has acquired some of the characteristics of that hostile world Cernuda had found waiting for him outside the garden. The landscape has lost its vitality, its sense of potential, and its ability to relate to the poet's

[30] See J. Ferraté, *La operación de leer* (Barcelona, 1962), 220-4, for an excellent analysis of this poem.

aspirations; the walls which had once seemed to protect him from the outside world have now themselves taken on a vague air of menace. This faded vision of the walled garden is a powerful expression of the effect of love's failure, for this was a central image of the adolescent dream, a symbol of the ideal harmony between self and world that he had sought to find through love. He even feels alienated from his own youth, which is now just a foresaken promise lost in a failed dream. The purpose behind this survey of the garden's pallid shadow in the past is to see what can be salvaged from that wrecked dream. What has survived is the image seen in the pool, which is not just a narcissistic reflection but an image of the desire born in that garden. The image that has remained is still only a dream, desire without an object, imprisoned within Cernuda until such time as it can be made incarnate in a lover, and for the moment he remains in a state of suspended animation, not dissimilar to his adolescent limbo, although now there is no fervorous expectation for the future. It is, however, most significant that the term *verdad* should be used for the image of desire, when this is compared to the cynical *mentira* applied to love in "Dejadme solo" in *Un río, un amor*. Despite the all-pervading sadness in "Veía sentado", the ideal of desire has been rescued from total disillusionment, even though it is once again confined to dreams.

In poems where the tone of bemused sadness is replaced by the violent voice of rebellion Cernuda seeks to lay bare the cause of the crushing disillusionment he has undergone. In "Diré como nacisteis" he concludes that the failure of the dreams of desire was the result of his innocent ignorance of the corruption and restricting conventions of society:

No sabía los límites impuestos,
Límites de metal o papel,
Ya que el azar le hizo abrir los ojos bajo una luz tan alta,
Adonde no llegan realidades vacías,
Leyes hediondas, códigos, ratas de paisajes derruidos.

Extender entonces la mano
Es hallar una montaña que prohibe,
Un bosque impenetrable que niega,
Un mar que traga adolescentes rebeldes. (p. 66)

In this rationalisation of the dream's failure, where the nightmare creatures of Cernuda's disturbed emotions are now revealed as the forces of society, he makes an important step forward in his sentimental education. By recognising that he was the innocent victim of his own unawareness of social realities, he is able to absolve the ideal of desire from the taint of failure and place all blame upon society's hostility to his dream. He makes a direct contrast between the empty, ugly reality of the social world and the "luz tan alta" of his desire; this contrast is, moreover, a value judgement. He is suggesting that his desire is morally superior to the corrupt values of society, since desire is natural and life-giving while social conventions are unnatural, inhuman, and life-denying. The tragedy is that the corrupt social world was infinitely more powerful than the defenceless adolescent tentatively seeking to fulfil his desire.

This vehement denunciation of society was written in the turbulent days following the abdication of Alfonso XIII, although Cernuda's hostility to social values is not primarily political but the result of a direct confrontation between his homosexuality and society's taboos.[31] The attack on social convention in "Diré como nacisteis" is an attempt to come to terms with the 'forbidden pleasures' of his desire through a pugnaciously defiant proclamation of what society condemns in him. He has inverted the moral censure applied to him and directed it at society, engaging the morally superior force of desire in open conflict with corrupt social values and even threatening the heterosexual world with destruction:

> Abajo, estatuas anónimas,
> Sombras de sombras, miseria, preceptos de niebla;
> Una chispa de aquellos placeres
> Brilla en la hora vengativa.
> Su fulgor puede destruir vuestro mundo. (p. 66)

At one time Cernuda regarded the element of rebellion, which first appears strongly in *Los placeres prohibidos*, as the most important motivating force in his poetry.[32] This is undoubtedly an over-simplification, but the defiance of society in these poems is one of the most decisive actions in the whole of *La Realidad y el Deseo*, for it means that Cernuda has chosen to accept his homosexuality. This, moreover, is a decision to accept himself by accepting that *truth* about himself he had discovered in the hidden garden of his adolescence. Through this act of self-affirmation he seeks also to give new hope and vitality to the crushed, mutilated personality left after the failure of love.

The influence of André Gide is a principal agent in this uncompromising decision to accept his homosexuality; as Octavio Paz has succinctly said: "Gide lo animó a llamar las cosas por su nombre".[33] This is a spiritual rather than a literary influence which makes itself felt in a similarity of ideas not textual coincidences.[34] Cernuda's respect and admiration for Gide are expressed in a long study of his writings, and in the poem "In memoriam A. G.", from *Con las horas contadas*, composed on the occasion of the novelist's death in 1951, he has also admitted that Gide helped him to come to terms with "un problema vital mío decisivo" in a way which Salinas, who had encouraged him in his reading, could never have suspected (*PL*, 246). One of Gide's books, read as a result of Salinas's encouragement, was *Morceaux choisis*, and he recalls how

[31] In 'Historial de un libro' Cernuda specifically relates his spirit of rebellion with the political state of Spain at this time (*PL*, 247-8). The scornful references in "Diré como nacisteis" to a king and the shadow of a king would seem to be allusions to Alfonso XIII and Primo de Rivera.

[32] ". . . el lado de sombra, la protesta, la rebelión. . . Yo creo que ahí reside el motivo principal de cuanto he escrito", letter from Cernuda to J. L. Cano, December 1953. *Apud* Cano, 'En la muerte de Luis Cernuda', *Revista de Occidente,* no. 12 (1964), 364-8.

[33] *Cuadrivio,* 187.

[34] A distinct stylistic resemblance is, however, visible in some of Cernuda's short stories. See "Sombras en el salón", *Hora de España,* no. XIV (1938), 39-66, and *Tres narraciones* (Buenos Aires, 1948).

here he discovered Lafcadio whom he saw as a symbol of youthful freedom. The singling out of Lafcadio from his early reading closely links the influence of Gide with *Los placeres prohibidos,* since in 1931 Cernuda published a newspaper article, "Carta a Lafcadio Wluiki", which echoes a number of the ideas found in this collection of poems.[35]

The general nature of Gide's influence may be gathered from this comment taken from his study of Gide written in 1946 :

> La figura trascendente de Gide no es la del hombre que por medio de la abstención y la renuncia busca lo divino, mas la del hombre que por medio del esfuerzo y la exaltación individual busca lo plenamente humano.[36]

Such an exaltation of "lo plenamente humano" is what Cernuda attempts in many of the poems of *Los placeres prohibidos* where uninhibited sensuality is made the supreme value and justification of life. Gide's morality of freedom from restraint is expressed most fully in *Les Nourritures terrestres* and here can be found some close point of contact with Cernuda.[37] Gide exalts the transcendental importance of what he calls *volupté* or *ferveur,* by which he means all forms of physical pleasure sought with a feverish delight in a luxuriant communion with Nature. This guiltless hedonism would clearly appeal to Cernuda since it corresponds closely to the *fervor* on which his adolescent dreams were based. There are, moreover, in *Les Nourritures terrestres* a number of parallels with his own experience, particularly in the ecstatic references to Seville and to the very gardens of the Alcázar, where a walled garden is the setting for an erotic episode.[38] In addition two significant echoes of this book occur in Cernuda's later writings : the statement in 'Palabras antes de una lectura' that "la realidad exterior es un espejismo y lo único cierto mi propio deseo de poseerla" strongly recalls Gide's idea that "chaque désir m'a plus enrichi que la possession toujours fausse de l'objet même de mon désir",[39] and the dictum "que *l'importance* soit dans ton regard, non dans la chose regardée" is approvingly glossed by Cernuda in his essay on Gide, specifically in the context of Gide's homosexuality.[40]

These two direct echoes of Gide are the hub of his influence on Cernuda; the exaltation of desire for its own sake and the moral corollary that it is the dignity and integrity of the desire, not its object, that give it virtue, help him to come to terms with the hostility of society towards the homosexual. In some of the

35 *Heraldo de Madrid,* 24-IX-31, 12. Reprinted in *Poesía y literatura II,* 217-22.

36 'André Gide', *Poesía y literatura,* 122.

37 Cernuda's familiarity with this work, even during the period of *Perfil del aire,* is shown by his reference to the phrase "la melancolía no es sino fervor caído" in connection with his early poems (*PL,* 240). This phrase is taken from *Les Nourritures terrestres:* "La mélancolie n'est que de la ferveur retombée", Gide, *Oeuvres Complètes* (Paris, 1933), vol. 2, 66. A relationship between *Los placeres prohibidos* and *Les Nourritures terrestres* has been noted by Müller, *Die Dichtung Luis Cernudas,* 64, note 10.

38 Gide, *Oeuvres Complètes,* vol. 2, 99-101.

39 *Poesía y literatura,* 196, and Gide, *loc. cit.* 63.

40 Gide, *loc. cit.,* 63, and 'André Gide', *Poesía y literatura,* 145.

poems of *Los placeres prohibidos* he is able to rehabilitate the ideal of desire without even feeling the need to defend it against social condemnation. In "Unos cuerpos son como flores" the transitoriness of love is accepted as an inevitable and perfectly natural phenomenon because it is the transcendent nature, not the duration of love, that is important. Love or desire are declared to be the force of life itself, "convirtiendo por virtud del fuego a una piedra en un hombre" (p. 71). This general identification of desire and life is transferred into personal terms in the poem "Como leve sentido" where Cernuda delicately suggests that the dream of desire is the motivating force of his existence :

Tu presencia está conmigo fuera y dentro,
Es mi vida misma y no es mi vida,
Así como una hoja y otra hoja
Son la apariencia del viento que las lleva. (p. 80)

This is, in effect, a return to his youthful declaration "vivo un solo deseo", except that it is made against the background of the unhappy experience of love in both *Los placeres prohibidos* and *Un río, un amor*, and reveals therefore a firmer, even more profound commitment to the erotic ideal.

This recuperation of the dream of desire from the failure it has suffered and the reassertion of love as a life-force are given an added dimension in the poem "Si el hombre pudiera decir", which, despite the cautious tone of its beginning, ends as a triumphant proclamation of the supreme value of love. The erotic ideal is here made more than a life-force, it is the expression and justification of Cernuda's very personality in which he is totally involved :

Si el hombre pudiera decir lo que ama,

. . . . .

La verdad de sí mismo
Que no se llama gloria, fortuna o ambición,
Sino amor o deseo,
Yo sería aquel que imaginaba;
Aquel que con su lengua, sus ojos y sus manos
Proclama ante los hombres la verdad ignorada,
La verdad de su amor verdadero.

. . . . .

Tú justificas mi existencia :
Si no te conozco, no he vivido;
Si muero sin conocerte, no muero, porque no he vivido. (pp. 70-1)

This is a most significant statement; *la verdad* is both the truth of love and the truth of himself, the essence of his character, so that by affirming his involvement with the erotic dream he is affirming himself. Such an affirmation goes far beyond the simple defiance of society in "Diré como nacisteis", for Cernuda, in full awareness of the nature of his desire and of the difficulties it must encounter, has staked all, his very identity, on this single aspect of his life. The dream of desire has become for him an existential necessity with which there can be no possible compromise, and the moment of perceiving this relationship between his life and the erotic ideal is the beginning of his search for himself through the search for love.

In the immediate context of *Los placeres prohibidos* the primacy accorded to love is part of the recovery from disillusionment and of the acceptance of his homosexuality. The idea that the experience of love is more important than its success or failure is clearly present in poems that deal with the memories of love, which are not bitter *olvidos*, as in *Un río, un amor*, but still retain an ambivalent attraction. In "Adónde fueron despeñadas" the lost lover, whom he calls "Corsario", is begged desperately by Cernuda to return, while in "Qué más da" just the memory of love is sufficient to dissipate the sadness created by its loss. Cernuda is also able now to use overtly homosexual erotic symbols, like the "Corsario" just mentioned, the "adolescente rumoroso" in "Quisiera saber por qué esta muerte", and the sailors who are presented as the archetypal objects of desire in "Los marineros son las alas del amor". Nevertheless, the restoration of belief in love and the defiant exhibition of its homosexual nature do not in themselves solve the problem of society's hostility to Cernuda's desire, which, in "Diré como nacisteis", he was forced to admit is "apto solamente en la vida sin muros" (p. 65).

The new aggressive mood in *Los placeres prohibidos* seeks a solution to this problem by giving desire elemental proportions and so freeing it from the constraint of social disapproval. Desire is made more powerful than the barriers with which the adolescent dreams had collided; images of desire from *Primeras poesías*, such as light and the sky, acquire a new stature to become "cielos relampagueantes" (p. 66) and "luz inextinguible" (p. 77), thus removing from such images the negative, degraded associations with which they had been burdened in *Un río, un amor*. In addition new erotic images of a similar powerful nature are introduced, such as the sea and the associated idea of drowning as a symbol of abandonment to love. In "Si el hombre pudiera decir", with an almost baroque delight in paradox,[41] the only true freedom is declared to be in the bonds of love, which brings complete self-abnegation, likened to the absorption of drift-wood by the sea. This idea harks back to the "afán de amor y olvido" of adolescence and is also reminiscent of the desire for fusion with the world to which Cernuda refers in 'Palabras antes de una lectura', but the primary aim of this elemental concept of love is to offer an escape from the hostile social world:

> Si un marinero es mar,
> Rubio mar amoroso cuya presencia es cántico,
> No quiero la ciudad hecha de sueños grises;
> Quiero sólo ir al mar donde me anegue,
> Barca sin norte,
> Cuerpo sin norte hundirme en su luz rubia. (p. 72)[42]

[41] Cano, *Poesía española del siglo XX*, 349, finds a parallel between this poem and a sonnet by Villamediana, "Esta flecha de amor con que atraviesa".

[42] The sea as an image of desire appears fleetingly in poem XII of *Primeras poesías*, and in the drowned man's flight into the open sea in "Cuerpo en pena". This image appears to have strong homosexual connotations; cf. the poems of Hart Crane and also the image of death by drowning in Lorca's *Diván del Tamarit*, especially "Gacela de la muerte oscura" and "Gacela de la huida".

The idea of communion with the natural world achieved through the new elemental concept of desire is developed in several poems. "Quisiera saber por qué esta muerte" is a reappraisal of desire as a cosmic life-force. The adolescent who provokes desire is a "huracán ignorante", the innocent vehicle for a violent force of nature, and a "recuerdo de siglos", the representative of an eternal spirit in the world. The experience of desire is likened to death, another image of self-abnegation, and the adolescent is described entirely through an enumeration of natural images :

Quisiera saber por qué esta muerte
Al verte, adolescente rumoroso,
Mar dormido bajo los astros negros,
Aun constelado por escamas de sirenas,
O seda que despliegan
Cambiante de fuegos nocturnos
Y acordes palpitantes,
Rubio igual que la lluvia,
Sombrío igual que la vida es a veces. (p. 73)

The view of desire as a cosmic phenomenon is taken a step further in "El mirlo, la gaviota" where it loses even the residual awareness of possible pain visible in the final line of the above quotation from "Quisiera saber por qué esta muerte". "El mirlo, la gaviota" is an entirely jubilant poem where desire is a "sueño inacabable" and a "filtro sempiterno" producing a rose-coloured vision of life, and where the sailors who are the objects of this desire transport Cernuda to a "mundo de espejismo". The opening stanza is a chaotic enumeration that gives a panoramic view of the natural world and of the life of man from childhood to death, to which the final stanza returns as Cernuda proclaims that desire will bring communion with Nature :

Creo en la vida,
Creo en ti que no conozco aún,
Creo en mí mismo;
Porque algún día yo seré todas las cosas que amo :
El aire, el agua, las plantas, el adolescente. (p. 79)[43]

This triumphant *credo* is the final restoration of faith in the erotic ideal and a restoration of Cernuda's own personality shattered by the disillusion of his youthful dreams. Belief in a future communion through love with the natural world also offers him a defence against the sense of alienation he experiences in the hostile social world. "El mirlo, la gaviota" is, in effect, a restatement of the

[43] The final line of this quotation is an echo of Empedocles: "For by now I have been born as boy, girl, plant, bird and dumb sea-fish", Kathleen Freeman, *Ancilla to the Pre-Socratic Philosophers* (Oxford, 1948), 65. Cernuda quotes this same fragment in 'Historial de un libro' (*PL,* 252). It is interesting that this allusion to Empedocles should appear in such an early poem since Cernuda was attracted to Pre-Socratic philosophy much later, when he was in the United States (*PL,* 275).

adolescent ideal of the *acorde total,* by which Cernuda completes the reconstruction of his inner world of *deseo.*[44]

It is in this quasi-pantheistic concept of desire that the influence of Gide can be seen most clearly, an influence whose nature can be gathered from some of Cernuda's remarks in his article 'Carta a Lafcadio Wluiki':

> Tu presencia me dice que debe amarse la vida y el aire y la tierra divinos que la rodean. Caminar con los pies desnudos para mejor sentir la aspereza confortadora de la tierra . . . / . . . Lo único real en definitiva es el hombre libre, que no se siente parte de nada, sino todo perfecto y único en medio de la naturaleza, sin costumbres impuestas y profanadoras.[45]

Lafcadio is the ideal of youthful beauty, like the adolescent in "Quisiera saber por qué esta muerte", and his presence produces the same sense of communion with the natural world. The concept of the "freeman" is the answer to the constraint of society; the man who exists in total sympathy with the natural world is free from obeisance to the "unnatural" customs of society. This strongly recalls the contrast made in "Diré como nacisteis" between the naturalness of desire and the unnatural character of society's laws. In this essay on Gide's Lafcadio is the basis for Cernuda's reappraisal of the nature of desire in *Los placeres prohibidos*; he has rejected the social world, and the repression it contains, to seek in a transcendent vision of the natural world the *vida sin muros* necessary for desire.

The reconstitution of desire as an elemental force emanating from Nature is, however, another attempt to evade reality. Having realised that his commitment to the erotic ideal is an existential necessity, Cernuda is again seeking to create what is essentially an artificial world protected from a hostile society. He has constructed another version of the hidden garden, now surrounded by what he hopes are stronger walls. He is seeking to build a bulwark against further disillusionment, as he makes clear in a statement contained in an article written only a few months after *Los placeres prohibidos*:

> No, no, amigo mío, no ponga su confianza en las personas; ahí están los animales, las plantas, las piedras, las cosas maravillosas, tan puras como la luz o las nubes, y que nunca decepcionan.[46]

Communion with the natural world offers a safe alternative to the strong possibility of failure inherent in a personal love. This is another example of Cernuda's evasive response to difficulties put in the way of his dreams, but his new pantheistic vision of the world is of a different order from the attempted escape to exotic paradises in *Un río, un amor,* since it foreshadows the idea of a superior reality hidden behind the everyday appearance of the world, developed

[44] The elemental, cosmic proportions given to desire in *Los placeres prohibidos,* and especially the idea of desire as death, evokes some similarity with the poetry of Vicente Aleixandre with whom Cernuda was friendly during this period (*PL,* 248), and it is quite possible that he may have been influenced by some of his friend's poetic ideas.

[45] *Poesía y literatura II,* 221-2.

[46] 'La escuela de los adolescentes', *Heraldo de Madrid,* 5-XI-31, 12.

a few years later in 'Palabras antes de una lectura'. He is claiming that the elemental concept of desire and the transcendent communion with Nature represent the true reality, while society is composed of *realidades vacías*.

But if Cernuda has turned his back on social reality he has also made the momentous decision to face up to his personal reality. With the help of Gide and the pantheistic concept of desire he liberates himself from any sense of guilt and creates instead a feeling of outrage against society based on a part ethical, part aesthetic value judgement. In *Los placeres prohibidos* there is an inherent declaration that his personal values are superior to those of the world about him, and the exhibition of those values – his homosexuality – is therefore an act of self-affirmation. He has discovered the truth of himself, the truth of love or desire, and is now concerned to protect this identity. The real rebellion of *Los placeres prohibidos* is the refusal to compromise his identity with inimical social conventions. Cernuda here begins his preoccupation with his personal integrity, which is also something he owes to Gide, as perhaps he himself realised when he wrote these words about the French novelist :

> Cualquiera opinión que se tenga del hombre y de la obra, no es fácil negar a ambos que nunca sacrificaron las exigencias íntimas a la consideración ajena, ni que su móvil principal no fuera siempre desinteresado. Así nos presenta una de las figuras ejemplares que pueden hallarse en la literatura contemporánea : la de uno que puso los intereses humanos por encima de los intereses de partido. Por haber sido Gide fiel a sí mismo, ha sido a la larga fiel al hombre.[47]

The Failure of Love

Cernuda's renewed commitment to the erotic ideal in *Los placeres prohibidos* and the transcendent dimension given to desire in those poems expose him to a potential catastrophe should his dreams fail again. *Donde habite el olvido* is the expression of such a disaster. The love affair which gave rise to many of these poems was of a different order to that of his earlier experience, which I have suggested was concerned with thwarted love; love now seems to have been fulfilled and then to have turned sour. Cernuda himself has admitted that this was a sordid affair (*PL*, 251). This failure of love cannot be blamed on the hostility of society, but is the result of the disparity between the ideal he had created and the harsh fact of his experience. He now discovers the reality of love as he had earlier discovered the reality of society. This collapse of what in *Los placeres prohibidos* had seemed the triumph of desire plunges Cernuda into the deepest despair, a despair all the more profound because of the restraint with which it is expressed. The shock, bewilderment and anger of earlier poems make way for an emotional devastation so complete that it gives to this collection a deceptively gentle air. Cernuda has been drained of an active emotional response for these are poems from the dead, poems described in the short preamble in prose as "el recuerdo de un olvido".[48]

[47] 'André Gide', *Poesía y literatura*, 160-1.

[48] "Recuerdo de un olvido" is the title of one of the poems in Manuel Altolaguirre's *Ejemplo* (Málaga, 1927), See Altolaguirre, *Poesías completas* (México, 1960), 40.

The presence of Bécquer in this collection is evident enough from the title and from the first poem, which is a gloss on the famous *rima* LXVI. Bécquer provides Cernuda with a model for expressing total disillusionment with intensity but without obtrusive emotionalism. The delicacy and evocativeness of the technique of the *chispa eléctrica* provide a mode of expression uniquely capable of conveying his numbed despair. Bécquer's influence also extends to the concept of love presented in these poems; Cernuda's love, like Bécquer's, is a violently destructive experience. Love is likened to fire or a knife wound, "vibrante fuego/ O filo inextinguible" (p. 92), "incesante filo contra el pecho" (p. 96), images which are also characteristic of Bécquer. Noting this similarity, J. L. Cano has linked Cernuda's concept of a tragic, savage love with the essay on Bécquer published by Cernuda in 1935, which emphasises Bécquer's involvement in a violent, bitter, tormented passion :

> Un agudo puñal de acerados filos, alegría y tormento es el amor; no una almibarada queja artificiosa. Una entrega total al torrente diverso de los días, su lirismo apasionado; no un divertido y eficaz esparcimiento al margen de la propia vida . . . / . . . hay una pasión horrible, hecha de lo más duro y amargo, donde entran los celos, el despecho, la rabia, el dolor más cruel . . . / . . . Pocos sentimientos tan hondos como ése. Y ésa es la verdadera imagen del amor que Bécquer conoció, sufrió y cantó.[49]

In the emotional intensity of these statements is a clear indication that Cernuda saw his own experience reflected in Bécquer's anguished poems. He too had fallen victim to precisely such a "pasión horrible", which, in an intrusion of his own feelings, he cynically calls the true image of love. It is such sentiments as these that are described in *Donde habite el olvido*, where love is presented as an impossible compound of egoism and vindictiveness, which can end only in disaster and mutual torment for those concerned. As the erotic ideal collapses yet again, the truth of love becomes once more a lie. This return to cynicism appears in its most trenchant form in the prose introduction to the poems where love is compared to the mating of hedgehogs. The embittered sarcasm of this tortured travesty of love devoid of all tenderness is made all the more caustic by the casual manner of its expression as a universally accepted idea :

> Como los erizos, ya sabéis, los hombres un día sintieron su frío. Y quisieron compartirlo. Entonces inventaron el amor. El resultado fue, ya sabéis, como en los erizos. (p. 86)

A similar cold despair appears in many of the poems. Poem XIV is dedicated to Concha Méndez and Manuel Altolaguirre and was written on the occasion of the death of their first child, who lived only for a few hours after birth.[50] As in "De qué país" from *Los placeres prohibidos*, the innocent newborn child is a symbol of the promise of what life might be in contrast to the impotence and

[49] 'Bécquer y el romanticismo español', *Cruz y raya,* no. 26 (1935), 54 and 63-4. Reprinted in Cernuda, *Crítica, ensayos y evocaciones* (Barcelona, 1970). See Cano, *Poesía española del siglo XX,* 334-5.

[50] This information is taken from a typed copy of this poem in the archives of Juan Guerrero Ruiz. See Silver, *"Et in Arcadia Ego",* 70, note 9.

disillusion which have proved for Cernuda to be its reality. The world into which the child has been born is a place of horror, degradation and corruption – reminiscent of the surrealist poems – which the child is then held to have rejected by dying, thus saving his innocence from being destroyed. The child had unknowingly brought with him into the world a truth, a vision of life as it ought to be if his innocence was to be preserved, and this is what Cernuda bitterly sees him as having abandoned :

> Tu leve ausencia, eco sin nota, tiempo sin historia,
> Pasando igual que un ala,
> Deja una verdad transparente;
> Verdad que supo y no sintió,
> Verdad que vio y no quiso. (p. 97)

Here again is the image of truth, used in *Los placeres prohibidos* for the dream of love, and now employed for the ideal of life the child represents, but it has become a futile dream which can never be fulfilled. In these calm, deceptively delicate lines is a statement of utter hopelessness.

The failure of love again produces a vision of the world warped by anguish and despair, although there is little presence of any exterior reality in these poems. Cernuda has almost returned to the repressed, enclosed situation of his adolescence, except that the feeling of incarceration is now greatly intensified. He is trapped in a nightmare existence by hostile forces and degraded images of his dreams, as the melancholic inscapes of his youth acquire a violent character learnt from the surrealist phase of his poetry. Nightfall is subtly personified as a creature of active menace, bringing the threat of time, while the sky and budding leaves that symbolised the hope of youth have been cruelly mutilated :

> Nocturno, esgrimes horas
> Sordamente profundas;
> En esas horas fulgen
> Luces de ojos absortos.
>
> Bajo el cielo de hierro
> Da hojas la amargura,
> Lenta entre las cadenas
> Que sostienen la vida.
>
> . . . . .
>
> Ya no es vida ni muerte
> El tormento sin nombre,
> Es un mundo caído
> Donde silba la ira. (pp. 91-2)

This cankered world is a projection of the realm of shattered dreams in which Cernuda is once again imprisoned, rather like the drowned man in the lifeless landscape of "Cuerpo en pena", although he now has a much clearer vision of his disillusioned state of mind.

Previous reverses suffered by the erotic ideal had been the result, in part, of conflict between the dream and the environment where the dream sought to realise itself, but Cernuda had resolved that problem by giving to desire elemental proportions capable of overcoming any hostile situation, and the new crisis he has encountered can therefore have no explanation other than that love itself is impossible. He finds that love has proved to be a form of subjugation, not the liberating experience for which he had hoped, not a blissful self-effacement in an elemental life-force. The broad horizons of his dreams narrowed in reality to claustrophobic limits and desire has become :

> . . . este afán que exige un dueño a imagen suya,
> Sometiendo a otra vida su vida,
> Sin más horizonte que otros ojos frente a frente. (p. 87)

Here is a suggestion that love failed because of the narcissistic character of the desire that inspired it. This possible explanation for love's failure can be supported by one of Cernuda's comments on the affair that gave rise to *Donde habite el olvido* :

> mi reacción había sido demasiado cándida . . . y demasiado cobarde. Son necesarios, además, algunos años, aunque no sabría decir cuántos, para aprender, en amor, a regir la parte de egoísmo que, no del todo conscientemente, arriesgamos en él. (*PL*, 251)

It would seem that Cernuda had manoeuvred himself into an impossible situation, seeking both self-effacement in love and also an affirmation of himself. What is more, the reality of love has been neither communion with the cosmic world nor triumphant self-justification. Poem XV declares that love is a prison created by egoism which makes any form of relationship impossible and traps the truth of the erotic ideal behind barriers of non-communication. The dream may still exist but it can never be exteriorised :

> Un deseo inmenso,
> Afán de una verdad,
> Bate contra la carne
> Como un mar entre hierros.
>
> . . . . .
>
> Entre piedras de sombra,
> De ira, llanto, olvido,
> Alienta la verdad.
>
> La prisión,
> La prisión viva. (p. 98)[51]

The failure of the love with which he had identified his life again reduces Cernuda to a state of spiritual death. In poem III he sees himself once more as

[51] Cf. "Nos desconocemos profundamente los unos a los otros. Nos separan irreparablemente espacios infranqueables, murallas de carne. Es inútil combatir contra ello." 'Bécquer y el romanticismo español', *Cruz y raya*, no. 26 (1935), 62.

having been swept away by the river of love and turned into an empty body, although his inner world of dreams has not been entirely destroyed :

> Soy eco de algo;
> Lo estrechan mis brazos siendo aire,
> Lo miran mis ojos siendo sombra,
> Lo besan mis labios siendo sueño. (p. 89)

Something of the dream of desire has remained, despite the Becquerian progressive dematerialisation of the senses by which it can be perceived, even though it is only an echo, a memory of what once it was or might have been. The persistence of desire trapped in the living prison of the poet's body is a major cause of pain in *Donde habite el olvido* as continuing desire clashes with the memory of its past failure. In poem X Cernuda sees himself as an angel thrust out of the eden of love into a world of misery where he becomes a wandering beggar "recordando, deseando/Recordando, deseando"; these two gerunds summarise the attitude of *nessun maggior dolore* that imbues so many of these poems. Love, in poem XVI, is declared by means of a series of sarcastically insincere negations to be a murderous dagger, a poison and a catastrophe, but then when memory intervenes that self-same distorted, disillusioned experience of love reawakens desire;

> Placer, amor, mentira,
> Beso, puñal, naufragio,
> A la luz del recuerdo son heridas
> De labios siempre ávidos;
> Un deseo que no cesa,
> Un grito que se pierde
> Y clama al mundo sordo su verdad implacable. (p. 99)

This is a statement of the basic emotional problem with which Cernuda is now confronted; love has failed yet he is still inextricably involved with the erotic ideal for which love was meant to be the fulfilment.

The continuing commitment to the dream of desire is made evident in poem XIII, which is addressed to the lost lover whom he calls "mi arcángel", a transcendent figure inheriting the place of the "Corsario" in *Los placeres prohibidos.* As in some of the poems of the previous collection, the memory of the "arcángel" has become an integral part of his existence, and is capable, momentarily, of lifting the depression caused by his physical absence. The memory of the lost lover in the second poem of *Donde habite el olvido* stimulates a renewed wish for self-effacement in love, again expressed through the image of drowning in the sea. This, however, is now seen ambivalently as a descent into an abyss and the lover himself has acquired a dubiously indeterminate character as an "ángel, demonio, sueño de un amor soñado". Many years later, in the poem "*Apologia pro vita sua*" from *Como quien espera el alba,* Cernuda recalled that this love affair aroused in him contradictory emotions akin to the classical paradox of *odi et amo,* which may be partly explained by the idea that it was an "amor soñado". This memory of love is both the ideal and its reality, an interacting mixture of hope and disillusion. The opposing sentiments provoked by painful memories and continuing desire are clearly expressed in poem X, where an attempt to reconstruct the ideal is frustrated because the only elements Cernuda possesses to carry out this task are his bitterness and sense of failure :

Pesa, pesa el deseo recordado;
Fuerza joven quisieras para alzar nuevamente,
Con fango, lágrimas, odio, injusticia,
La imagen del amor hasta el cielo,
La imagen del amor en la luz pura. (p. 94)[52]

It is not only the memory of lost love that pains Cernuda, he is grieved just as strongly by the recollection of the innocent dreams of his adolescence. A concern with lost innocence is even more pronounced in these poems than in his surrealist poetry. It now seems to him that all his dreams were in vain and that the promise of his youth has been irrevocably betrayed by his experience. The memory of the indolent, sheltered life of his adolescence when the erotic ideal was conceived is now a source of acute pain as he contrasts what might have been with what has in fact happened to him. Poem VII is an excellent example of these sentiments, and of the masterly economy of expression in the allusive technique employed in *Donde habite el olvido* :

Adolescente fui en días idénticos a nubes,
Cosa grácil, visible por penumbra y reflejo,
Y extraño es, si ese recuerdo busco,
Que tanto, tanto duele sobre el cuerpo de hoy.

Perder placer es triste
Como la dulce lámpara sobre el lento nocturno;
Aquél fui, aquél fui, aquél he sido;
Era la ignorancia mi sombra.

Ni gozo ni pena; fui niño
Prisionero entre muros cambiantes;
Historias como cuerpos, cristales como cielos,
Sueño luego, un sueño más alto que la vida.

Cuando la muerte quiera
Una verdad quitar de entre mis manos,
Las hallará vacías, como en la adolescencia
Ardientes de deseo, tendidas hacia el aire. (p. 91)

This delicate poem is a clear statement of the painful nostalgia Cernuda feels

[52] Cernuda has explained this poem in the following way: "Creo que, tras del fracaso de la experiencia amorosa, el poeta trata de reconstruir su imagen del amor. Para lo cual usa los materiales únicos de que dispone, fango, etc. . . . bien deleznables e inadecuados. Hay pues sarcasmo y necesidad de creer en el amor, al mismo tiempo." Letter to the present writer dated 3-VIII-62.

for the time of his adolescence; his youth is seen now, without its accompanying melancholy and repression, as the halcyon days of his life. In his memory his adolescent self has become idealised as an ethereal creature leading, in a near timeless world, a latent existence that recalls the original title of his first book of poems, *Perfil del aire*. It is a bitter paradox that the memory of this tenuous former self should provoke such pain in him now that he has acquired, with experience, corporeal substance. Cernuda is still using the image of "cuerpo" to stress the physical nature of the torment caused by the failure of the dream of desire. This simple contrast is then continued throughout the poem with the deft evocation of the enclosed environment and vicarious dreams of adolescence, and the pained awareness that he is separated irredeemably from the age of innocence. The final stanza is an expression of bitter irony; the adolescent dream, which was meant to be the truth of his existence, has been destroyed leaving only empty, futile desire. Here is the seat of Cernuda's pain, his yearning continues but he knows from experience that his questing hands will not find the truth they seek. This poem is, moreover, a specific return to the world of *Primeras poesías*, so succinctly evoked in the third stanza, and as such it is an admission by Cernuda that the edifice of the life he had tried to build on these adolescent foundations has been destroyed in the conflict with reality.

The double burden of the memories of lost love and of the lost adolescent dream provoke an extreme reaction : the wish to erase memories completely in a state of oblivion, the *olvido* of the collection's title. This is a solution of despair, an extreme example of Cernuda's evasive reaction when the dream clashes with reality, and a manifestation in personal terms of the iconoclasm that had appeared in his surrealist poems. In poem XI, one of the finest compositions in the collection, he deliberately turns his back on both the suffering and the joy he has experienced, seeking to evade all memories in a total forgetfulness of the dreams of youth and of the still-open wound of desire. Unlike Bécquer, whom in this poem he equals in intensity, he is unable to gain a cynical comfort from the thought "siquiera padecer es vivir"; having been reduced to a state of spiritual death by the failure of love he strives to erase the last spark of life left to him, his memory. This, by an emotively potent duplication, becomes the oblivion of the *olvido* into which his dreams have been transformed :

Aún va conmigo como una luz lejana
Aquel destino niño,
Aquellos dulces ojos juveniles,
Aquella antigua herida.

No, no quisiera volver,
Sino morir aún más,
Arrancar una sombra,
Olvidar un olvido. (pp. 94-5)

The abandonment of all hope contained in this wish to escape into oblivion is made the more emphatic by the calm, firm resolution of its expression. It is a wish for death as an escape from the pain of life, but a death of emotional response not physical death, although it does come close to this in the opening poem as a result of the close links with Bécquer's *rima* LXVI. Here Cernuda seeks the peace of the graveyard, described as "los vastos jardines sin aurora" in a terrible travesty of his adolescent dreams, where all that will remain of his existence will be a tombstone hidden amongst the nettles. Bécquer in *rima* LXVI is pained that his life should end with an inscriptionless stone, but for Cernuda this would be a welcome release from his torment of desire and memory. He longs for a condition where pain and pleasure will be no more than words, incapable of inflicting suffering, and where he himself will achieve an enigmatic freedom in a dematerialised existence :

Donde al fin quede libre sin saberlo yo mismo,
Disuelto en niebla, ausencia,
Ausencia leve como carne de niño. (p. 78)[53]

The suggestion that death will bring a return of childhood innocence and also give him the freedom he had once sought in love indicates the depth of Cernuda's bitterness. Yet this is not a conventional death-wish; the fifth poem of *Donde habite el olvido* makes clear that what he wants is an indolent, vestigial existence, a limbo-like state where feeling and memory have been numbed :

Quiero con afán soñoliento,
Gozar de la muerte más leve
Entre bosques y mares de escarcha,
Hecho aire que pasa y no sabe.

. . . . .

Voy a morir de un deseo,
Si un deseo sutil vale la muerte;
A vivir sin mí mismo de un deseo,
Sin despertar, sin acordarme,
Allá en la luna perdido entre su frío. (pp. 89-90)

This is the extreme situation to which the failure of love has brought him; the erotic ideal, which was meant to be a vehicle for self-affirmation, has been the means of reducing him to a state of spiritual and emotional death, has been, in fact, the instrument that has destroyed his personality. Cernuda's despair can go no further than his wish to expunge from himself the last remnants of his dreams in order to protect himself from further failure. The wish for *olvido* is a voluntary resolve to negate the entire world of *deseo* which he had struggled to express and fulfil in his four previous collections of poems, and as such it marks the end of an era in his development.

Donde habite el olvido is the end of a cycle begun with the dreams of adolescence in *Primeras poesías*, a cycle that contains the story of Cernuda's youth. These first five sections of *La Realidad y el Deseo* are the record of the experi-

[53] There is a clear echo here of Baudelaire's "Correspondances" : "Il est des parfums frais comme des chairs d'enfants."

ence that provides the basis for the theory of the conflict between *realidad* and *deseo*, first developed only two years after *Donde habite el olvido* was written, and they are, therefore, the pediment upon which the whole of Cernuda's poetry stands. These early poems set out the ideal of an existence in complete harmony with the world and then translate that ideal into erotic terms. The collision of the erotic dream with social reality in the surrealist poems establishes him as a spiritual exile, and, in turn, leads to the defiant proclamation of his homosexuality. In addition, the identification of the erotic ideal with his personality and the consequent defiance of society in order to preserve what he regards as his true identity are decisive actions that determine in large part the way in which Cernuda's later poetry will develop. *Primeras poesías* holds the key to Cernuda's ideal view of the world and *Los placeres prohibidos* is a statement of the uncompromising stand he will take in defence of this ideal and of his own integrity.

The first five books of *La Realidad y el Deseo* also provide concentrated examples of Cernuda's tendency to seek evasive solutions when confronted with difficulties. The retreat into dreams and the hidden garden of adolescence, the terrestrial paradises of *Un río, un amor*, the elemental ideal of *Los placeres prohibidos*, and the wish for oblivion in *Donde habite el olvido*, all provide evidence for the view of Cernuda as a man of glass who withdraws fearfully from all contact with reality. But these prominent evasive characteristics are not indications of an effete personality, they are symptoms of Cernuda's commitment to his ideal and of his refusal to compromise. When the dream collides with reality he seeks to retreat from failure to somewhere where the dream can flourish. Even the search for *olvido* shows by its utter despair the degree of involvement with the dream of love. These early poems are the story of a series of attempts to assert and fulfil the ideal; in adolescence where it is thwarted by its own impotence, in the surrealist poems where it is crushed by social convention, and in *Donde habite el olvido* where love itself fails. It is a story of constant failure and constant renewal, of unbending commitment to the ideal. These are the poems of youth in which emotions are more powerful than the ability to control them, and it is to this overwhelming experience of his youth that Cernuda will continually return in later years to investigate what it has made him.

III

THE HIDDEN GARDEN

> Y yo de tierra mala trazo un huerto
> Sellado para el mundo todo,
> Que huraño lo contempla concertando hundirlo.
>
> ("Silla del rey", *Vivir sin estar viviendo*, p. 266)

The strong evasive element in Cernuda's character, which emerges from the series of attempts in his early poems to withdraw from reality into a private world of his own making, continues in his mature work, although the evasion tends to acquire more complex forms. The hidden garden of his adolescence, that paradigm of the world as it ought to be, is left behind him with his youth, but the idea that the garden represented stays with him as he seeks persistently to insulate his inner world of *deseo* against the depredations of reality. The development of the idea of a hidden garden through the terrestrial paradises of *Un río, un amor* to the elemental, cosmic view of desire in *Los placeres prohibidos* finally acquires a clear ideological basis in the theories of 'Palabras antes de una lectura' which state Cernuda's aim of finding a transcendental plane of existence where the division between the objective and the subjective dimensions of the world is eliminated. The ways by which he seeks to attain this transcendent mode of being in his mature poems are several and various; some are straightforward attempts at evasion, others like the search for a personal salvation in love and in poetry have a more positive intent. I shall in this chapter examine the subsidiary attempts to bring together the divided worlds of *realidad* and *deseo,* leaving the major themes of love and poetry to be examined separately.

In 'Palabras antes de una lectura' Cernuda makes a clear distinction between the world's deceitful appearance and the hidden *idea divina,* the *imagen completa del mundo,* which is the true reality. A similar attitude expressed with a more illuminating terminology recurs some ten years later in the contrast made between visible and invisible realities in the course of a definition of metaphysical poetry :

> . . . hay cierta forma de lirismo, no bien reconocida ni apreciada entre nosotros, que atiende con preferencia a lo que en la vida humana, por dignidad y excelencia, parece imagen de una inmutable realidad superior. Dicho lirismo, al que en rigor puede llamársele metafísico, no requiere

> expresión abstracta, ni supone necesariamente en el poeta algún sistema filosófico previo, sino que basta con que deje presentir, dentro de una obra poética, esa correlación entre las dos realidades, visible e invisible, del mundo.[1]

Cernuda further asserts that the three poets whose work this definition describes, Manrique, Aldana, and the anonymous author of the "Epístola moral a Fabio", arrive at the conclusion that "la fantasmagoría que nos cierne, conforme al testimonio de los sentidos, sólo adquiere significación al ser referida a una vislumbre interior del mundo suprasensible".[2] Here, reflected in these comments on the three "metaphysical" poets, is a much clarified statement of the philosophical attitude of 'Palabras antes de una lectura'; it is also Cernuda's ideal to transcend the false visible world and gain communion with a superior, hidden spiritual reality. This perception of a higher realm of existence offers him the possibility of escape from the oppressive alienation of his life in society into a state of harmony between himself and the world, such as he has always desired. This is another way of achieving the fusion with the whole body of creation of which he speaks in 'Palabras antes de una lectura'.

Such attitudes as these evoke some affinity with mystical experience, and Cernuda himself, in the prose poem "El acorde" written towards the end of his life, has referred to a recurring experience of a mystical nature, although this is of a non-religious order, being a sense of fusion with the cosmos not with God:

> ¿Como si se abriese una puerta? No, porque todo está abierto: un arco al espacio ilimitado, donde tiende sus alas la leyenda real. Por ahí se va, del mundo diario, al otro extraño y desusado. La circunstancia personal se une así al fenómeno cósmico, y la emoción al transporte de los elementos.
>
> El instante queda sustraído al tiempo, y en ese instante intemporal se divisa la sombra de un gozo intemporal, cifra de todos los gozos terrestres, que estuvieran al alcance.[3]

A similar experience of an intoxicating wonder and newness in the world, which produced a state of "acorde con la vida", is described in another late prose poem, "Mañanas de verano", which refers to an incident in Cernuda's childhood and thus helps to relate this experience to his poetry.[4] The feeling of seeing things as though for the first time is reminiscent of some of the adolescent experience described in *Primeras poesías* and awakens a particular echo of the *acorde total* in "Ninguna nube inútil". I would suggest, therefore, that the mystical experience outlined in "El acorde" is not only linked with the philosophical speculations of the essays 'Tres poetas metafísicos' and 'Palabras antes

[1] 'Tres poetas metafísicos', *Poesía y literatura,* 57. This essay dates from 1946.

[2] *Ibid.*

[3] *Ocnos,* 192-3. A typescript of "El acorde" amongst Cernuda's papers in Seville is dated: "México 12 VIII– 11-XI-1956".

[4] *Ocnos,* 39-41. A typescript of "Mañanas de verano" amongst Cernuda's papers in Seville is dated: "México 9-10 VIII 1956", thus making it almost exactly contemporaneous with "El acorde".

de una lectura' but can be traced back to Cernuda's first perception of the world through the innocent eyes of adolescence. The mystical fusion with the cosmos is but a more complex explanation of the experience of harmony with the world Cernuda underwent in that hidden garden of his youth. It is another manifestation of the wish to escape from an oppressive reality into an ideal existence.

However, the feeling of harmony with the world, of an intensity sufficient to be described as mystical, occurs only infrequently in Cernuda's poetry; in fact, as an actual experience it appears in only two poems, "Río vespertino" from *Como quien espera el alba* and "El nombre" from *Vivir sin estar viviendo*. A passage towards the end of "Río vespertino" describes an experience of union between past, present and future in a single timeless moment akin to the absence of temporality referred to in "El acorde" :

En la paz vespertina, más humilde
Que el júbilo animal a la mañana,
Lo renunciado es poseído ahora,
Cuando la luz su espada ya depuso
En el tiempo sin tiempo, consumando
La identidad del día y de la noche.
El viento fantasmal entre los olmos
Las hojas idas mueve y las futuras. (p. 228)

Although there is little sense of ecstasy here, this is clearly an experience of a mystical order, as is indicated by an echo of a dictum from San Juan de la Cruz's *Avisos y sentencias espirituales*.[5] But these sentiments occupy only a small part of a long, complex poem dealing with a wide range of thematic material. "El nombre" describes an experience of lesser intensity, limited to a sense of oneness with the natural world, which evokes a reminiscence of Juan Ramón Jiménez's poem "Arboles hombres" from *Romances de Coral Gables*, a reminiscence that is disturbing in view of the pronounced distaste the mature Cernuda had acquired for Jiménez's poetry :

Hasta parece el hombre,
Tú quieto, entre los otros,
Un árbol más, amigo
Al fin en paz, la sola
Paz de toda la tierra. (p. 245)

While the attainment of a cosmic harmony may be the ideal for which Cernuda strives, the limited reference to actual mystical experience indicates that this remains for the most part only an ideal. Cernuda almost always exists in the

[5] St. John's dictum "niega tus deseos y hallarás lo que desea tu corazón" is quoted in 'Tres poetas clásicos', *Poesía y literatura*, 52. This essay dates from 1941, the poems of *Como quien espera el alba* were written between 1941 and 1944. The idea of the fusion of day and night brings an echo of Hölderlin's "Brot und Wein" : "Ja ! sie sagen mit Recht, er söhne den Tag mit der Nacht aus."

condition which, in "El acorde", he calls *otredad*, that is the feeling of being separated from the world, and the experience of separation rather than that of union provides the dynamic element in his vision of the world. It is the sense of *otredad* that keeps him striving throughout his life to find ways of achieving a communion between himself and the world.

Cernuda's attitude to the concept of the *acorde* is clearly displayed in the poem "El árbol" from *Vivir sin estar viviendo.* The contemplation of an oriental plane tree of great age in the Fellows' Garden of Emmanuel College, Cambridge (*PL*, 269), awakens a sharp consciousness of man's subjection to time. The garden, walled and silent, evokes an immediate echo of the hidden garden of adolescence, and the two hundred year old tree, which has escaped the flux of time, casts a "sombra edénica". The students in the garden are also unconscious of time but remind the poet of his own lost youth and force on him the bitter recognition of the inevitability of this loss, for him, and for them. But the tree is free from such disillusion; it is the "ser de un mundo perfecto donde el hombre es extraño" (p. 244), existing in complete harmony with the world while man is condemned to alienation.

The fusion of self with world in a quasi-mystical *acorde* is for Cernuda the "testimonio de lo que pudiera ser el estar vivo en nuestro mundo",[6] a taste of that integrated existence he always sought. The search for the *acorde* takes several forms and becomes the most complex of all the attempts to live in a private world. After the catastrophe of *Donde habite el olvido* Cernuda feels an overwhelming need to find a set of beliefs that can provide a frame-work of meaning for his shattered life, and the possibility of communion with a transcendent reality offers him the external support he so urgently requires. The proposition of the existence of a superior world appears under different guises: as a belief in the old gods of pagan antiquity, as a wish for death, engendered by the shock of the Civil War and exile, as a search for solace in more orthodox religious faith, and as an idealisation of Spain that later becomes absorbed into a similarly idealised view of Mexico. Each of these attempts to substantiate the existence of a superior reality is a further indication of the strong evasive tendency in Cernuda's character, but they are also symptoms of his commitment to his own values, to himself, and they therefore become negative manifestations of the concern with personal integrity that is the axis on which all his mature poetry turns.

The Ancient Gods

In *Invocaciones*, the collection of poems following *Donde habite el olvido*, Cernuda remains in the numb, limbo-like state of indolence produced by his disastrous experience of love. In the poem "Himno a la tristeza" he claims sadness as his muse while he surveys the collapse of his youthful illusions and the disappearance of his youth itself:

> La soledad poblé de seres a mi imagen
> Como un dios aburrido;

[6] "El acorde", *Ocnos*, 193.

Los amé si eran bellos,
Mi compañía les di cuando me amaron,
Y ahora como ese mismo dios aislado estoy,
Inerme y blanco tal una flor cortada. (p. 123)

The parallel here with the opening lines of poem III from *Donde habite el olvido*, "Esperé un dios en mis días/Para crear mi vida a su imagen", indicates how *Invocaciones* bears the same relationship to the preceding collection as do many of the poems of *Los placeres prohibidos* to *Un río, un amor*; Cernuda is again seeking to piece together what can be salvaged from the shattered fragments of his dreams. But he has now been forced into a much more fundamental reappraisal of himself, his aspirations and his relationship to the world about him, based on the theories set out in 'Palabras antes de una lectura'. These invocations are to those elements of his life and character with which he feels a special bond : the ideal of desire, his childhood, and his vocation as a poet, and also to the new concept of a superior, invisible reality.

However, the reassessment of his values in the light of the new idea of a transcendent reality brings only a lament for the separation between himself and his vision of a divine world of harmony. Cernuda now firmly takes on the mantle of an elegiac poet. The analysis of the failed aspirations of his youth is prompted by the need to come to an understanding of his past experience, a task which is now begun in earnest, and which is provoked by the necessity to find a broad faith to replace his lost dreams and establish a sense of belonging, now so painfully absent. "Himno a la tristeza" contains a wish for communion with some superhuman being who will console man for the torment of life :

Luchan algunos por fijar nuestro anhelo,
Como si hubiera alguien, más fuerte que nosotros,
Que tuviera en memoria nuestro olvido;
Porque dulce será anegarse
En un abrazo inmenso,
Vuelto niebla con luz, agua en la tormenta;
Grato ha de ser aniquilarse,
Marchitas en los labios las delirantes voces. (pp. 124-5)

This is reminiscent of the desire for self-effacement in love expressed in the image of drowning in *Los placeres prohibidos*, but now that the elemental, personalised ideal of love has failed Cernuda seeks a more objective justification for his existence. He wishes now for a union with the cosmic world such as that described in 'Palabras antes de una lectura'; indeed, the lines "dulce será anegarse/En un abrazo inmenso" strongly recall the desire expressed in that essay "de salir de mí mismo, anegándome en aquel vasto cuerpo de la creación".[7] This is clearly revealed as an evasive desire, a means of escape from the "delirantes voces" of emotional pain, while the use of the subjunctive and of expressions of probability indicate that it is no more than another dream.

The idea of a superior reality, which the poems of *Invocaciones* attempt to

[7] *Poesía y literatura,* 196.

define, harks back to the elemental view of the natural world in *Los placeres prohibidos*, but this has now acquired a quasi-religious dimension that brings it closer to pantheism. The *idea divina del mundo* referred to in 'Palabras antes de una lectura' is most evident in the two poems dealing with the theme of the ancient gods that Cernuda borrowed from Hölderlin. He has said that he learnt from the German poet a new vision of the world and a new poetic technique (*PL*, 254); the first of these claims is easier to substantiate than the second. He had a close affinity with Hölderlin, sharing the same pantheistic vision of Nature, the same sense of a tragic destiny, the same conviction that society was hostile to the Poet, and, above all, the same nostalgia for a lost Golden Age of harmony. Yet he has declared that he discovered Hölderlin's poetry when *Invocaciones* was more than half completed (*PL*, 253), and it would seem, therefore, that this is not the case of submission to an influence but of an encounter with a kindred spirit who helped him clarify ideas he had already established. Stylistically Hölderlin would have provided Cernuda with an example of a poetic language using long sense periods in extensive poems that develop a theme in depth. One critic has pointed out that the German's language obeys a rhythm of ideas rather than a metric rhythm,[8] and this is certainly a characteristic that begins to enter Cernuda's poetry at this time.

Cernuda's deep affinity with Hölderlin is also linked with the concept of the *poder daimónico* developed in 'Palabras antes de una lectura' where the German poet is used as an example of someone possessed by such a force and driven to destruction by it. This daemonic power is related with the division of reality into two levels and with the mystical idea of cosmic union; it is part of the superior, invisible reality lying behind the illusory appearance of the world and through contact with this mysterious power the poets can bring together the human and supernatural elements of life in "una armonía superior a los poderes de la comprensión humana".[9] Such a concept postulates the existence of a hidden, all-embracing life-force in the world, an idea that is clearly present in the pantheistic vision of Nature contained in *Invocaciones*, although it can be traced back to *Los placeres prohibidos* and to "Los fantasmas del deseo", the final poem of *Donde habite el olvido*. In this latter poem Cernuda rejects the personalised erotic dreams of his youth in favour of a view of desire as a telluric life-force which offers the possibility of communion with the elemental world. This attitude is taken further in "Soliloquio del farero", from *Invocaciones*, where Cernuda uses the symbol of the lighthouse-keeper to investigate the solitude that has resulted from the failure of his youthful dreams. In this early example of the objectivising technique of projecting his experience onto an imaginary personage he concludes that solitude has a positive value, being both a reflection of, and a means of communion with the natural forces of the world; in 'Palabras antes de una lectura' he refers to "esa soledad esencial suya donde

[8] L. S. Salzberger, *Hölderlin* (Cambridge, 1952), 55.

[9] *Poesía y literatura*, 199-200. See also 'Hölderlin', *Cruz y raya*, no. 32 (1935), 117. In 'Palabras antes de una lectura', *loc. cit.*, 200, Cernuda quotes some of Goethe's ideas on "lo demoníaco" from his conversations with Eckermann. An earlier allusion to a "poder demoníaco" which rules man's destiny occurs in 'La escuela de los adolescentes', *Heraldo de Madrid*, 5-XI-31, 12.

[el poeta] cree escuchar las divinas voces".[10] Solitude is seen as a return to the pristine dreams of childhood that had been betrayed by the search for a personalised erotic ideal :

> Por ti [soledad] me encuentro ahora el eco de la antigua persona
> Que yo fui,
> Que yo mismo manché con aquellas juveniles traiciones;
> Por ti me encuentro ahora, constelados hallazgos,
> Limpios de otro deseo,
> El sol, mi dios, la noche rumorosa,
> La lluvia, intimidad de siempre,
> El bosque y su alentar pagano,
> El mar, el mar como su nombre hermoso. (p. 107)

Cernuda is here trying to recapture the sense of oneness with the world he had felt as a child, but there is no ecstasy of cosmic union in this poem. This is an expression of hope rather than belief, and a hope accompanied by a nagging doubt of its impracticality. Solitude may bring an awareness of the cosmic world, but it is also a form of protection against the destructive contact with other people. The lighthouse-keeper's justification for his solitude is hollow casuistry :

> Soy en la noche un diamante que gira advirtiendo a los hombres,
> Por quienes vivo, aun cuando no los vea;
> Y así, lejos de ellos,
> Ya olvidados sus nombres, los amo en muchedumbres. (p. 108)[11]

This is an admission of defeat, a sad statement of Cernuda's incapacity to enter into personal relationships and a declaration of his feelings of *otredad*, on a social level, which the pantheistic view of the world is meant to eliminate, but, in fact, accentuates.

The concept of the *poder daimónico* takes on a more specific manifestation in the theme of the ancient gods which appears in the last two poems of *Invocaciones*, although the presence of the gods here is heralded by an occasional mention in earlier poems, such as the "Egloga" and the "Oda", and "De qué país" from *Los placeres prohibidos* where the young child grieves for broken statues of forgotten gods. In the introductory note to his translations of some of Hölderlin's poems, published at the time he was writing *Invocaciones*, Cernuda emphasises the relationship between the theme of the ancient gods and the pantheistic vision of the world :

> Siempre extrañará a alguno la hermosa diversidad de la naturaleza y la horrible vulgaridad del hombre. Y siempre la naturaleza, a pesar de esto,

[10] *Poesía y literatura,* 195.

[11] These sentiments recall a phrase found amongst Hölderlin's papers during the time of his madness: "Only now I understand human beings, since I live far from them and in solitude", *apud* M. Hamburger, *Poems of Hölderlin* (London, 1943), 88. The idea of love for the mass of men may also be an echo of Cernuda's flirtation with Communism during this period.

> parece reclamar la presencia de un ser hermoso y distinto entre sus perennes gracias inconscientes. De ahí la recóndita eternidad de los mitos paganos, que de manera tan perfecta respondieron a ese tácito deseo de la tierra con sus símbolos religiosos, divinos y humanizados a un tiempo mismo.[12]

This view of pagan myth echoes the idea expressed in 'Palabras antes de una lectura' that poetry is a link between the human and supernatural worlds. He also saw these myths as part of the invisible reality hidden behind the appearance of the world, the symbols of a mode of existence in communion with Nature, in contrast to the social structures of modern man which have lost the link with the natural world. The ancient gods had for Cernuda, as for Hölderlin, an ethical, religious rôle, which takes them beyond being a mere literary device; they are personifications of love, poetry, strength and beauty, the symbols of values and beliefs lost or ignored by modern man.[13]

Cernuda was clearly attracted to the ancient gods as part of his attempt to rebuild a viable set of beliefs. The view of pagan myth he found in Hölderlin helped him to authenticate and give form to his vague pantheistic ideas, and also provided him with the sense of belonging he so desperately needed. But this poetic faith in the ancient gods contained a tragic dimension, for it committed him to a spiritual exile whose only recompense was a participation in "una divinidad caída y en un culto olvidado".[14] He could really belong neither to the lost classical age of harmony nor to his own time, and, like his lighthouse-keeper, he was consoling himself with casuistry. He could only echo Hölderlin's lament in "Brot und Wein" for the disappearance of the gods from the world :

> Aber Freund ! wir kommen zu spät. Zwar leben die Götter,
> Aber über dem Haupt droben in anderer Welt.

Cernuda himself recognised the dangers inherent for him in this nostalgia for the gods in a prose poem written many years after *Invocaciones*, but referring to his childhood discovery of Greek myth :

> Que tú no comprendieras entonces la causalidad profunda que une ciertos mitos con ciertas formas intemporales de la vida, poco importa : cualquier aspiración que haya en ti hacia la poesía, aquellos mitos helénicos fueron quienes la provocaron y la orientaron. Aunque al lado no tuvieses alguien para advertirte del riesgo que así corrías, guiando la vida, instintivamente, conforme a una realidad invisible para la mayoría, y a la nostalgia de una

[12] 'Hölderlin', *Cruz y raya*, no. 32 (1935), 115.

[13] "El amor, la poesía, la fuerza, la belleza, todos estos remotos impulsos que mueven al mundo, a pesar de la inmensa fealdad que los hombres arrojan diariamente sobre ellos para deformarlos o destruirlos, no son simples palabras; son algo que aquella religión supo simbolizar externamente a través de criaturas ideales, cuyo recuerdo aún puede estremecer la imaginación humana . . . piénsese que en nuestra poesía . . . los mitos griegos son únicamente un recurso decorativo; pero nunca eje de una vida perdida entre el mundo moderno y para quien las fuerzas secretas de la tierra son las solas realidades, lejos de estas otras convencionales por las que se rige la sociedad." 'Hölderlin', *loc. cit.*, 115-16.

[14] *Ibid*, 116.

> armonía espiritual y corpórea rota y desterrada siglos atrás de entre las gentes.[15]

Here the classical myths are clearly linked with the concept of a hidden, superior reality, but they are also related to the motivation of poetic experience, which is likewise involved with that invisible world of harmony referred to in 'Palabras antes de una lectura'. This statement by the mature Cernuda points to the conclusion that his faith in the ancient gods is, besides being an evasive nostalgia for a lost Golden Age, also a symptom of his commitment to a set of values which are tragically not those of the mundane world in which he must live. He has chosen spiritual exile in order to preserve the integrity of those values.

Despite Cernuda's profound concern with pagan myth at this time, the ancient gods have a definite presence in only the last two poems of *Invocaciones*, "Himno a la tristeza", where sadness is seen as the gods' gift to man,[16] and "A las estatuas de los dioses", which is an even deeper elegy for the disappearance of the gods from the modern world. Yet even if the gods themselves are absent in other poems these are all deeply imbued with the pagan spirit described in Cernuda's note to his translations from Hölderlin. In particular the idealised figures of the protagonists in "A un muchacho andaluz" and "El joven marino" recall those semi-divine beings who reflect the beauty of the natural world. "A las estatuas de los dioses" neatly encapsulates Cernuda's attitude to the gods :

> Reflejo de vuestra verdad, las criaturas
> Adictas y libres como el agua iban;
> Aún no había mordido la brillante maldad
> Sus cuerpos llenos de majestad y gracia.
> En vosotros creían y vosotros existíais;
> La vida no era un delirio sombrío.
>
> . . . . .
>
> Hoy yacéis, mutiladas y oscuras,
> Entre los grises jardines de las ciudades,
> Piedra inútil que el soplo celeste no anima,
> Abandonados de la súplica y la humana esperanza.
>
> . . . . .
>
> En tanto el poeta, en la noche otoñal,
> Bajo el blanco embeleso lunático,
> Mira las ramas que el verdor abandona
> Nevarse de luz beatamente,
> Y sueña con vuestro trono de oro
> Y vuestra faz cegadora,
> Lejos de los hombres,
> Allá en la altura impenetrable. (pp. 125-6)

Although forgotten and humiliated in an alien, degraded world, the gods still

15 "El poeta y los mitos", *Ocnos,* 35-6.
16 The same idea is found in Hölderlin's poem "Die Heimat".

represent an age of joy, innocence, and harmony, when love was still possible. The use of the term "verdad" in connection with this pagan Eden before the Fall shows that the gods represent a new "truth" which has been found to replace the old, failed one. But although the poet has kept faith with the gods, the world in which he lives has lost its faith, and his continuing belief acquires an air of madness which separates him from his fellow men, while at the same time consoling him for this alienation.

The spirit of the pagan gods remains strong in the pantheistic ideas of the poems in *Las nubes*, reflecting the continuing influence of Hölderlin, but the incidence of the theme is greatly reduced in *Como quien espera el alba*. In this collection only three poems refer to the gods or to the classical world, "El águila", "Ofrenda" and "Urania", and only the first of these is of real significance.[17] In this poem the gods are decadent, tired of their immortality and amusing themselves with the antics of man, while in the following poem, "Las ruinas", Cernuda declares his rejection of "eternos dioses sordos". Only one later poem sustains a tone of faith in the gods; this is "El elegido" from *Con las horas contadas*, but it has a Mexican background of human sacrifice in which a youth is offered to the gods, and his beauty so preserved for ever. While in "Las edades" from *Vivir sin estar viviendo* the gods are depicted as statues in a museum, where they are humiliated by the gaze of the incredulous and crumble with the passing of time; here the gods are dead, and far from being the expression of a nostalgic faith, this poem is a meditation on the meaning of life.

It is surprising that the ancient gods should have such a small physical presence in Cernuda's poetry, since they represent more clearly than any other theme the very characteristic feeling of belonging to another world. He is noticeably careful to refrain from direct classical allusion, and the gods are never named. The only classical personage ever identified is the muse Urania. Even when referring to a particular myth, as in the case of Ganymede in "El águila", the names are concealed. Such reticence avoids the theme degenerating into a mere literary device and also the particular danger of awakening echoes of the Hellenism of the *modernista* poets. For Cernuda, who the gods are is less important than the values they represent. For him, as for Hölderlin, the gods are the symbols of a value judgement he has made about the world in which he lives, a judgement that has resulted in his rejection of that world. The gods provide Cernuda with an objective basis for his reappraisal of his situation in the world, and give clarity and definition to the pantheistic ideas embodied in the concept of the daemonic power. They are thus able to disappear from his poetry when they have served their purpose, but through the values which they represent their spirit remains inextricably woven into the fabric of his mature poems.

In *Invocaciones* Cernuda is not content to leave his criticism of the modern world implicit in his declaration of faith in the ancient gods; addressing his familiar demon in "La gloria del poeta" he castigates the debased values of

[17] "El águila" recalls Hölderlin's "Ganymed". Cf. also "Urania" and "An die Göttin der Harmonie".

contemporary society with an unmitigated fury reminiscent of Hölderlin's attack on the German people in *Hyperion* :

Los hombres tú los conoces, hermano mío;
Mírales cómo enderezan su invisible corona
Mientras se borran en la sombra con sus mujeres al brazo,
Carga de suficiencia inconsciente,
Llevando a comedida distancia del pecho,
Como sacerdotes católicos la forma de su triste dios,
Los hijos conseguidos en unos minutos que se hurtaron al sueño
Para dedicarlos a la cohabitación, en la densa tiniebla conyugal
De sus cubiles, escalonados los unos sobre los otros.

Mírales perdidos en la naturaleza,
Cómo enferman entre los graciosos castaños o los taciturnos plátanos.
Cómo levantan con avaricia el mentón,
Sintiendo un miedo oscuro morderles los talones;

. . . . .

Oye sus marmóreos preceptos
Sobre lo útil, lo normal y lo hermoso;
Oyeles dictar la ley al mundo, acotar el amor, dar canon a la belleza
inexpresable,
Mientras deleitan sus sentidos con altavoces delirantes;
Contempla sus extraños cerebros
Intentando levantar, hijo a hijo, un complicado edificio de arena
Que negase con torva frente lívida la refulgente paz de las estrellas.

(pp. 113-4)[18]

The above quotation, with its enumeration and repetition, length of line and long sense periods, is an example of the discursive style of these poems and of the loss of intensity which such a style can produce as it succumbs to the "garrulería y ampulosidad" Cernuda himself criticised in *Invocaciones* (*PL*, 253). The attack on the sacred convention of the family is obviously motivated by Cernuda's homosexuality, but it is objectivised by being made from the point of view of man's disengagement from Nature. The inhabitants of the "densa tiniebla conyugal" are alienated from the natural world because they have deliberately eschewed the values it represents. It is they who have cast down the statues of the gods and destroyed the Golden Age of innocence. Cernuda here is returning to the attitude that his misfortunes are the fault of society, at the same time as broadening the ethical basis of this judgement. However, now there is no sense of exultancy, no threat of destruction from an avenging thunderbolt as in "Diré como nacisteis". He is trapped in this debased society where, tragically, it is those who have lost contact with the true, hidden reality of the daemonic

[18] A source for the figure of the demon in this poem is suggested by a reference in the rough draft of 'Palabras antes de una lectura', among Cernuda's papers in Seville, to a "Satán bellísimo" treading on the body of Job in a picture by William Blake; this would seem to be the well-known "Satan Smiting Job with Sore Boils". Here is a further dimension to the concept of the *poder daimónico* or *demoníaco*.

power, who dictate the form love and beauty should take and so corrupt the values on which he has based his life.

The disassociation from contemporary society is expressed most strongly in the hostile attitude to Christianity hinted at in the disdainful reference to Catholic priests in "La gloria del poeta". In Cernuda's eyes at this time Christianity was as debased as the corrupt materialist society it served, and the Christian God was "el exangüe dios cristiano/A quien el comerciante adora para mejor cobrar su mercancía" (p. 117). Yet this hostility is based on deeper reasons than a scorn for society; in the prose poem from *Ocnos* where Cernuda recalls his childhood discovery of the Greek myths he emphasises the effect on his conventional religious beliefs of the sad contrast he found between the idealised creatures in the myths and the martyred figure of Christ:

> . . . en tus creencias hondas y arraigadas se insinuó si no una objeción racional, el presentimiento de una alegría ausente. ¿Por qué se te enseñó a doblegar la cabeza ante el sufrimiento divinizado, cuando en otro tiempo los hombres fueron tan felices como para adorar, en su plenitud trágica, la hermosura?[19]

Again Cernuda's attitude is the result of an ethical/aesthetic value judgement; the worship of Christ is a cult of suffering, the worship of the ancient gods is a cult of beauty. His concept of the divine is the idealised sensuality of the "muchacho andaluz" who represents a positive value opposed to the depressing negation he finds in Christianity:

> . . . . nunca he querido dioses crucificados,
> Tristes dioses que insultan
> Esa tierra ardorosa que te hizo y deshace. (p. 106)

Cernuda's faith in the ancient gods and in the pantheistic vision of the world which they represent is a protection for his personal values and a solace for his alienation in society, but this faith is essentially another escapist dream, another version of the hidden garden of his adolescence. He is continuing to dream of the world as it ought to be, yet a significant change of aspect has taken place in this dream; the aspirations of his early poetry were directed towards the future, now his gaze is directed towards an irretrievable past. The mood of elegy which lays so heavily on the poems of *Invocaciones* is sufficient indication of Cernuda's own awareness of the impracticality of his new faith. The belief in the ancient gods is even more of a retreat from reality than any of his earlier attempts at evasion, although, paradoxically, it is partly as a result of this belief that he is able to clarify his view of the world. He has been forced to make a definitive acceptance of his alienation in society, yet the consolation of a communion with the daemonic power of Nature remains only a tantalising ideal which can be vaguely perceived but not fully experienced. However, the belief in the ancient gods also has the positive function of objectivizing Cernuda's personal conflict

[19] *Ocnos*, 35.

with the world. The erotic aspirations of his early poems are now depersonalised and transferred to an ethical/aesthetic plane as the conflict between *realidad* and *deseo* is expanded to become a clash between two antagonistic systems of values. Cernuda's poetic faith in the ancient gods is another means of affirming his identity against a hostile society whose laws "alguien como Hölderlin no puede jamás reconocer, a menos de negarse a sí mismo y desaparecer".[20]

Death as a Salve for Life

The new dream Cernuda had tried to construct in *Invocaciones* is interrupted in 1936 by the violent intrusion of reality in the form of the Spanish Civil War, although, unlike many of his contemporaries, he avoided direct political commitment in his attitude towards the war. He was able to absorb his reactions to the war into the essentially tragic view of the world established in *Invocaciones*, and, while sympathizing with the Republic, he could stand above the partisan struggle to lament the violation of Spain by her own sons.[21] To a considerable extent the pantheistic idea of the daemonic power of Nature is transferred to Spain herself, which takes on the role of the Earth Mother. In the poems concerned with the war and the first painful years of exile the elegiac tone of *Invocaciones* acquires a sharper note of pessimism, which is strengthened by the new influence of Leopardi (*PL*, 259). The Italian poet's profound disillusion, his belief in the vanity of life and lament for lost ideals, find a clear response in Cernuda's reactions to the Spanish catastrophe.

"Noche de luna", the opening poem of *Las nubes*, sets the mood for the Spanish elegies of this collection.[22] The moon is seen as an adolescent goddess, now forgotten by man, who continues to watch impassively over the Earth. In a view of history, strongly reminiscent of Leopardi, she has surveyed the confused and often sordid development of the human race in a land un-named but obviously Spain, and observed how all man's dreams and struggles have been rendered futile by the passing of time.[23] The final stanza forecasts the disappearance of man from the Earth, which will then be as dead and as sterile a world as the moon. The deep sense of tragedy and the belief in the impotence of life, which this poem expresses as a reflection of the Civil War, are greatly accentuated by the experience of exile. In "El ruiseñor sobre la piedra", the final poem of *Las nubes*, Cernuda, now in exile, surveys the aspirations of his life and sees them collapse one after the other until the earth, Spain herself, is snatched from him by the war and he loses the last repository of his ideals :

[20] 'Hölderlin', *loc. cit.*, 116.

[21] Cernuda's attitude to Spain at this time owes much to a rereading of the poetry of Unamuno and Antonio Machado (*PL*, 259).

[22] Cernuda had originally intended to give the title *Elegías españolas* to the poems written at the time of the Civil War; see note to "Elegía a un poeta muerto", *Hora de España,* no. VI (1937), 36. The rough draft of "Noche de luna", amongst Cernuda's papers in Seville, has the title "Elegía a la luna de España".

[23] Cf. Leopardi's poems "Bruto minore" and "Inno ai Patriarchi". "Noche de luna" is also reminiscent of Hölderlin's "Die Frieden" and awakens echoes of Unamuno's "Aldebarán", illustrating the variety of literary parallels in Cernuda's mature poems.

Hay quienes aman los cuerpos
Y aquellos que las almas aman.
Hay también los enamorados de las sombras
Como poder y gloria. O quienes aman
Sólo a sí mismos. Yo también he amado
En otro tiempo alguna de esas cosas,
Mas después me sentí a solas con mi tierra,
Y la amé, porque algo debe amarse
Mientras dura la vida. Pero en la vida todo
Huye cuando el amor quiere fijarlo.
Así también mi tierra la he perdido. (p. 180)

It has been suggested that exile would not be the shock for Cernuda that it was for other poets, since alienation was the norm of his existence before the Civil War,[24] but in the poems concerned with his first reactions to exile there are those characteristic symptoms of shock – indolence and emotional numbness – associated with earlier crises. He sees himself completely friendless and isolated in an alien world, "así está el chopo/Entre encinas robustas" (p. 157), living a limbo-like existence, "perdido, lejos, entre sueño y vida" (p. 145). The poem "Impresión de destierro" is an excellent example of this profound melancholy. Quietly, without rhetoric, Cernuda creates here a most moving statement of the crushing sadness of exile; the mere mention of the word "España, densa como una lágrima cayendo", is sufficient to provoke "un cansancio sin nombre". Everything in the poem conspires to produce an air of dusty unreality and meaningless existence. The setting is a tea-party of old gentlemen and old ladies in a drawing room with old-fashioned furniture in the Old Temple in London. The tea-party had taken place a year before, to emphasise the consciousness of time, and the depressing persistence of its memory. Dust, greyness and silence cover everything, even the feathers in the old ladies' hats, with a stultifying atmosphere of fatigue. Out of the silence comes the one word of irrepressible sadness, "España", dropped like a stone in the void. In the street outside, when the tea-party is over, a man with a foreign accent speaks the lines which suddenly summarize all the bitterness and emotional desolation in this poem :

'¿España?', dijo. 'Un nombre.
España ha muerto'. (p. 165)

Nothing is alive in this poem; the man with the foreign accent is like someone returned from the dead, carrying the crushing weight of his tombstone on his shoulders, and at the end of the poem he disappears like a ghost into the shadows whence he had come.

In the disastrous events of the Civil War and the lifeless existence of exile Cernuda feels he has lost control over his destiny. This feeling is reflected in an acute consciousness of time; exile coincides with his passing the mid-point of man's allotted span. "La visita de Dios" begins with a Dantesque allusion and

[24] J. L. Aranguren, *Crítica y meditación* (Madrid, 1955), 182.

a statement of his lost youth. Time is now seen as a destructive force, threatening man's puny desires with the vastness of eternity :

> Pasada se halla ahora la mitad de mi vida.
> El cuerpo sigue en pie y las voces aún giran
> Y resuenan con encanto marchito en mis oídos,
> Mas los días esbeltos ya se marcharon lejos;
>
> . . . . .
>
> El tiempo, ese blanco desierto ilimitado,
> Esa nada creadora, amenaza a los hombres
> Y con luz inmortal se abre ante los deseos juveniles.
>
> (pp. 147-9)

Time is the one active element in the life of exile, indeed, it is time that provides the dynamic for the poems of exile. The awareness of time turns Cernuda in on himself, looking more to the past than to the future, and seeking in his memories a vicarious existence in the vacuum of exile. The analysis of himself imposed by exile ultimately leads him to the self-knowledge he needs to come to terms with his new situation, but his initial reaction is a product of the shock created by the cataclysmic upheaval in his life. In a characteristically evasive reaction he seeks to escape from this new set of painful circumstances into the oblivion of death.

The intense pessimism which prompts this death-wish is apparent even in poems that seem to contain some element of hope. Cernuda has specifically related the poem "Lázaro" to the apparent brightening of the political situation in Europe at the time of the Munich agreement in the Autumn of 1939, which produced in him a feeling that he likens to being reborn after having died (*PL*, 260). These sentiments are projected onto the figure of the risen Lazarus, using the *Doppelgänger* technique learnt from Robert Browning, but the hopeful image of resurrection is tempered by the terrible sense of unreality of life in exile.[25] The risen Lazarus is brought grudgingly back into life from the peaceful oblivion of the grave where he had been free from the pain and torment of existence. With a bitterness and cynicism again reminiscent of Leopardi, he laments his return to the hell of life :

> Quise cerrar los ojos,
> Buscar la vasta sombra,
> La tiniebla primaria
> Que su venero esconde bajo el mundo
> Lavando de vergüenzas la memoria.
> Cuando un alma doliente en mis entrañas
> Gritó, por las oscuras galerías
> Del cuerpo, agria, desencajada,
> Hasta chocar contra el muro de los huesos
> Y levantar mareas febriles por la sangre.
>
> . . . . .

[25] Cf. Browning's poem "An epistle containing the strange medical experience of Karshish, the Arab physician", from *Men and Women*.

Sentí de nuevo el sueño, la locura
Y el error de estar vivo,
Siendo carne doliente día a día. (pp. 161-2)

Lazarus has not been brought fully back to life, only returned to a spiritually dead existence from which he thought he had escaped. The bread and fruit of his home-coming feast taste bitter, and he sees himself as "un muerto/Andando entre los muertos", recalling that man with a foreign accent in "Impresión de destierro" who seemed to have returned from the dead. Even though "Lázaro" ends with the hope of a genuine resurrection in Christ, the poem as a whole is overshadowed by the sense of life's futility that is engendered by exile.

The idea of death as an escape from life first appears in *Invocaciones*. The drowning of the sailor in "El joven marino" creates in Cernuda a wish to die so that he too may find freedom from the debased world of man. The sailor's death is described as an erotic experience, an act of consummation with the elemental force of the sea, which finds an echo in the desire to be absorbed in "un abrazo inmenso" expressed by Cernuda in "Himno a la tristeza". In "La gloria del poeta" he appeals to his familiar demon to end his life because only death can bring fulfilment to the poet and release the "melodía prometida", a musical image reminiscent of the idea of harmony associated with the theories of the *poder daimónico*. In *Invocaciones*, therefore, death is presented as a means of regaining the lost communion with the hidden, transcendent reality of the world.[26] The element of pessimism in such an attitude to death is inevitably strengthened in the poems of the war and exile, where the conviction that death is the only consolation for life would have been reinforced by Cernuda's reading of Leopardi.[27]

The Civil War naturally focuses Cernuda's attention on the theme of death, but the concept of death as an escape from life is kept separate from the presence of violent death in the war. He sees the destruction of life in the war as the creation of hatred provoked by the "caínes sempiternos" (p. 176), as he characterises the Nationalist forces in an image which reflects his reading of Antonio Machado at this time. The distinction between these two kinds of death, one a consolation for life, the other a violent product of hatred, is drawn clearly in a primitive version of the elegy for Lorca, now preserved amongst Cernuda's papers in Seville :

Grato es a veces recordar la muerte

. . . . .

Cuando nada puede consolarnos
La terrible desdicha de estar vivo.

. . . . .

[26] In 'Palabras antes de una lectura', *loc. cit.*, 200, death is spoken of as bringing "una enigmática libertad" to poets possessed by the daemonic power. Cf. the concept of death in Hölderlin's "Stimme des Volks".

[27] This is a recurring theme in Leopardi's poetry; see for example "Sopra un basso rilievo antico sepocrale".

No es esa muerte ésta que ahora se levanta,
Con hierros vestida y una baba sangrienta
Entre los fríos dientes,
Recorriendo la tierra a grandes pasos.

Es el odio, Federico, es el odio.
La muerte es el odio mismo.
Es la fuerza del odio quien la engendra
En el verde regazo de la tierra.[28]

These lines help to clarify the attitude towards death in *Las nubes* and also help to explain why the war seems to disturb the pantheistic beliefs of *Invocaciones*. If hatred is engendered in the bosom of the earth then some strange and bitter fruits have been produced by the elemental world of Nature in which Cernuda had sought communion.

The idea of death as a consolation for life appears in a number of poems; in "Soñando la muerte" it is the "única realidad clara del mundo", the only hope in a crumbling world; in the second "Elegía española" Cernuda sees death as the "única gloria cierta que aún deseo", while in the first "Elegía española" death is referred to as "la patria más profunda". It is difficult not to read a sardonic intention in such statements, particularly the latter one, contained in poems which lament the mutilation of Spain by the war. The idea of death as the only possible reality in life fits well with a belief in the futility of existence, although this attitude can also be accommodated within the view of death as a means of gaining communion with the daemonic spirit in the world, which is first put forward in *Invocaciones*. The imagery used in connection with death is reminiscent of that associated with Cernuda's pantheistic vision of the world. In "Soñando la muerte" death is a "sombra eterna" and a "vasta sombra", possessing almost elemental proportions; it is also described as a "sombra enigmática", recalling the "enigmática libertad" attributed to death in 'Palabras antes de una lectura'. In "A Larra con unas violetas" death becomes "El fiel y último encanto de estar solo", echoing the idea of solitude in "Soliloquio del farero". In "Lázaro" death is again "la vasta sombra" and in addition "la tiniebla primaria/Que su venero esconde bajo el mundo", which immediately recalls the concept of the transcendent reality hidden behind the appearance of the world. In his critical essay on Jorge Manrique, written a few years after the poems of *Las nubes*, Cernuda sees death as the moment when the visible and invisible realities coincide, bringing perfection and meaning to life.[29] Such a philosophic view may help to explain the death-wish in so many of the poems of the war and early exile, as the idea of death as a consolation for life is absorbed into the vision of the world set out in 'Palabras antes de una lectura' and *Invocaciones*, yet there is also a strong element of bitterness in this assumption by Cernuda of the old Romantic desire to escape from life into death. The death wish may be consistent with his philosophical ideas at this time, but it is

[28] From a manuscript in the possession of don Angel Mª. Yanguas Cernuda. The punctuation has been added by the present writer.
[29] 'Tres poetas metafísicos', *Poesía y literatura,* 62-4.

also a reflection of the pessimism engendered by the war and exile, and it is, moreover, the ultimate evasion.

In *Como quien espera el alba*, with the first shock of exile overcome, the death-wish disappears as Cernuda seeks to come to terms with his new situation. As his consciousness of time grows more acute, and he grows older, he becomes aware of his own mortality and death is regarded as the "dura compañera" of life (p. 197). This changed attitude to death is expressed most forcefully in "Río vespertino" with a clear echo of Quevedo's "Avisos de la muerte":

Ajado en toda cosa está el encanto,
El fruto deseado amarga ahora
Y un círculo de sombra encierra al día.
Con tácita premura en cada ciclo
La primavera acerca más la muerte
Y adondequiera que los ojos miren
Memoria de la muerte sólo encuentran. (p. 227)[30]

In 'Historial de un libro' this desperate sense of life's inevitable decline into death is directly related to the effects of the vicarious existence of exile: "la consecuencia de ese vivir es que nada se interpone entre nosotros y la muerte; desnudo el horizonte vital, nada percibía delante sino la muerte" (*PL*, 274). Death thus ceases to hold an attraction for Cernuda, especially as his consciousness of time increases in latter collections; this ultimate escape route is closed as his initial pessimistic reaction to the war wanes and he becomes concerned with the task of self-affirmation imposed by the alien environment of exile.

The Solace of Christianity

Any orthodox religious belief in Cernuda's poetry must appear strange when set beside his rejection of sad, crucified gods and his nostalgia for the world of pagan antiquity. A faith in the ancient gods is so clearly in accord with his character that it is not surprising to find that the Christian sentiments expressed in some of the poems of *Las nubes* are coloured by his earlier beliefs and assimilated into his system of values. The attempt to find hope in Christianity is concentrated in the poems written under the stress of the first shock of exile and is then subdued as the shock wears off. Cernuda himself has seen that the inevitable conclusion to be drawn from the appearance of a Christian belief in such circumstances is that this represents a desperate and essentially superficial search for faith which is abandoned when the pressures motivating it are eased.[31]

[30] There is an echo here of Quevedo's "Avisos de la muerte": "y no hallé cosa en que poner los ojos / que no fuese recuerdo de la muerte." Noted by J. Olivio Jiménez, 'Emoción y trascendencia del tiempo en la poesía de Luis Cernuda', *La caña gris*, nos. 6-8 (1962), 61.

[31] ". . . mis creencias, como las campanas en la leyenda de la ciudad sumergida, sonando en ocasiones, me han dado pruebas a veces, con su intermitencia, de que acaso eran también legendarias y fantasmales; pero acaso también de que subsistían ocultas. Así tras de largos períodos inoperantes, en momentos de *Sturm und Drang*, después de la guerra civil, por ejemplo, o durante la peripecia amorosa que refieren los "Poemas para un cuerpo", surgían a su manera, según mi necesidad. Por eso mismo ¿no parecerán sino reflejo egoísta de esa necesidad mía de ellas, sin que merezcan propiamente el nombre de creencias?" (*PL*, 276-7).

Despite the hostility to Christianity expressed in *Invocaciones*, the first hint of concern for a conventional religious belief appears in this collection. The proposition of a superhuman being in "Himno a la tristeza" is rather vague and obviously related to the concept of the *poder daimónico*, but the poem does nevertheless postulate the existence of a person watching over man : "alguien, más fuerte que nosotros/Que tuviera en memoria nuestro olvido." A similar ill-defined, yet personal deity is invoked in "No es nada, es un suspiro", although referred to only as a shadow or as "tú", with no capitalization. This god, who is either ignorant of or indifferent to man's fate, is presented as merely the creation of man himself, a projection of his desires and anxieties :

> . . . tú que eres
> Nuestro afán, nuestro amor,
> Nuestra angustia de hombres;
> Palabra que creamos
> En horas de dolor solitario. (p. 110)

There can be little doubt that this word is "God", a word which Cernuda is reluctant to use in view of the unfriendly references in other poems, but if God is a word created at times of solitary pain then the appearance of religious sentiments in the poems of early exile needs no further explanation.

The only reference to a personal deity in the poems written during the Civil War occurs in "A un poeta muerto" in another reticent allusion to a superhuman being :

> . . . alguna mente creadora inmensa,
> Que concibe al poeta cual lengua de su gloria
> Y luego le consuela a través de la muerte. (p. 134)

However, in the primitive version of this poem, already referred to, there is a strong nostalgia for the comfort of religion and an overt reference to the Christian God :

> Mas entre el odio desbordado
> Un pensamiento me consuela;
> Queda Dios, Federico, otra extraña palabra,
> Cifra de las restantes,
> De amor o de maldad,
> De piedad o blasfemia.[32]

Although the removal of such a direct concern with Christianity from the final version of the poem does reveal a degree of inhibition on Cernuda's part towards the expression of a conventional religious belief at this time, the primitive version of "A un poeta muerto" does demonstrate that the attempt to find solace in Christianity was already present at the height of the Civil

[32] From a manuscript amongst Cernuda papers in Seville; the punctuation has been added by the present writer.

War. But it is exile which brings these nascent religious sentiments into the open; Cernuda has recorded that in Glasgow and later in Cambridge it was his custom, before going to sleep at night, to read a few verses from the King James' Bible (*PL*, 264). The first direct appeal to God is made in "La visita de Dios", which is in part an account of the difficulties of life in exile, of spiritual desolation and of acute consciousness of time, giving point to Cernuda's admission that his religious beliefs appear only at moments of stress. The same necessity for belief caused by exile is found in "Atardecer en la catedral", where the cathedral becomes a haven of peace from the cares of life :

Aquí encuentran la paz los hombres vivos,
Paz de los odios, paz de los amores,
Olvido dulce y largo, donde el cuerpo
Fatigado se baña en tinieblas.

. . . . .

No hay lucha ni temor, no hay pena ni deseo.
Todo queda aceptado hasta la muerte
Y olvidado tras de la muerte, y adorando,
Necesidad del alma exenta de deleite. (pp. 154-5)

The church offers another avenue of evasion from the anguish of existence; the oblivion of faith is similar to that ascribed to death in other poems, and also recalls the indolent limbo for which there is a recurring longing throughout Cernuda's poetry. Moreover, Christianity provides a solution to the threat of time and the limitation of life by death, when death is seen from a negative viewpoint.

The attempt to find solace in a conventional religious belief represents another effort by Cernuda to overcome his sense of alienation, now greatly intensified by exile, as the poem "Cordura" makes clear :

Duro es hallarse solo
En medio de los cuerpos.
Pero esa forma tiene
Su amor : la cruz sin nadie.

Por ese amor espero,
Despierto en su regazo,
Hallar un alba pura
Comunión con los hombres. (p. 157)

The image of the empty cross brings to mind his distaste for sad, crucified gods, and it would seem that this faith is in the Holy Ghost, the Risen Christ, rather than the Crucified Martyr.[33] This new means of establishing a sense of belonging is, however, assimilated into Cernuda's earlier attitudes : in "Lázaro" the

[33] Silver, *"Et in Arcadia ego"*, 112, sees "Cordura" as a meditation on love, and the "cruz sin nadie" as symbolising the agony of desire. This would seem an unlikely interpretation.

image of "truth", used previously for love and for the pantheistic vision of the world, is applied to the Living Christ, as Lazarus accepts his return to life "por una verdad en aquellos ojos entrevista", while in "Atardecer en la catedral" the religious sentiment is described in nature images reminiscent of the *poder daimónico* :

Llanto escondido moja el alma,
Sintiendo la presencia de un poder misterioso
Que el consuelo creara para el hombre,
Sombra divina hablando en el silencio.

Aromas, brotes vivos surgen,
Afirmando la vida, tal savia de la tierra
Que irrumpe en milagrosas formas verdes,
Secreto entre los muros de este templo,
El soplo animador de nuestro mundo
Pasa y orea la noche de los hombres. (p. 155)

The close connection between Cernuda's idea of Christianity and his previous beliefs is established beyond doubt by the statement in "La visita de Dios" that God represents the same values of truth, beauty and justice as those ascribed to the ancient gods :

Mira las tristes piedras que llevamos
Ya sobre nuestros hombros para enterrar tus dones :
La hermosura, la verdad, la justicia, cuyo afán imposible
Tú sólo eres capaz de infundir en nosotros.
Si ellas murieran hoy, de la memoria tú te borrarías
Como un sueño remoto de los hombres que fueron. (p. 149)

This Unamunesque God's dependence on man for His existence recalls that word created by man in moments of solitary pain in "No es nada, es un suspiro", and this concept of Christianity also brings to mind the "amor de justicia imposible" which was the ancient gods' gift to man in "Himno a la tristeza".[34] This God has, moreover, a "divina indiferencia", the same impassiveness attributed to the ancient gods. The attempt to find a stabilising faith in Christianity is an act of despair made when all else seems to have failed, a despair made apparent in the question addressed to the God of "La visita de Dios" : "si el amor no eres tú, ¿quién lo será en tu mundo?"

Subsequent echoes of a religious sentiment in Cernuda's poetry are few. In *Como quien espera el alba* a hope for consolation in God appears in "*Apologia pro vita sua*", but this is again an Unamunesque God created by man from his own anguish. The *romancillo* "Nochebuena cincuenta y una", included in *Con las horas contadas*, evokes distant echoes of Lope de Vega's *villancicos*, but does not express the traditional sentiments of this genre. The Infant Christ in

[34] A similar idea is to be found in Hölderlin's poem "Der Rhein" : "Und bedürfen / Die Himmlishchen eines Dings, / So sinde Heroen und Menschen / Und Sterblische sonst."

Cernuda's poem is too weak to combat the misery of the world to which He has come again. Yet this melancholy lament for the impotence of the ideal of love the Infant Christ represents does contain a strong nostalgia for faith. "Nochebuena cincuenta y una" almost immediately precedes the "Poemas para un cuerpo" which Cernuda has specifically mentioned in connection with a resurgence of religious belief (*PL*, 271). However, only two poems of this series contain religious references, and one of these is very ambiguous. The opening poem is entitled "Salvador", but this saviour could be either Christ or the lover himself, while the appeal to God in "El amante espera" is another act of despair, since God remains the only source of help left.

The reaction against such a superficial belief in Christianity is to be found even within *Las nubes*; "La adoración de los Magos" is an allegory of the search for faith and of the failure to find it. Melchior, the leader of the Magi, sees the star as the herald of "la verdad divina", which he hopes will bring peace and fulfilment, the recovery of lost youth and a victory over death, although his hope is expressed without much conviction : "si yo vivo/ Bien puede un Dios vivir sobre nosotros." After the deprivations of their long and difficult journey, the Magi's discovery of the Infant Christ not in a palace but in a ruined hut shatters all their hopes. They find merely a human child, subject, like them, to life's pain and death's inevitability. The Magi are like the beggars in the poem "Linterna roja" from *Un río, un amor* who were reduced to their wretched state through seeking an impossible ideal. The truth for which the Kings searched would have solved the problems of their lives, but their discovery of human misery, of which they were previously unaware, effectively destroys their lives. One dies, presumably Melchior who had hoped to escape death; another is dethroned, most probably Balthazar, the believer in *Realpolitik*; the third lives out his life in melancholy solitude, a fitting end for the hedonist Gaspar. The message of this poem seems clear : only disaster awaits those who seek the impossible.

It is, however, not Christ who is impossible but the Magi's expectation of what the god they seek will be able to do, and the poem is not, therefore, entirely despairing. The King's disillusionment is viewed with an intense nostalgia for faith, apparent in the statement "Buscaron la verdad, pero al hallarla/ No creyeron en ella", contained in the epitaph to the poem. Despite this mitigation of the Kings' apostasy, this poem points strongly to the conclusion that Cernuda has recognised the dangers of a religious faith becoming a form of evasion. "La adoración de los Magos", with its tripartite division of Cernuda's character amongst the Magi, is an outstanding example of the acute powers of self-analysis acquired in the enforced isolation of exile; there is, in consequence, an inference that it is a parable of Cernuda's own search for solace in religion. Yet, not all the people in the poem succumb to disillusionment; an old shepherd who had seen the Kings on their journey many years before is completely unmoved by talk of new gods, he is content with life and enjoys an enviable communion with the natural world :

> Buscaban un dios nuevo, y dicen que le hallaron.
> Yo apenas vi a los hombres; jamás he visto dioses.

¿Cómo ha de ver los dioses un pastor ignorante?
Mira el sol desangrado que se pone a lo lejos. (p. 174)

The shepherd who draws his spiritual sustenance from Nature possesses the sense of fulfilment the Magi lacked and never found. He has always lived in the way the Kings had wished to do after their disillusion : "y quisimos ser hombres sin adorar a dios alguno" (p. 173). The shepherd exists in that ideal harmony with the world for which Cernuda longed, and his presence in the poem demonstrates that as the hope of Christianity is dimmed the attraction of the natural world recovers some of its force.

The despairing experience of the Three Wise Men develops in "Las ruinas", the second poem of *Como quien espera el alba*, into an outright rejection of the God of Christianity, and, for that matter, of all other gods. The poem begins with a long evocation of an ancient city, which, although ruined, has survived the passage of time, while the people who inhabited it have vanished almost without trace.[35] The contrast between the permanence of man's creations and man's own transience leads to a reproach to God for having made man mortal while giving him a thirst for eternity. This is, in effect, a plea to be redeemed from such a situation, but the appeal is immediately brushed aside by the pronouncement that God does not exist; he is again just a word created by man in his grief.[36] After this statement of apostasy Cernuda declares that man can live without supernatural beliefs providing he can accept the transitoriness of life and its corollary of death :

Esto es el hombre. Aprende pues, y cesa
De perseguir eternos dioses sordos
Que tu plegaria nutre y tu olvido aniquila.
Tu vida, lo mismo que la flor, ¿es menos bella acaso
Porque crezca y se abra en brazos de la muerte?

Sagrada y misteriosa cae la noche,
Dulce como una mano amiga que acaricia,
Y en su pecho, donde tal ahora yo, otros un día
Descansaron la frente, me reclino
A contemplar sereno el campo y las ruinas. (pp. 188-9)

As in "La adoración de los Magos" the abandonment of religious faith brings a return of sympathy for Nature, but it is now Cernuda himself who finds peace in the natural world. Like the Magi he is seeking to be just a man without a god to worship. He now feels strong enough to stand alone without external support

[35] This is reminiscent of Leopardi's "La ginestra". It is possible that Cernuda may have had in mind the ruins of Itálica, rather than Leopardi's Pompeii.

[36] A similar denial of God's existence, provoked by acute consciousness of time, appears in "Escrito en el agua", a prose poem in the first edition of *Ocnos,* (London, 1942), 43-4. "Escrito en el agua" was omitted from the second edition of *Ocnos,* (Madrid, 1949), to avoid censorship difficulties. See C. D. Ley, *Spanish Poetry Since 1939* (Washington, 1962), 17. This prose poem was also omitted from the third edition of *Ocnos,* but it has been collected in *Crítica, ensayos y evocaciones* (Barcelona, 1970), 197-8.

and to endeavour to come to terms with life. The recantation of "Las ruinas" thus ushers in the great poems of self-analysis in *Como quien espera el alba.*

Cernuda's brief attempt to find consolation in religion is little more than a reaction to the shock of exile and another attempt to retreat into a refuge from reality. Christianity offers him the vision of a supernatural hidden garden where all is harmony. But he turns to God only as a last resort. Some Spanish critics have tended to emphasise the religious poems of *Las nubes,* and the view has even been expressed that the cult of the ancient gods indicates a repressed Christian faith.[37] Yet, as Octavio Paz has pointed out, Cernuda is a completely unchristian writer since he lacks a sense of sin.[38] His attitude to God is summed up in two lines from "*Apologia pro vita sua*" :

> He vivido sin ti, mi Dios, pues no ayudaste
> Esta incredulidad que hizo triste mi alma." (p. 206)

This is more than the nostalgia for faith of the agnostic; it is an affirmation of a belief in the quiescence of the deity. This recognition of God's impassivity means in effect that man must seek solace in himself, which is what Cernuda proceeds to do in the poems of his exile.

Spain, Sansueña, Mexico

Cernuda's concern with Spain as a theme is naturally concentrated in *Las nubes,* then recedes into the background as the shock of exile wears off. Yet Cernuda's own observation that his involvement with Spain gradually subsided into indifference is not exactly true.[39] He had an ambivalent love-hate relationship with his country, and nostalgia for Spain can exist side by side with bitter criticism. Although he could, at times, wish to eschew all ties with Spain, he remained in fact inextricably bound to his native land through its language and culture, and his own vocation as a poet. His preoccupation with Spain is thus closely related to the concern with identity which is provoked by exile. The theme of Spain also reflects some of Cernuda's basic ideas and undergoes several stages of transformation beyond the simple level of patriotism or nostalgia, since his view of Spain at the time of the Civil War is already coloured by the pantheistic attitudes of *Invocaciones,* and this begins a process of idealisation that embraces both his nostalgia for childhood and the discovery of Mexico.

The initial despairing reaction to the Civil War, vehemently expressed in that terrible phrase, "España ha muerto", from "Impresión de destierro", is tempered by a series of poems in which Spain, although ravaged by the war, lives on in spirit as an idealised vision assimilated to the view of the world developed in *Invocaciones.* This process of idealisation is clearly visible in the two "Elegías españolas" from *Las nubes.* The first of these elegies, written at the

[37] J. L. Aranguren, *Crítica y meditación* (Madrid, 1955), 206. Francisco Brines, 'Ante unas poesías completas', *La caña gris,* nos. 6-8 (1962), 130-2.
[38] *Cuadrivio,* 187-8.
[39] *PL,* 258 and 268. See also J. L. Cano, 'En la muerte de Luis Cernuda', *Revista de Occidente,* no. 12 (1964), 366.

height of the war, personifies Spain as an eternal spirit which represents the essence of the country and its people :

Háblame, madre;
Y al llamarte así, digo
Que ninguna mujer lo fue de nadie
Como tú lo eres mía. (p. 135)[40]

This apostrophe to a maternal goddess grieving over the destruction of her land and the fratricidal struggle of her sons reveals both the depth of Cernuda's involvement with Spain at this time and the way in which the new preoccupations created by the Civil War are absorbed into his personal system of values. Spain herself has now become the repository of the life-force Cernuda had discovered in the elemental natural world of *Invocaciones.* The second elegy seems to refer to the end of the war and the beginning of physical separation from Spain. The Nationalist victory is seen as a defeat for the idealised vision of Spain, which is also here closely linked with the dreams of Cernuda's youth, yet within this lament the further apostrophe of Spain as "Tú . . . / Tierra, pasión única mía", completes by this amorous reference the transfer to Spain of the pantheistic concept of the earth. The vocabulary used about Spain is very reminiscent of that associated with the *poder daimónico.* The first elegy speaks of the eternal spirit of Spain as "remota y enigmática" and as a "cuerpo inmenso", while in the second elegy Cernuda speaks of "la verdad de tu alma pura", using again the key idea of "truth" applied to all his other ideals.

This transcendent vision of Spain is carried a stage further in the long meditation on the monastery of El Escorial in "El ruiseñor sobre la piedra", where the monastery, the "hermana de los dioses" and the expression of "designios inmortales", embodies the eternal spirit invoked in the two "Elegías españolas". The monastery is both symbol and part of the undying truth of the ideal Spain, an image of perpetual harmony which is a source of consolation to Cernuda trapped in the time-ravaged, discordant existence of exile :

Así te canto ahora, porque eres
Alegre, con trágica alegría
Titánica de piedras que enlaza la armonía,
Al coro de montañas sujetándola.
Porque eres la vida misma
Nuestra, mas no perecedera,
Sino eterna, con sus tercos anhelos
Conseguidos por siempre y nuevos siempre
Bajo una luz sin sombras.

Y si tu imagen tiembla en las aguas tendidas,
Es tan sólo una imagen;

[40] A typescript of this poem amongst Cernuda's papers in Seville is dated "25-27 Febrero 1937". The fourth edition of *La Realidad y el Deseo* contains a misprint in the second line quoted above: "Y al *hallarme* así . . ." I have corrected this in accord with the text of the third edition (Mexico, 1958), 139.

Y si el tiempo nos lleva, ahogando tanto afán insatisfecho,
Es tan sólo como un sueño;
Que ha de vivir tu voluntad de piedra,
Ha de vivir, y nosotros contigo. (p. 182)

In this poem, where the idea of Spain has developed beyond a maternal spirit into a complete idealisation, the patriotic concern awakened by the Civil War is completely absorbed into Cernuda's system of aesthetic values. The monastery is also a symbol of beauty and the poem is as much about the nature of art as it is about Spain; the immediately personal preoccupations of earlier poems have here been objectivised. Moreover, in "El ruiseñor sobre la piedra" the mood of elegy which begins the poem develops by the final stanza quoted above into a hymn of triumph for recovered faith as a new idealised vision of Spain emerges from the ashes of the Spain destroyed in the war.

The idealisation of Spain is completed by the use of the legendary name Sansueña in the so-called fragments of a dramatic poem, "Resaca en Sansueña".[41] The reality of Spain is here completely superceded by myth, although the spikenards, magnolias, palm trees and whitewashed houses which indicate an Andalusian setting, give specific characteristics to the myth. The vision of a Mediterranean paradise can be traced back to *Invocaciones* and to the edenic portrait of Andalusia set out in the essay 'Divagación sobre la Andalucía romántica'.[42] Yet Cernuda's Sansueña is not an idealised reality, but a dream world, the *locus amoenus* of the "Egloga" given a more specific topography. Sansueña is another version of the lost Golden Age of the ancient gods whose spirit remains alive in the beauty, innocence and indolence of the inhabitants there:

El aroma del mar vasto y denso suspende
Los mortales dormidos bajo un clásico encanto,
Y modela los cuerpos con fuertes líneas puras,
Y en las venas infiltra las pasiones antiguas.

Con la gracia inocente de esbeltos animales
Se mueven en el aire estos hombres sonoros,
Bellos como la luna, cadenciosos de miembros,
Elásticos, callados, que ennoblecen la fuerza.

[41] The most well-known use of the symbol of Sansueña occurs in Fray Luis de León's "Profecía del Tajo", line 24. Fr. José Llobera S. J. (ed.), Fray Luis de León, *Obras poéticas* (Cuenca, 1931), 145-6 nn., gives examples of the use of this term as part of the "geografía legendaria caballeresca". I am indebted to Dr. A. A. Heathcote for his assistance on this topic.

[42] "Confesaré que sólo encuentro apatecible un edén donde mis ojos vean el mar transparente y la luz radiante de este mundo; donde los cuerpos sean jóvenes, oscuros y ligeros; donde el tiempo se deslice insensiblemente entre las hojas de las palmas y el lánguido aroma de las flores meridionales. Un edén, en suma, que para mí bien pudiera estar situado en Andalucía." *Cruz y raya,* no. 37 (1936), 10.

Las mentiras solemnes no devoran sus vidas
Como en el triste infierno de las ciudades grises.
Aquí el ocio es costumbre. Su juventud espera.
La hermosura se precia. No alienta la codicia. (p. 150)

Although the total intention of this complex poem is somewhat obscure, the idealising process which Spain has undergone is nonetheless clear : the idea of the eternal spirit of Spain has been transferred to the myth of Sansueña, then assimilated into the system of values represented by the ancient gods and the idealised vision of Andalusia. Confronted with the ruin of Spain by the war and the Nationalist victory, Cernuda has created a dream to console him in the alien world of his exile.

The concept of Sansueña must be set against the deep repugnance provoked by the urban, industrial environment of Glasgow in the early years of exile. The sordid ugliness of the cold, grey, nordic world to which he had been banished, bitterly described in such poems as "Cementerio en la ciudad" and "Gaviotas en los parques", adds insult to the injury of exile. Cernuda explained his attitude to Glasgow many years later in a prose poem included in *Ocnos* where he attacks the city's physical ugliness and spiritual sterility :

> Divinidad de dos caras, utilitarismo, puritanismo, es aquella a que pueden rendir culto tales gentes, para quienes pecado resulta cuanto no devenga un provecho tangible. La imaginación les es tan ajena como el agua al desierto, incapaces de toda superfluidad generosa y libre, razón y destino mismo de la existencia.[43]

The total contrast between the Calvinistic materialism of Scotland and the indolence and beauty of Sansueña's inhabitants is clearly expressed in "El ruiseñor sobre la piedra" where the entirely non-utilitarian, beautiful structure of El Escorial is opposed to the soul-destroying pragmatism of a nordic world :

¿Qué es lo útil, lo práctico,
Sino la vieja añagaza diabólica
De esclavizar al hombre
Al infierno en el mundo?

Tú, hermosa imagen nuestra,
Eres inútil como el lirio.
Pero ¿cuáles ojos humanos
Sabrían prescindir de una flor viva?

Junto a una sola hoja de hierba,
¿Qué vale el horrible mundo práctico
Y útil, pesadilla del norte,
Vómito de la niebla y el fastidio? (p. 181)

[43] "Ciudad caledonia", *Ocnos*, 135-6.

Here Cernuda has translated the exile's sense of alienation into ethical/aesthetic terms, underlined by the Biblical allusion to the lilies of the field; the nordic world is unacceptable because it is precisely the "triste infierno de las ciudades grises" from which the inhabitants of Sansueña had been saved. The mythical Andalusian paradise is very clearly another manifestation of the hidden garden syndrome, a vision of Spain as she ought to be, a dream created when reality has failed; yet, while this is a haven from the inimical world of exile, the combination of ethical and aesthetic values which Sansueña represents shows that the evasive tendencies inherent in the dream are subordinated to a positive concern with affirming Cernuda's beliefs. His attitude to Spain, and, in particular, the creation of Sansueña, reflect the problems of alienation caused by exile; the myth he makes of Spain is matched to his values and identity as a counterbalance to the antagonistic, incompatible world to which he has been banished.

After its prominence in *Las nubes* the theme of Spain recedes into the background in the calmer mood of *Como quien espera el alba* where it is absorbed into an intense nostalgia for childhood and adolescence. Even references to the sordid environment of exile are few in this collection where Cernuda begins in earnest the process of self-analysis, preoccupying himself more with his inner world. The problems of exile do become more pressing in *Vivir sin estar viviendo,* although they seem to have been temporarily relieved by the prospect of a new life in a new world, as a result of his move to the United States of America. But the feeling of optimism, expressed in the poem "Otros aires" from this book, is shortlived; America, especially after the discovery of Mexico, is just as alien an environment as Glasgow. Although it improved his material comfort, America was unable to satisfy his spiritual needs. In El Greco's portrait of Fray H. F. Paravicino in an American museum he finds a fellow exile trapped like him in an empty, futile existence surrounded by the spiritually dead inhabitants of another nordic nightmare:[44]

> El norte nos devora, presos en esta tierra,
> La fortaleza del fastidio atareado,
> Por donde sólo van sombras de hombres. (p. 291)

While in the poem significantly entitled "Limbo" he castigates the society that treats art with patronising philistinism and declares that he can have no place amongst those who see a poet's work as a curiosity or as an addition to their material possessions.

Disillusion with the United States provokes no compensatory idealised vision of Spain, since this function is now taken over by Mexico. In any case the wounds of exile are now beginning to heal and the mythic Sansueña is losing its attraction. The meditation on this legendary Spain in the poem "Ser de Sansueña" begins with a startling expression of doubt, "acaso allí estará", which firmly demonstrates that a spiritual detachment is now being added to Cernuda's physical separation from his native land. Sansueña has, moreover, turned in this poem from a Mediterranean paradise into a land of impossible

[44] This painting is in the Museum of Fine Arts, Boston, Massachussetts, J. A. Coleman, 'The Meditative Poetry of Luis Cernuda', Ph.D. Dissertation (Columbia University, 1964), 239.

contrasts, strongly reminiscent of Antonio Machado's *España de charanga y pandereta*. The Earth Mother of *Las nubes* has become a step-mother who has abandoned her sons, and Cernuda laments that he is a "compatriota,/Bien que ello te repugne, de su fauna". The price of belonging to such a country has been a stateless existence in an alien, hostile world:

> Y ser de aquella tierra lo pagas con no serlo
> De ninguna : deambular, vacuo y nulo,
> Por el mundo, que a Sansueña y sus hijos desconoce. (p. 263)

This poem is, in part, another Spanish elegy, a lament for the passing of the period in the sixteenth century when Spain dominated the world and all her contradictions were fused together in a "gloria monstruosa". The grotesque caricature which Cernuda makes of modern Spain as a betrayal of the glorious past is an indication of the love/hate relationship he has with his native country, while the use of the name Sansueña in this context reveals a disenchantment with the myth he had created in *Las nubes*. Yet the lines quoted above concerning the empty existence imposed on those evicted from this mythical Spain clearly illustrate the existential relationship linking Cernuda with his native country. His Spanish background is part of his identity, which is diminished in the condition of exile, and his concern with Spain is another facet of the preoccupation with finding a sense of belonging, which lies behind the various attempts to seek solace examined so far.

As the passing years of exile loosen the bond between Cernuda and Spain, his nostalgia for his homeland centres more and more on the Andalusia of his childhood rather than the ideal of Sansueña. This is part of the activity of "buscando recuerdos/En el trágico ocio del poeta" (p. 180), which is one of the means by which he pursues his self-analysis. Memories of childhood appear prominently in *Como quien espera el alba,* evoking the sharp elegiac emotion of *nessun maggior dolore* as Cernuda looks back at his lost innocence and lost sense of communion with the world in the hidden garden of his youth :

> El susurro del agua alimentando,
> Con su música insomne en el silencio,
> Los sueños que la vida aún no corrompe,
> El futuro que espera como página blanca.
>
> Todo vuelve otra vez vivo a la mente.
> Irreparable ya con el andar del tiempo,
> Y su recuerdo ahora me traspasa
> El pecho tal puñal fino y seguro.
>
> Raíz del tronco verde, ¿quién la arranca?
> Aquel amor primero, ¿quién lo vence?
> Tu sueño y tu recuerdo, ¿quién lo olvida,
> Tierra nativa, más mía cuanto más lejana? (p. 192)[45]

[45] There is a strong affinity between "Tierra nativa" and Hölderlin's poem "Die Heimat", which was one of the poems Cernuda translated in *Cruz y raya,* no. 32 (1935), 121, entitling it "Tierra nativa".

This pained remembrance of the past, part dream, part memory, has still an idealised colouring, but it is largely stimulated by the concern for identity provoked by the experience of exile. The past not only offers recollections of happiness in the empty life of exile, but is also a component in his investigation of himself as his analysis tends to gravitate to the time when his dreams and character were first formed. This attitude is expressed plainly in the poem "Hacia la tierra" where a wish to be absorbed in the bosom of the earth is related to a desire to return to his life's starting point now that all dreams seem to have failed :

Posibles paraísos
O infiernos ya no entiende
El alma sino en tierra.
Por eso el alma quiere,

Cansada de los sueños
Y los delirios tristes,
Volver a la morada
Suya antigua. (p. 218)

The examination of childhood and adolescence is the principal theme of the majority of the prose poems in *Ocnos,* especially those contained in the first edition of 1942, which were written between 1940 and 1942.[46] The obviously obsessive nature of the theme at this time explains why it should be concentrated into a separate volume and expressed in prose, which would be a vehicle more suited to directly autobiographical material than verse.[47] But this examination of his formative years also has a place among Cernuda's poetry, and the close links between the prose and verse poems of this time can be demonstrated by the similarity between the poem "Jardín antiguo" from *Las nubes* and the prose poem of the same title contained in *Ocnos*. Both poems are evocations of the old Moorish garden in the Alcázar of Seville, the hidden garden of *Primeras poesías* where the adolescent Cernuda had dreamed of the future promised by desire. In the poem from *Las nubes* the man on the threshold of middle age expresses a wish to return to the walled garden to hear again the murmur of the fountain, the bird-song and rustling leaves. He wants to recapture his youth, but knows that this is impossible, the "sueño de un dios sin tiempo", and time is the one commodity which exists in plenty in exile. The prose poem from *Ocnos* is an exact parallel, another elegy for the loss of youth's dream which repeats the wish to return to the past as an escape from an alien environment :

[46] In 'Historial de un libro' (*PL,* 263) Cernuda says that the period from Autumn 1941 to Spring 1942 was one of intense literary production.

[47] Cf. "Ahí [en la prosa] recuerdos, retratos, paisajes, pueden aliarse mejor con el yo que los ofrece, y no exigen en tanta medida como sí lo exige el verso, cierta despersonalización, fundiendo al poeta con su medio de expresión . . . En la prosa, por poética que sea, hay algo menos severo, y permite a lo accidental del personaje humano afirmarse directamente tras las palabras, causando menos enojo." 'Juan Ramón Jiménez', *Bulletin of Spanish Studies,* no. XIX (1942), 174.

> Más tarde habías de comprender que ni la acción ni el goce podrías vivirlos con la perfección que tenían en tus sueños al borde de la fuente. Y el día que comprendiste esa triste verdad, aunque estabas lejos y en tierra extraña, deseaste volver a aquel jardín y sentarte de nuevo al borde de la fuente, para soñar otra vez la juventud pasada.[48]

The presentation of this nostalgia for childhood through the image of the hidden garden reveals the profoundly escapist tendency in this theme. It is, in effect, a wish to return to the womb, to go back to the moment of the dream's conception when self and world appeared to be in harmony. This is an impossible desire, as Cernuda himself recognises, and as the memory of his youth in Seville continues to pain him his reaction to the memory becomes increasingly sardonic. "Primavera vieja" from *Como quien espera el alba* recounts another journey back in the mind to his native city only to find that he would be now an alien being in that idyllic environment and its remembrance brings merely a bitter recognition of the impotence of the dream created there :

> En el rincón de algún compás, a solas
> Con la frente en la mano, un fantasma
> Que vuelve, llorarías pensando
> Cuán bella fue la vida y cuán inútil. (p. 208)

In *Vivir sin estar viviendo* the evasive quality of Cernuda's concern with his youth is made abundantly evident in the poem "El éxtasis", which he has described as "un ejemplo flagrante de *wishful thinking*",[49] where he proposes that death will be a paradise of regained youth and adolescent dreams fulfilled. "Viendo volver" repeats the sentiments of "Primavera vieja", as, in a *dédoublement* of himself, he returns to the past to contemplate the youth he once was, and finds that he is again alienated from his former self. The man is painfully aware of the disenchantment awaiting the youth, and withdraws lest the latter realise that life is simply "una burla delicada". The same sardonic reaction to the memories of youth continues in "Lo más frágil es lo que dura", from *Con las horas contadas*, where the smell of orange blossom becomes an objective correlative for the insubstantial experience of youth, which is nonetheless declared to be the irreducible essence of his existence. The poem ends with this bitter comment :

> Y ves que es lo más hondo
> De tu vivir un poco
>
> De eso que llaman nada
> Tantas gentes sensatas :
>
> Un olor de azahar,
> Aire. ¿Hubo algo más? (p. 303)

[48] *Ocnos*, 55.

[49] Letter from Cernuda to Philip Silver dated 21-II-61, *apud* Silver *"Et in Arcadia ego"*, 126, note 22. In this letter Cernuda states that the title of his poem comes from John Donne's "The Extasie", and also that the setting of his reunion with his youthful self is a deliberate echo of Garcilaso's "Egloga primera", lines 394-407.

His youth, the foundation of his personality, had the promise of orange blossom, but it has borne no fruit, and all that he ever possessed was this unfulfilled promise whose memory has remained to taunt him as old age approaches.[50] The persistent remembrance of his adolescence is perhaps the most tragic element in Cernuda's mature poetry, for of all the paradises of which he dreamed this is the only one he ever experienced, only to have it carried away by the irrevocable passage of time.

The profound sense of alienation and the various attempts to overcome this, which occupy much of the poetry of Cernuda's exile, are brought to an end by the discovery of Mexico. The encounter with an Hispanic environment after the long years spent in Anglo-Saxon countries is the subject of the series of prose poems *Variaciones sobre tema mexicano*, although it has little presence in Cernuda's verse, which seems to have been reserved mainly for treating the love affair he experienced in Mexico. Only the occasional poem of *Con las horas contadas* has a Mexican background, like "El viajero" or "Otra fecha", for example, but these poems do express his ecstatic reaction to the discovery of a world that seemed to be a mirror image of his native Andalusia. He found in the air, light and palm trees of Mexico a recreation of that friendly environment of his youth in Seville which had haunted him by its absence during his exile in England and the United States, and this reintegration into a world with which he could feel a sense of identification offered a possible resolution to his problems of identity :

Aires claros, nopal y palma,
En los alrededores, saben,
Si no igual, casi igual a como
La tierra tuya aquella antes.

También tú igual me pareces,
O casi igual, al que antes eras :
En el casi sólo consiste,
De ayer a hoy, la diferencia. (p. 301)

Despite such expressions of reservation, this is a major reversal of the attitudes predominant in the poetry of exile up to this time. The alienation of Cernuda's inner world of dreams from the external world of reality has been abolished; *realidad* and *deseo* seem finally to have coincided, although he hardly dares to believe in this precarious fulfilment of his aspirations :

El mundo
Mágico que llevabas
Dentro de ti, esperando
Tan largamente, afuera
Surge a la luz. Si ahora

[50] Philip Silver, *"Et in Arcadia ego"*, 78, seems to suggest that this poem lacks any element of pain, but it would be more in accord with Cernuda's character if the final rhetorical question were to be read as ironic.

Tu sueño al fin coincide
Con tu verdad, no pienses
Que esta verdad es frágil,
Más aún que aquel sueño. (pp. 294-5)

Variaciones sobre tema mexicano describe in more detail this miraculous discovery of a world propitious for his dreams. In contrast to the limbo-like existence amidst the practical, industrial society of his exile, he found in Mexico a world that was truly alive, inhabited by people who had the same dignified indolence and animal grace as the ideal creatures who had peopled the mythic realm of Sansueña.[51] The vision of a terrestrial paradise, first formulated in the hidden garden of *Primeras poesías* and the pastoral idyll of the "Egloga", then expanded in the exotic dream-worlds of *Un río, un amor*, and further developed in the theme of the ancient gods and the idealisation of Andalusia, at last becomes reality. One of the prose poems of *Variaciones sobre tema mexicano* describes a Mexican patio as "un rinconcillo andaluz", a recreation of that hidden garden which was the central image of his dreams. As in the walled garden of the Alcázar in Seville, the Mexican patio enables him to feel in accord with the world, bringing a recovery of that communion with the world he had experienced as a child :

> Viendo este rincón, respirando este aire, hallas que lo que afuera ves y respiras también está dentro de tí; que allá en el fondo de tu alma, en su círculo oscuro, como luna reflejada en agua profunda, está la imagen misma de lo que en torno tienes; y que desde tu infancia se alza, intacta y límpida, esa imagen fundamental, sosteniendo, ella tan leve, el peso de tu vida y de su afán secreto.
>
> El hombre que tú eres se conoce así, al abrazar ahora al niño que fue, y el existir único de los dos halla su raíz en un rinconcillo secreto y callado del mundo. Comprendes entonces que al vivir esta otra mitad de la vida acaso no haces otra cosa que recobrar al fin, en lo presente, la infancia perdida, cuando el niño, por gracia, era ya dueño de lo que el hombre luego, tras no pocas vacilaciones, errores y extravíos, tiene que recobrar con esfuerzo.[52]

In another of the Mexican prose poems the feeling of having regained the *acorde total* of childhood and early adolescence is carried further when the experience of love in Mexico creates that quasi-mystic fusion between self and world which Cernuda describes in the prose poem "El acorde" from *Ocnos* :

> En un abrazo sentiste tu ser fundirse con aquella tierra; a través de un terso cuerpo oscuro, oscuro como penumbra, terso como fruto, alcanzaste la unión con aquella tierra que lo había creado. Y podrás olvidarlo todo menos ese contacto de la mano sobre un cuerpo, memoria donde parece latir, secreto y profundo, el pulso mismo de la vida.[53]

[51] "Dignidad y reposo", "Lo nuestro", and "Mercaderes de la flor", *Variaciones sobre tema mexicano* (Mexico, 1952), 21-3, 25-6, and 30-1, respectively.
[52] "El patio", *ibid.*, 63-4.
[53] "La posesión", *ibid.*, 67.

In Mexico Cernuda found a resolution for his experience of alienation, which he had sought earlier in his belief in the ancient gods, in his wish for death at the time of the Civil War, in Christianity during the first years of exile, and in the idealised vision of Spain. The discovery of his dream world in Mexico and the experience there of the love for which he had almost abandoned hope was the climactic moment of his life and the justification of the painful existence he had led until then. Mexico did offer him the quasi-mystic experience of love and the recapture of the idyllic world of his childhood, but it also provided him with an environment where he felt he could at last be himself. One of the prose poems of *Variaciones sobre tema mexicano* describes his discovery of Mexico as an experience of rebirth, a feeling that he had come home to a land that truly reflected his values and affirmed his identity :

> Por unos días hallaste en aquella tierra tu centro, que las almas tienen también, a su manera, centro en la tierra. El sentimiento de ser un extraño, que durante tiempo atrás te perseguía por los lugares donde viviste, allí callaba, al fin dormido. Estabas en tu sitio, o en un sitio que podía ser tuyo; con todo o con casi todo concordabas, y las cosas, aire, luz, paisaje, criaturas, te eran amigas. Igual que si una losa te hubieran quitado de encima, vivías como un resucitado.[54]

Cernuda's Mexican experience reveals, in fact, that his successive attempts to reach a transcendent level of existence are not concerned with evading reality, but are the symptoms of a concern with self-affirmation. The image of the hidden garden, in all its manifestations, is not in essence just a place of retreat from the world but a haven from hostile suroundings where Cernuda can preserve his identity. The hidden garden syndrome analysed in this chapter is thus not the indication of an effete personality incapable of living in the real world, but a sign of Cernuda's refusal to compromise his personal truth in a world he felt would betray or destroy him.

[54] "Centro de hombre", *ibid.*, 70-1.

IV

THE POET AND POETRY

La expresión de mi ser contradictorio,
Que se exalta por sentirse inhumano,
Que se humilla por sentirse imposible.

("Silla del rey", *Vivir sin estar viviendo*, p. 265)

The concern with the nature of poetry and the status of the poet, which becomes an insistently recurring theme in Cernuda's mature work, is, besides being a reflection of his symbolist background, a sign of commitment to his vocation. Since his youth Cernuda had seen poetry as his primary occupation, a justification for his existence;[1] in the long years of exile poetry assumed an even greater importance as a staff of life. Poetry itself, which has the fundamental aim of revealing the transcendent *imagen completa del mundo*, is the source of a possible consolation for the pain of life, another means of gaining the longed-for *acorde*. Yet it is as a poet that Cernuda finds himself brought into direct collision with the society that forms his audience and is the judge of his achievement. The contrast between the exalted rôle of poetry and the poet's conflict with society creates in Cernuda a typically ambivalent attitude which sees the poet both as the redeemer of the world and as a *poète maudit*. In one respect the theme of poetry forms part of the hidden garden syndrome analysed in the previous chapter, for it offers a refuge from the alien environment of exile and the possibility of creating a private world where reality and desire are one. But this evasive element in the theme is absorbed into the function that poetry exercises as a means of self-expression.

Although Cernuda appears to have been conscious of his existential involvement in his poetry from the beginnings of his literary career, in his early poems this awareness is present only in the conventional symbolist motifs of *Primeras poesías* and the occasional consciousness of being a poet which shows itself in *Un río, un amor*. However, when he reaches the process of self-reappraisal undertaken in *Invocaciones*, poetry becomes inevitably one of the most important of the values upon which he tries to rebuild his shattered world. It is thus at precisely this time that he makes an attempt to set out a theory of poetry in the essay 'Palabras antes de una lectura'. The central element of this theory, the

[1] In 'Historial de un libro' (*PL*, 239) Cernuda claims that even in 1927 "comenzaba a entrever que el trabajo poético era razón principal, si no única, de mi existencia".

conflict between *realidad* and *deseo*, has already been examined, but several other aspects remain to be considered.

Cernuda sees poetry as an expression of a mysterious "fuerza daimónica" that is the guiding force in the world, and poetry thus becomes a means of access to the life force, while the poet is made into a *vate*, a mediator between man and the daemonic power. The poet is gifted with the perception of "el misterio de la creación, la hermosura oculta del mundo", able to see the truth hidden behind appearance and unite the divided visible and invisible realities in the world.[2] In poetry the poet finds the real truth about life and about himself, as Cernuda clearly states in an essay written a few years before 'Palabras antes de una lectura':

> . . . un poema es casi siempre un fantasma, algo que se arrastra en busca de su propia realidad. Ningún sueño vale nada al lado de esta realidad, que se esconde siempre y sólo a veces podemos sorprender. En ella poesía y verdad son una misma cosa.[3]

Another statement made almost thirty years later echoes the idea of the need for the poet to discover the hidden mystery of life, demonstrating a continuity of thought and a dedication to this principle:

> Al leer hoy *Les Fleurs du Mal*, el espectáculo que Baudelaire nos hace compartir está tan vivo, pasado un siglo, como cuando él lo vivía y contemplaba. Para conseguir eso el poeta ha de considerar cada instante de su existir como si en él pudiera encerrarse el momento supernatural, el momento que esconde al misterio, ya que su tarea es desentrañar a éste y, haciéndolo suyo, revelarlo.[4]

The belief that the poet should regard each moment of his life as though it contained the key to life's enigma is linked with another persistent and fundamental element in Cernuda's view of poetry: the concern with the relationship between the temporally circumscribed existence of the individual and the eternal spirit of life itself. In 'Palabras antes de una lectura' Cernuda declares that the poet's aim is to halt the flux of time, and that poetry is engendered by the ensuing struggle with time. This is part of the poet's search for the eternal reality beneath the transitory appearance of the world, which is focussed in particular on his pursuit of beauty, since beauty is part of the daemonic power but manifests itself in ephemeral forms. These ideas lead to what is referred to as an "inevitable" definition of poetry:

> . . . la poesía fija a la belleza efímera. Gracias a ella lo sobrenatural y lo humano se unen en bodas espirituales, engendrando celestes criaturas, como en los mitos griegos del amor de un dios hacia un mortal nacieron seres semi-divinos. El poeta, pues, intenta fijar a la belleza transitoria del mundo que percibe, refiriéndola al mundo invisible que presiente, y al desfallecer y

[2] 'Palabras antes de una lectura', *loc. cit.*, 200-1.
[3] 'El espíritu lírico', *Heraldo de Madrid*, 21-I-32, 12.
[4] 'Baudelaire en el centenario de *Las Flores del Mal*', *Poesía y literatura II*, 145.

quedar vencido en esa lucha desigual, su voz . . . llora enamorada la pérdida de lo que ama.[5]

Such a definition clearly owes something to Antonio Machado's poetics, but it is also highly coloured by Cernuda's idiosyncratic view of the world.[6] Poetry is a means of access to the invisible reality, the transcendent realm symbolised by the ancient gods; it is a means of creating the ideal state of the *acorde*. Yet the task of breaking through temporality into eternity is too great for the poet's puny strength, and the poet is condemned to lament the dominance of Time, and by extension, the schism between *realidad* and *deseo*. The tragic view of the poet's task is at the basis of the great elegiac poems of Cernuda's maturity. It is, above all, interesting to note that the wish to halt the flux of time is, in effect, the same as the wish to gain the state of the *acorde*, but here there are no illusions about the inescapable failure awaiting such a desire.

The poet is also a tragic figure because of his conflict with society; his connection with the daemonic power gives him the status of a prophet, an interpreter of the divine law, but contemporary society has chosen to ignore the sacred mysteries. The poet is isolated, without a public to heed his words or compensate him for his vain struggle with time, yet driven to write because he is possessed by the daemonic power. This Romantic view of the poet as a victim of Fate and society is strongly underlined by the attitude taken towards Bécquer in an essay roughly contemporaneous with 'Palabras antes de una lectura' :

> Su destino todos lo conocemos : enfermedad, pobreza, infortunio. Pero no nos lamentemos de ello ahora : sería farisáico. A nuestro lado puede repetirse en alguien más aquel destino ya cumplido en otros; no nos importaría. Mientras la sociedad esté organizada de la manera que lo estuvo entonces y lo está hoy, el infortunio de Bécquer es y será posible.[7]

The Romantic element in Cernuda's concept of the poet is further emphasised by the declaration in 'Palabras antes de una lectura' that the poet is a revolutionary, a man imprisoned in society like other men, but who is incapable of accepting this and continually tries to break down the walls of his cell.[8] Cernuda sees the struggle with society as an essential characteristic of modern poetry, and one that has a positive and salutary effect, since it obliges the poet who has

[5] *Loc. cit.*, 199-200.

[6] Cernuda has compared Machado's poetics and concept of time with some remarks of an Arab mystic quoted by Louis Massignon, *Estudios sobre poesía española contemporánea,* 116 n. These same remarks of the Arab mystic are also quoted in 'Palabras antes de una lectura', *loc. cit.*, 199, and, in the following form, on a band round the first edition of *La Realidad y el Deseo* (Madrid, 1936):

> Hallach, teólogo musulmán, pasaba un día con sus discípulos por una calle de Bagdad, cuando les sorprendió el sonido de una flauta exquisita. "¿Qué es eso?", le pregunta uno de sus discípulos. Y el responde : "Es la voz de Satán que llora sobre el mundo."
>
> Satán llora sobre el mundo porque quiere hacerlo sobrevivir a la destrucción. Ha sido condenado a enamorarse de las cosas que pasan y por eso llora.

[7] 'Bécquer y el romanticismo español', *Cruz y raya,* no. 26 (1935), 56.

[8] *Loc. cit.*, 197.

broken with his social environment to seek strength entirely within himself. Cernuda's comment on Wordsworth is illuminating on this point :

> La grandeza de Wordsworth resulta precisamente de su lucha individual para conseguir unidad de espíritu. De ahí que sus poemas expresen la reacción del hombre que se afana por sobrevivir en una sociedad donde no hay sitio para él, y eso hace de Wordsworth, juntamente con Blake, el primer poeta inglés moderno.[9]

This existential dimension given by Cernuda to the poet's struggle with society takes his concept of the poet beyond the purely Romantic idea of the poet as victim and *vate.* What the poet seeks is his personal salvation through poetry, pursuing in poetry a transfigured level of existence. This is the experience Cernuda felt he shared with poets like Wordsworth and Bécquer; it was as a poet that he was forced to confront the society in which he lived, and it was through his poetry that he struggled to overcome the ensuing conflict. *La Realidad y el Deseo* is the record of Cernuda's own "lucha individual para conseguir unidad de espíritu".

The Struggle with Time

The idea that poetry's aim is to eternalize ephemeral beauty is a direct product of Cernuda's acute consciousness of temporality, part of his desperate need to find "una pausa de amor entre la fuga de las cosas" (p. 148). The poet's thirst for eternity is aroused above all by beauty because the abstract concept of beauty is eternal even though its physical manifestations are transitory. Here is the root of both the poet's glory and his tragedy. The duality in this attitude to beauty is clearly evident in the poem on the myth of Ganymede, "El águila", from *Como quien espera el alba.* The tragic relationship between beauty and time is particularly marked in respect of the erotic ideal of youthful beauty. The adolescent Ganymede is destined to lose his beauty, but Zeus, who delivers the monologue that forms the poem, raises him to Olympus, making him immortal to preserve his beauty. It is suggested that beauty is the human reflection of the gods and that its ephemerality is therefore an injustice :

Tú no debes morir. En la hermosura
La eternidad trasluce sobre el mundo
Tal rescate imposible de la muerte.

. . . . .

¿Es la hermosura,
Forma carnal de una celeste idea,
Hecha para morir? Vino de oro
Que a dioses y poetas embriaga,
Abriendo sueños vastos como el tiempo,
Quiero hacerla inmortal. (p. 186)

[9] *Pensamiento poético en la lírica inglesa* (*siglo XIX*) (Mexico, 1958), 61.

Here is a poetic restatement of the assertion in 'Palabras antes de una lectura' that the poet's task is to fix transitory beauty and relate it to the invisible, eternal world, bringing together the human and divine planes of life. These lines also demonstrate how an acute consciousness of time provides the dynamic for this attitude: the eternity glimpsed in beauty offers just a faint possibility of redeeming man from his transient existence.

The relationship between beauty and time is the subject of one of Cernuda's most well-known poems, "Violetas" from *Las nubes*. This delicate poem, perhaps inspired by violets which were a forerunner of spring in the harsh English winter of exile, contrasts the fragility of these humble blooms with the immortal beauty reflected in them. The violets symbolise the promise of youth and vitality that is born anew each spring free from time. The glimpse of eternity offered by the flowers is a redemption from the oblivion of death and, moreover, the memory of what the violets represent lives on in the mind of the poet:

> Al marchar victoriosos a la muerte
> Sostienen un momento, ellas tan frágiles,
> El tiempo entre sus pétalos. Así su instante alcanza,
> Norma para lo efímero que es bello,
> A ser vivo embeleso en la memoria. (pp. 177-8)[10]

The violets' momentary escape from the flux of time arouses in the poet that state of "embeleso" which Cernuda uses to describe the experience of harmony between self and world. The state of timelessness further awakens a reminiscence of the childhood innocence of time to which Cernuda continually looks back with elegiac nostalgia. However, Cernuda is here a spectator of the moment of eternity contained in the violets, and the freedom from time he perceives in the flowers is in tacit contrast to his own subjection to temporality, which is why the poem creates a mood of elegy and not exultancy. But if the poet can eternalize beauty in his work, even though he himself is mortal, something of him will continue to exist in the poetry, which is independent of its creator. Poetry offers an escape from a life curbed by time and a glimpse of that state of *acorde* which is always Cernuda's goal.

The problems raised by the fragility and transience of beauty are confronted from a different angle in "El ruiseñor sobre la piedra" where the monastery of El Escorial is both a symbol of Spain and of the artistic achievement of man. The monastery is an image of beauty, the creation of a sensibility that despises practical things and is diametrically opposed to the ethic of usefulness, which Cernuda sees as the dominant characteristic of the environment of his exile. The Escorial is as useless as the lily, a biblical allusion that emphasises the moral value-judgement made in this poem.[11] The worship of things practical and use-

[10] The inevitable comparison between Cernuda's concept of beauty and that of Keats has been made by J. L. Cano, *Poesía española del siglo XX* (Madrid, 1960), 339-43.

[11] Similar sentiments and the same biblical allusion occur in the short story "El sarao", written in 1942 and therefore nearly contemporaneous with "El ruiseñor sobre la piedra": "[Lotario] Nunca hubiera sido útil a los demás, y él mismo se reiría de la idea. Pero no por eso dejaba de tener valor su existencia. ¿No nos preocupamos demasiado de lo útil

ful enslaves man, whereas beauty, free from such subservience, offers to man a glimpse of freedom:

> ¿Qué es lo útil, lo práctico,
> Sino la vieja añagaza diabólica
> De esclavizar al hombre
> Al infierno en el mundo?
>
> . . . . .
>
> Lo hermoso es lo que pasa
> Negándose a servir, Lo hermoso, lo que amamos,
> Tú sabes que es un sueño y que por eso
> Es más hermoso aún para nosotros. (p. 181)

Society's abandonment of beauty for the cult of practicality is one consequence of the loss of contact with the daemonic power in the world. But the freedom of beauty from social bonds gives to the creator of beauty a freedom that is all the greater because beauty is also capable of negating the threat of time. The assertion that beauty is a dream and therefore even more beautiful could be taken as ironic, yet this can also be given a positive interpretation. Beauty may only be a dream, but by dedicating his life to a dream that is of greater virtue than reality, a man makes an act of faith which itself ennobles him. Beauty, and the pursuit of beauty in the artifact, can redeem the wretchedness of human existence.[12]

The poet's concern with beauty is one of the ways he is brought into conflict with society. In "El ruiseñor sobre la piedra" Cernuda refers to "el trágico ocio del poeta"; idleness is the poet's occupation, and this, in a practical society, is a sin, all the more so in the puritanical world of Glasgow.[13] Yet while the idle concern for beauty alienates the poet from society, his poetry offers him, as a compensation, a measure of self-sufficiency. Cernuda's ideal concept of the poet is expressed in the image of the nightingale in the title of the poem; the nightingale, like the monastery, sings purely for itself, impelled by its love of beauty and with no desire for recognition. Although it too is engaged in a useless occupation, it possesses the divine solitude also given to the poet, and its song is a means of communion with the heavens:

> Tú conoces las horas
> Largas del ocio dulce,
> Pasadas en vivir de cara al cielo
> Cantando el mundo bello, obra divina,

11 continued
y lo práctico, olvidándonos de vivir? Quizá sea incomprensible hoy para nosotros la verdad de aquellas palabras divinas: 'Reparad los lirios del campo, cómo crecen que no trabajan ni hilan; mas os digo que ni Salómón en su gloria fue vestido así como uno de ellos'." *Tres narraciones* (Buenos Aires, 1948), 145.

[12] Cf. "Aunque dentro de su alma existe acaso la creencia de que las cosas no son como él dice que las ve, no importa: conviene embriagar la razón y transformar la mísera realidad de los hombres, que tan divina pudiera ser sólo con añadirle un poco de exaltación." 'Cervantes', *Poesía y literatura II*, 34-5.

[13] Cf. "Ocio", *Variaciones sobre tema mexicano,* 45-7.

Con voz que nadie oye
Ni busca aplauso humano,
Como el ruiseñor canta
En la noche de estío,
Porque su sino quiere
Que cante, porque su amor le impulsa.
Y en la gloria nocturna
Divinamente solo
Sube su canto puro a las estrellas. (p. 182)

The ideal situation of self-sufficiency is developed in "Silla del rey", from *Vivir sin estar viviendo,* another poem in the trilogy on Philip II,[14] although a more complex work than "El ruiseñor sobre la piedra" because it is expressed through the mouth of the king himself and has that subtle blend of objective and subjective elements with which Cernuda creates his monologues by historical or legendary characters. The king, watching the building of the Escorial from his chair on the hill above the site, sees the monastery as an expression of his Catholic faith and centralising political ideals. But the Escorial is here again an artistic creation, and on this level the poem becomes concerned with Cernudas' own preoccupations. The king's observation, used as a rubric for this chapter, that the monastery represents his own contradictory personality leads to a meditation on the relationship between his work, time and society, and he declares that what he is creating is a haven from the world protected from temporal changes by spiritual power :

Y yo de tierra mala trazo un huerto
Sellado para el mundo todo,
Que huraño lo contempla concertando hundirlo.

. . . . .

Mi obra no está afuera, sino adentro,
En el alma; y el alma, en los azares
Del bien y el mal, es igual a sí misma :
Ni nace, ni perece. Y esto que yo edifico
No es piedra, sino alma, el fuego inextinguible. (p. 266)

Here is another appearance of the image of the hidden garden, now applied to the process of artistic creation as a sign of the ideal state of self-sufficiency which poetry can bring to the poet. What is more, while these lines are in part concerned with the artifact's freedom from the flux of time, they also emphasise that an artist's work is an expression of himself, and therefore what is termed the construction of a soul is really an act of auto-creation. The attempt to capture eternity in art is, thus, also a means of gaining personal immortality. The artist incorporates himself into the "fuego inextinguible", an image reminiscent

[14] It was Cernuda's declared intention that "El ruiseñor sobre la piedra", "Silla del rey" and "Aguila y rosa", from *Con las horas contadas,* should form a trilogy. See the note to the publication of "Aguila y rosa", *Papeles de Son Armadans,* no. XIX (1957), 57.

of terms used to describe the daemonic power. Art again provides an access to the transcendent *acorde*.

The poet's struggle to break free of temporality is a major concern in "Las ruinas" from *Como quien espera el alba*. The contrast made in this poem between the survival of the classical ruins and the disappearance of the men who built them, symbolises the root of man's tragedy: while himself subject to time and death, he can create what is immune to time. It is unjust that mortal man should be driven through life by a thirst for eternity. The solution Cernuda proposes here for the problem of beauty's transience is to regard beauty as though it were eternal, thereby denying its transitoriness. This is associated with the reproach to God in this poem:

> Todo lo que es hermoso tiene su instante, y pasa.
> Importa como eterno gozar de nuestro instante.
> Yo no te envidio, Dios; déjame a solas
> Con mis obras humanas que no duran:
> El afán de llenar lo que es efímero
> De eternidad, vale tu omnipotencia. (p. 188)

This is a declaration of outstanding importance. The challenge to God, who is immortal, is made in full knowledge of man's puniness; beauty is ephemeral, so are the works of man, and the desire to give them eternity, which is the poet's mission, is, by implication, doomed to failure. Nonetheless, Cernuda has staked his very existence on this point. The "afán", the will to try, is what is significant, since this amounts to an act of faith in himself. The struggle to redeem beauty from the flux of time, which is at the basis of Cernuda's theory of poetry, is linked in "Las ruinas", even more clearly than in "Silla del rey", with the identification Cernuda makes between himself and his poetic activity, which becomes a means of affirming and justifying his existence.

The Status of the Poet: Redeemer and Victim

The idea of the poet as a prophet interpreting the divine law is inherent in the concept, set out in 'Palabras antes de una lectura', that poetry is an expression of the daemonic power; only the poet can hear divine voices, only he can perceive the mystery of creation. In "La gloria del poeta", from *Invocaciones*, poetry is compared to the action of a child throwing stones into a lake in order to see the ripples spread across its smooth surface like the "reflejo de una gran ala misteriosa" (p. 115), while in "Noche de luna", the first poem of *Las nubes*, it is this strange and powerful force that enables the poet to find rest in a transitory world and dream of eternal beauty:

> Algo inmenso reposa, aunque la muerte aceche.
> Y el mágico reflejo entre los árboles
> Permite al soñador abandonarse al canto,
> Al placer y al reposo,
> A lo que siendo efímero se sueña como eterno. (p. 131)

The poet also, of course, acquires prophetic stature from his association with the ancient gods. However, the most extensive treatment of the view of the poet as a *vate* occurs in the elegy to Lorca, "A un poeta muerto". As the reticence of the title suggests, this poem is a meditation on the status of the Poet, in a generalised sense, even though it was directly inspired by the death of a much-loved friend. Because Cernuda uses the personal and particular tragedy to make a statement about the tragic destiny he feels is the lot of any poet, he has produced in "A un poeta muerto" a poem whose significance surpasses that of most of the elegies for Lorca produced by other poets of his generation.

Lorca is seen both as the victim of an uncomprehending and inimical society, and as a communicant with the daemonic power. He was the representative of the supreme glory of life, since, as a poet, he was able to give expression to the mysterious motivating force of the world. The poet is here defined as "aquel que ilumina las palabras opacas/Por el oculto fuego originario"; but this, the poet's glory, is also his tragedy, since he is consumed by the primal fire. His only consolation is in death, an idea that links this concept of the poet with the death-wish studied in the previous chapter:

> Para el poeta la muerte es la victoria;
> Un viento demoníaco le impulsa por la vida. (p. 133)

This Romantic view of the poet as someone driven to destruction by an implacable destiny owes much to Cernuda's interest in Hölderlin at this time, and to the ideas of 'Palabras antes de una lectura', but in the final stanza of the poem the concept of the poet is taken beyond that of someone possessed by the daemonic power:

> . . . este ansia divina, perdida aquí en la tierra,
> Tras de tanto dolor y dejamiento,
> Con su propia grandeza nos advierte
> De alguna mente creadora inmensa,
> Que concibe al poeta cual lengua de su gloria
> Y luego le consuela a través de la muerte. (p. 134)[15]

The Becquerian "ansia divina" in these lines, already mentioned in connection with Cernuda's brief attempt to find solace in Christianity, makes the poet into an interpreter of the divine will for whom death brings a consummation with the harmony that is absent in the world of man. In "A un poeta muerto" the implications of this exalted view of the poet are subdued by the dominant tone of pessimism in the poems of the Civil War, but in later years, as the divine presence, whether pagan or Christian, recedes into the background, the pro-

[15] Cf. Vicente Aleixandre's poem "El poeta" from *Sombra del paraíso*:

> inmensa lengua profética que lamiendo los cielos
> ilumina palabras que dan muerte a los hombres.

Cf. also Hölderlin's poems "Rousseau", "Dichterberuf", "Heimkunft" and "An die Parzen", this later poem is one of those translated by Cernuda, *Cruz y raya*, no. 32 (1935), 122.

phetic status of the poet as an intermediary with the gods develops into the idea that the poet is himself a creator.

The beginnings of such a development can be found in "Río vespertino", from *Como quien espera el alba*, where Cernuda examines the function of the poet, using the image of a blackbird, in parallel to the nightingale which is a symbol for the poet in "El ruiseñor sobre la piedra". The blackbird is another creature blessed with self-sufficiency, singing only for itself, unlike man who is burdened with the task of expressing the whole human condition :[16]

Está todo abstraído en una pausa
De silencio y quietud. Tan sólo un mirlo
Estremece con el canto la tarde.
Su destino es más puro que el del hombre
Que para el hombre canta, pretendiendo
Ser voz significante de la grey,
La conciencia insistente en esa huida
De las almas. Contemplación, sosiego,
El instante perfecto, que tal fruto
Madura, inútil es para los otros,
Condenando al poeta y su tarea
De ver en unidad el ser disperso,
El mundo fragmentario donde viven.
Sueño no es lo que al poeta ocupa,
Mas la verdad oculta, como el fuego
Subyacente en la tierra. Son los otros,
Traficantes de sueños infecundos,
Quienes despiertan en la muerte un día,
Pobres al fin. ¿De qué le vale al hombre
Ganar su vida mientras pierde el alma,
Si sólo un pensamiento vale el mundo? (p. 226)[17]

The self-sufficient blackbird, in harmony with nature, exists in that eternal present of the "instante perfecto" also found in the quasi-mystical union between self and world to which Cernuda aspires. Man is separated from this ideal mode of existence by his consciousness of time and his involvement in society. The poet's prophetic status, his burden of the "voz significante" which singles him out from the herd, is here a cause of regret since it prevents him attaining that total freedom symbolised in the blackbird. Yet despite this ambivalent attitude, this passage from "Río vespertino" clearly reveals several of Cernuda's fundamental ideas about the rôle of the poet. The meaningfulness the poet conveys derives from the task of perceiving the unity hidden behind the fragmentary elements of life; he is a seeker of the truth, pursuing the true reality which lies behind the appearance of the world. This is a poetic restate-

[16] Cf. "El mirlo", *Ocnos,* 139-40.

[17] In addition to a biblical allusion, the rhetorical question here also contains an echo of San Juan de la Cruz: "Un solo pensamiento del hombre vale más que todo el mundo", *Avisos y sentencias espirituales,* no. 32.

ment of the theories of 'Palabras antes de una lectura' related in particular to the link between poetry and the daemonic power, alluded to here by the simile of subterranean fire. However, a new dimension is added by the use of the term "la verdad oculta", the same image of "truth" used in connection with several attempts to gain the ideal state of the *acorde*. The implication here that poetry is another means to this end is confirmed beyond all doubt by the biblical allusion and the echo of San Juan de la Cruz in the rhetorical question closing the passage quoted above.

The concept of the poet as the creator of unity out of formlessness has moved some distance beyond the idea of him as a familiar of the gods, and this development is carried a stage further in "El poeta", from *Vivir sin estar viviendo*. This poem is an expression of Cernuda's gratitude to Juan Ramón Jiménez, who was a major influence on his early poems, for having revealed to him the wonder and the mystery of poetry.[18] In this acknowledgement of his debt to Jiménez, Cernuda describes in some detail the conception of poetry he himself had come to hold in his mature years :

> Con reverencia y con amor así aprendiste,
> Aunque en torno los hombres no curen de la imagen
> Misteriosa y divina de las cosas,
> De él, a mirar quieto, como
> Espejo, sin el cual la creación sería
> Ciega, hasta hallar su mirada en el poeta.
>
> . . . . .
>
> . . . y nadie sino tú puede decirle,
> A aquel que te enseñara adónde y cómo crece :
> Gracias por la rosa del mundo.
>
> Para el poeta hallarla es lo bastante,
> E inútil el renombre u olvido de su obra,
> Cuando en ella un momento se unifican,
> Tal uno son amante, amor y amado,
> Los tres complementarios luego y antes dispersos :
> El deseo, la rosa y la mirada. (pp. 252-3)

Here is the idea that the poet is someone in the closest contact with reality, the true reality of both the visible and the invisible worlds, someone who can perceive the *verdad oculta*. Such an attitude recalls the idea expressed in 'Palabras antes de una lectura' that the tangible world is a mirage while the only real element is the desire to possess it, and also brings to mind the definition of metaphysical poetry as the expression of the superior reality hidden behind the invisible world. But in "El poeta" the poet is seen as more than just an intermediary in the creative process, a "medium" for divine revelation, although the simile of the mirror does maintain him in a passive rôle; in this poem he is

[18] The opening stanza of "El poeta" alludes to Cernuda's first contact with Jiménez in September 1925. See 'Los dos Juan Ramón Jiménez', *Poesía y literatura II*, 110.

brought close to being the creator of the world, for without him the true, invisible reality of the world would not be revealed. This element in the poet's function leads to another statement of poetry's relationship with the experience of the *acorde*, expressed here in the image of "la rosa del mundo". The rose is, of course, a central element of symbolist iconography, and thus related to the reference to Jiménez, but it also awakens an echo of the image of the rose and the fire in Aldana's "Epístola a Arias Montano", an image which Cernuda himself has referred to in connection with the fusion of form and content in Aldana's poem.[19] Cernuda's own concept of poetry is thus brought close to his idea of "metaphysical" poetry, which he sees typified in Aldana's work. However, the comparison made between the experience of artistic creation and the fusion of love, the lover and the beloved at the moment of coition brings an inevitable equation between the discovery of "la rosa del mundo" and the quasi-mystic *acorde*, since it is precisely this erotic simile Cernuda employs to describe the union between self and world.[20] As José Olivio Jiménez has pointed out the three elements in the final line of "El poeta", desire, the rose and the eye of the poet contemplating it, represent "los tres protagonistas del drama metafísico : el hombre, la realidad trascendente y el impulso desde aquél hacia éste".[21] The fusion of these three elements in the poetic experience can momentarily create that *instante perfecto* of a transcendent existence outside time which Cernuda always desires. Thus the poet moves beyond the status of a prophet to become a mystic.

The beatific attitude of "El poeta" turns to exultant triumph in "Silla del rey" where Cernuda's artist/king, Philip II, in a declaration of arrogant blasphemy, proclaims himself the redeemer of the world :

Cuando Alguno en Su nombre regresara al mundo
Que por El yo administro, encontraría,
Conclusa y redimida, la obra ya perfecta;
Intento de cambiarla ha de ser impostura,
Y a Su impostor, si no la cruz, la hoguera aguarda. (p. 267)

It has been suggested that the portrait of Philip II presented in this poem is a criticism of power and that therefore Cernuda is in disagreement with the sentiments expressed here,[22] yet, despite the unsympathetic display of arrogance, such a view of the poet is not too distant from the ideas of "El poeta". I suggest that the arrogance is part of the characterisation of Philip II and that behind this mask Cernuda is putting forward his own belief that the poet ought to be the redeemer of the world. This view of the poet is a logical conclusion of the

[19] See the "Epístola moral a Arias Montano", lines 439-444. These lines are quoted by Cernuda in 'Tres poetas metafísicos', *Poesía y literatura,* 69.

[20] "Plenitud que, repetida a lo largo de la vida, es siempre la misma : ni recuerdo atávico, ni presagio de lo venidero : testimonio de lo que pudiera ser estar vivo en nuestro mundo. Lo más parecido a ella es ese adentrarse por otro cuerpo en el momento del éxtasis, de la unión con la vida a través del cuerpo deseado." *Ocnos,* 193.

[21] 'Emoción y trascendencia del tiempo en la poesía de Luis Cernuda', *La caña gris,* nos. 6-8 (1962), 81.

[22] Silver, *"Et in Arcadia ego",* 205, note 15.

development of the prophetic status of the poet first set out in *Invocaciones*, but it is also an isolated case; the only other example of the poet seen as a redeemer occurs in the poem "Mozart" from *Desolación de la Quimera*. Such an idea would seem to be the product of *folie de grandeur* stemming from the poet's association with the daemonic power and the mystical dimension of his experience.

The concept of the poet as the creator of a superior reality insulated by its spiritual power from the sordid world of common man belongs to that evasive side of Cernuda's character already examined in connection with the symbol of the hidden garden; poetry offers another means of access to a transcendent mode of existence. The poet's exalted rôle as a mystic and a redeemer is, however, balanced by a view of the poet as the victim of a hostile and uncomprehending society blind to the world's divine dimensions. In the social context the poet is isolated by his prophetic status which makes him as alien in the modern world as the gods with whom he communes. The first direct confrontation between the poet and society appears in "La gloria del poeta" as part of the process of reappraisal of belief undertaken in *Invocaciones*. The critical comment in this poem, directed against society's spiritual poverty and disassociation from the natural world, is focused specifically on the problems encountered by the poet. The graceless phantoms who form this degraded society dictate the conventions under which the poet must live, providing the norm for beauty and thus usurping his function in the world. Isolated among alien creatures whom he refers to as "los seres con quienes muero a solas" (p. 114), Cernuda is nagged by the fear that after his death his work will be appropriated by this society which will one day produce :

El solemne erudito, oráculo de estas palabras mías ante alumnos
  extraños,
Obteniendo por ello renombre,
Más una pequeña casa de campo en la angustosa sierra inmediata a
  la capital. (p. 114)

In this bitter vision of the academic who derives material benefit from his explications of the work of a poet who was in total disagreement with the society that academic serves, there is an implicit desire on the part of Cernuda for recognition on his own terms. Such a desire is inherent in the complaint that he is isolated, and becomes more overt when this is repeated in greater detail in "Himno a la tristeza" :

Viven y mueren a solas los poetas,
Restituyendo en claras lágrimas
La polvorienta agua salobre,
Y en alta gloria resplandeciente
La esquiva ojeada del magnate henchido,
Mientras sus nombres suenan
Con el viento en las rocas,
Entre el hosco rumor de torrentes oscuros,
Allá por los espacios donde el hombre
Nunca puso sus plantas. (p. 124)

It is not by accident that the Muse of sadness should be described in this poem as "amor de justicia imposible". Cernuda is objecting that the poet is denied the recognition from society merited by his exalted rôle in the world, while, as an added insult, the future can only offer him oblivion. Here is a statement of the tragic dilemma confronting the poet: he is gifted to perceive the divine truth of the world but is imprisoned in a society that has forsaken the daemonic power, yet, while he rejects that society's values, he needs the recognition only that society can give him. No solution seems possible for this conflict with society, and, although the attitudes of *Invocaciones* hold some faint foreshadowing of the arrogance that will later appear in "Silla del rey", there is also a sense of the poet's powerlessness that sets this view of his status in society at a polar extreme from the concept of the poet as a redeemer.

The experience of the Civil War and exile produces an even bleaker aspect to Cernuda's view of the poet's relationship with society. In *Las nubes* Lorca and Larra become symbolic figures who represent the artist as a tragic victim of a philistine environment. He sees Lorca in "A un poeta muerto" as a martyr, but a martyr in the cause of poetry, someone who represented vitality amid the arid climate of Spain and who thus aroused the envy of his compatriots, whom Cernuda, after the manner of Antonio Machado, characterises with the mark of Cain. Lorca died simply because he was a poet, the victim of envy, ignorance and fear of the unknown in Spanish society. The blame is laid against the Spanish people as a whole, without distinction between Republican or Nationalist:

> El odio y destrucción perduran siempre
> Sordamente en la entraña
> Toda hiel sempiterna del español terrible,
> Que acecha lo cimero
> Con su piedra en la mano.
>
> Triste sino nacer
> Con algún don ilustre
> Aquí, donde los hombres
> En su miseria sólo saben
> El insulto, la mofa, el recelo profundo
> Ante aquel que ilumina las palabras opacas
> Por el oculto fuego originario. (p. 132)

In "A Larra con unas violetas", written to mark the centenary of Larra's death in 1937, the nineteenth-century satirist is seen as another victim of the spiritual vacuum of Spanish society. The real reason for his suicide is presented as his despair as a writer, not the failed love affair; to one of Larra's most well-known remarks, Cernuda adds his own caustic gloss: "Escribir en España no es llorar, es morir" (p. 142). As with Lorca, he uses Larra to make a generalised statement about the writer's position in society, a position that is impossible and intolerable because of society's hostility. Larra's death, like Lorca's, is seen as a salve for the pain of life, and death is the only salvation available to the artist, bringing him a final communion with the daemonic power. There can be little doubt that Cernuda in these two poems is identifying himself with Lorca and Larra, although they are cast as conventional elegies and do not employ the *Doppelgänger* technique he begins to develop at this time. The extreme degree of bitterness is a tacit sign of Cernuda's belief that he shared a similar tragic destiny.

In *Como quien espera el alba* Cernuda returns to the theme of the poet as a victim of society with his poem "Góngora". From the vantage point of the early 1940s he surveys the incomprehension and humiliation Góngora suffered during his lifetime, the critical hostility of the literary establishment for three centuries after his death, and the final bitter irony of his rehabilitation in 1927. Góngora's rediscovery after the centuries of indifference is regarded as an example of society's hypocrisy, and as an act of appropriation of the poet by society which Cernuda had feared for himself in "La gloria del poeta". The academic who profits from the poet's work is attacked with even greater ferocity than before, while the poem ends with a sardonic litany, containing distant echoes of Baudelaire's *Les litanies de Satan*, which holds out no hope that Góngora's fate will not be repeated in others :

> Ventaja grande es que esté ya muerto
> Y que de muerto cumpla los tres siglos, que así pueden
> Los descendientes mismos de quienes le insultaban
> Inclinarse a su nombre, dar premio al erudito,
> Sucesor del gusano, royendo su memoria.[23]
>
> . . . . .
>
> Gracias demos a Dios por la paz de Góngora vencido;
> Gracias demos a Dios por la paz de Góngora exaltado;
> Gracias demos a Dios, que supo devolverle (como hará con nosotros)
> Nulo al fin, ya tranquilo, entre su nada. (p. 194)

The intense bitterness of this powerful poem is emphasised by the change which has occurred in the attitude towards death as a release from the pain of life; the compensation now offered to the poet is oblivion, not an escape into a transcendent existence of communion with the guiding force of the universe. Góngora is another example of the injustice of the poet's lot in the world, and the depth of feeling here leads inevitably to the conclusion that Cernuda has identified himself with Góngora. Góngora is now set beside Lorca and Larra as a symbolic figure of the artist as victim, although the greater degree of objectivity, particularly evident in the description of the humiliations of Góngora's life, brings this poem closer to the *Doppelgänger* compositions and imparts a much greater impact to this denunciation of society's hostility to the poet.

As Cernuda's exile continues and his consciousness of the passing of time grows sharper the concern with the poet's relationship with society acquires a

[23] There is here, perhaps, an unpleasant allusion to Dámaso Alonso, with whom Cernuda later came into conflict. See 'Carta abierta a Dámaso Alonso', *Insula,* no. 35 (1948), and also "Otra vez con sentimento" from *Desolación de la Quimera.*

more personal focus and it becomes clear that what he seeks from society is recognition. Exile separates him even further than before from any possible audience for his work, and this becomes a source of acute anxiety as he realises that poetry is the only means he possesses of creating a lasting justification for his existence. The accentuation, due to exile, in his sense of being isolated in an alien environment is stated openly in the complaint contained in "Río vespertino" :

Aquéllos son los más, tienen la tierra
Y apenas si un rincón queda asignado
Para el poeta, como muerto en vida.
Es la patria madrastra avariciosa,
Exigiendo el sudor, la sangre, el semen
A cambio del olvido y del destierro. (p. 227)

The idealised vision of Spain the Earth Mother has turned into the sour image of a step-mother, shutting off Cernuda from that sense of belonging to his native country to which he had tried to cling in exile, but underlying this intense feeling of alienation is the assumption that he has been unjustly denied the recognition he deserves. The same complaint is repeated in "Un contemporáneo" from *Vivir sin estar viviendo* with a sardonic force heightened by the off-hand colloquial tone with which Cernuda presents a portrait of himself set in the words of a fictional acquaintance who had known him in Cambridge. This acquaintance, after having dismissed Cernuda's writings as valueless, asks whether it is possible for a poet to be unknown during his lifetime and then find fame after his death. The answer is a totally pessimistic negative; the poet who fails to gain recognition when alive will be brought only a continuation of this oblivion by death :

¿Acaso hubo exceso en el olvido
Que vivió día a día? Hecho a medida
Del propio ser oscuro, exacto era; y a la muerte
Se lleva aquello que tomamos
De la vida, o lo que ella nos da : olvido
Acá, y olvido allá para él. Es lo mismo. (p. 257)

Cernuda's belief in society's hostility to the poet would seem to make of him a *poète maudit*. Octavio Paz has made the point that the *poète maudit* is included within the social order against which he rebels, while Cernuda feels himself excluded, and Paz further comments that he does not lament this but returns blow for blow the attacks of society.[24] This last remark seems an over-simplification, for while it is true that he feels himself excluded from society, he also has a desperate wish to belong and be recognised for his poetry. His problem is that he cannot belong to a philistine society without betraying himself. Cernuda has said that it is an affectation for the poet to adopt the posture of a "poeta incomprendido", since this is the natural and inevitable condition for the

[24] *Cuadrivio,* 187.

poet,[25] but, as the bitter complaint of "Un contemporáneo" demonstrates, he is not always able to maintain this philosophical detachment. The contrast between the concept of the poet as *vate* and redeemer and the idea of the poet as a victim of a hostile society is as acute as the division between *realidad* and *deseo*. The poet is alienated from society by his vocation and no compromise is possible, yet he needs the recognition only society can give. This dilemma becomes even more marked when poetry is considered as an expression of Cernuda's own personality.

Poetry as a Means of Self-Redemption

The autobiographical nature of Cernuda's poetry makes of his work an extension of himself, all the more so because he is not content merely to record his experience but rigorously analyses it in an effort to reach a deeper understanding of himself. Yet the poem can acquire a separate existence from that of its creator and is capable of continuing to exist when he is dead. For Cernuda this is a simple corollary of his theory that man is able to create eternal beauty while he himself is mortal. The far-reaching implications of this idea, that the poet can achieve some measure of personal immortality through his creations, provide a possible source of consolation for Cernuda in the abandonment and solitude which he finds is the price he has to pay for being a poet. The first tentative statement of this attitude occurs in "A Larra con unas violetas" :

> Libre y tranquilo quedaste al fin un día,
> Aunque tu voz sin ti abrió un dejo indeleble.
> Es breve la palabra como el canto de un pájaro,
> Mas un claro jirón puede prenderse en ella
> De embriaguez, pasión, belleza fugitivas,
> Y subir, ángel vigía que atestigua del hombre,
> Allá hasta la región celeste e impasible. (p. 142)

The comparison here between the writer's words and the song of a bird is reminiscent of the image of the nightingale and the blackbird which Cernuda uses as a symbol of the poet, but the most significant element in these lines is the idea of the word as a guardian angel providing testimony to the writer's life. His work is seen as the surviving witness of his existence, and the use of the verb "atestigua" implies that the evidence a writer's work gives of his life must be the true evidence about him. Although this idea is hedged about with a pessimistic diffidence, since the work retains only the "dejo" and the "jirón" of the man and merely provides a testimony of his life to the impassive gods above the world, it does reveal a major element in Cernuda's private concern with poetry : the desire to create himself in poetry by discovering and expressing the truth of himself through poetry.

The view of poetry as an attestation of the poet's life is developed in particular in *Como quien espera el alba* as a response to the problems of alienation created by exile. In "A un poeta futuro" Cernuda examines his own isolation

[25] *Estudios sobre poesía española contemporánea*, 59.

and the incomprehension his work has met in the course of a monologue addressed to a young poet of the future in whom he hopes he might at last find someone who could understand the aspirations he has put into his poetry. He now posits for himself the possibility of survival in his work which he had earlier offered as a consolation to Larra :

> Yo no podré decirte cuánto llevo luchando
> Para que mi palabra no se muera
> Silenciosa conmigo, y vaya como un eco
> A ti, como tormenta que ha pasado
> Y un són vago recuerda por el aire tranquilo.
>
> . . . . .
>
> Escúchame y comprende.
> En sus limbos mi alma quizá recuerde algo,
> Y entonces en ti mismo mis sueños y deseos
> Tendrán razón al fin, y habré vivido. (pp. 201-2)

Despite the burden of sadness in these lines, which comes from the bitter acceptance that he can hope for no recognition during his lifetime, there is a more positive hope here than that held out to Larra; Cernuda, at least, can find for himself the possible expectation that his poetry will survive as his personal testimony in the world of man. These closing lines also clearly demonstrate how completely Cernuda has identified himself with his poetry. His work is an expression of himself which can offer to his dreams and desires a surviving existence, albeit a vicarious one. It is perhaps to such an existence in poetry that he refers in 'Palabras antes de una lectura' when he speaks of "una enigmática libertad" achieved by a poet after he has died.[26] The possibility of the artifact attaining a life freed from the mortal existence of its creator is referred to in the poem "Magia de la obra viva" which describes an oriental temple decorated with reliefs sculpted by an artist whose indolence awakens an immediate correspondence with Cernuda himself. These reliefs have survived their creator's disappearance, acquiring a life of their own, so that a peasant, in the uncertain light of dawn, can believe he sees two horsemen galloping across the surface of the lake in which the temple is reflected. Cernuda ends the poem with a pious wish : "Quién le diera a tus versos . . ./Vivir sin ti y sin nadie, con vida entera y libre" (p. 214). Here is an echo of that ideal situation of self-sufficiency symbolised in the images of the nightingale and the blackbird, but the diffident expression of this desire for a totally free existence for his work reveals that "Magia de la obra viva" is an example of the wishful-thinking in which Cernuda can indulge on occasions. This is especially so since the idea of a life "sin nadie" contradicts the hope of "A un poeta futuro" that his work will find an audience in that young poet to come. "A un poeta futuro" demonstrates that, unlike the nightingale or the blackbird, Cernuda needs a public.

In the exultant, arrogant mood of "Silla del rey" a more positive statement can be made about the poet's relationship to his work. Philip II's declaration

[26] *Loc. cit.*, 200.

that the Escorial is the expression of his own contradictory character is expanded on in the following lines :

> Una armonía total, irresistible, surge;
> Colmena de musical dulzor, resuena todo;
> Es en su celda el fraile, donde doma el deseo;
> En su campo el soldado, donde forja la fuerza;
> En su espejo el poeta, donde refleja el mito.
>
> Sé que estas vidas, por quienes respondo,
> En poco servirían de no seguir unidas
> Frente a una gran tarea, grande aunque absurda. (pp. 265-6)

This tripartite character of priest, soldier and poet, although an allusion to Baudelaire, recalls the comment in the essay 'Tres poetas metafísicos' : "si en Manrique hallamos el arquetipo del héroe y en Aldana el del santo, en el poeta anónimo sevillano hallamos, pura y simplemente, el del hombre".[27] There is also an echo of the three personalities of Cernuda's Magi : the priest corresponding to Melchior, the soldier to the pragmatic Balthazar, and the poet to the indolent Gaspar. These are the three life-styles to which, in different degrees, Cernuda himself feels an attraction, and at this point in "Silla del rey" he is clearly visible behind the mask of his regal *Doppelgänger*. Moreover, the idea that the Escorial, the metaphor for artistic creation, is capable of fusing these disparate personalities, recalls the tripartite union of "deseo", "rosa" and "mirada" achieved in poetry, as described in "El poeta". In "Silla del rey" the poet who has become a redeemer contains within himself that integration of separate and disparate elements which poetry provides. The act of artistic creation brings coherence to the fragmented tripartite personality of the Philip II who is Cernuda's kindred spirit, and by implication Cernuda's poetry becomes the means by which he gives a cohesive significance to his own complex personality, fulfilling the description of the poet's concern which is given in "Río vespertino" as "su tarea/De ver en unidad el ser disperso" (p. 226). Poetry thus becomes a vehicle for self-affirmation.

The total involvement Cernuda feels for his poetry springs from the fact that poetry offers him a way of achieving the complete expression of his personality that is denied him by the hostility of society. This is one reason for his preoccupation with poetic theory and his scrupulous selection and handling of influences. His work must be an exercise in both personal and artistic integrity if it is to present a true likeness of himself. Concern with integrity is the subject of the poem "Aplauso humano", whose title is a clear echo of Hölderlin's "Menschenbeifall", one of the poems Cernuda translated in 1935,[28] but he treats a more personal problem than the poet's struggle with the values of the market-place.

[27] *Poesía y literatura*, 71. In 'Baudelaire en el centenario de *Las Flores del Mal*', *Poesía y literatura II*, 140, Cernuda quotes the following comment by Baudelaire: "Entre los hombres sólo son grandes el poeta, el sacerdote y el soldado; el hombre que canta, el hombre que sacrifica y que se sacrifica."

[28] *Cruz y raya*, no. 32 (1935), 121.

"Aplauso humano" is one of the few poems where he directly confronts his homosexuality, a topic which is approached here specifically via his poetry. His poems reveal him as a homosexual, but he accepts the scorn of society this brings him, and refuses to evade this aspect of his personality in order to foster public approval of his work :

Ahora todas aquellas criaturas grises
Cuya sed parca de amor nocturnamente satisface
El aguachirle conyugal, al escuchar tus versos,
Por la verdad que exponen podrán escarnecerte.

. . . . .

La consideración humana tú nunca la buscaste,
Aún menos cuando fuera su precio una mentira,
Como bufón sombrío traicionando tu alma
A cambio de un cumplido con oficial benevolencia.

(pp. 216-217)

Cernuda's determined refusal in this poem to betray himself in return for an easier existence is a clear confession of the basic, personal reason for the mutual hostility between himself and society. But, most importantly, this resolve to maintain his personal integrity is linked inextricably with his vocation as a poet, since it is through his poetry that he can affirm his personal truth, that concept of *verdad* which recurs again and again as a key-note in his work. A more objectivised statement of this attitude is contained in the poem "Góngora" where Cernuda sees the Golden Age poet's retirement from the Court to his native Cordoba as the result of a decision to free himself from compromise with the shallow, vulgar society of his time and to dedicate himself to his poetry. He rejected the possibility of public acceptance in favour of preserving his integrity and finding in his poetry a solace for his isolation :

Ya restituye el alma a soledad sin esperar de nadie
Si no es de su conciencia, y menos todavía
De aquel sol invernal de la grandeza
Que no atempera el frío del desdichado . . .[29]

. . . . .

Pero en la poesía encontró siempre, no tan sólo hermosura, sino ánimo,
La fuerza del vivir más libre y más soberbio . . . (p. 193)

Góngora's withdrawal from the world into the haven of his poetry, which Cernuda clearly admires, could be construed as another demonstration of the evasive tendency in Cernuda's view of life. Yet Góngora withdraws from the

[29] Cf. Cernuda's comments on the anonymous poet of the "Epístola moral a Fabio": "para un alma desmedida, si quiere ser sincera consigo misma, acaso sólo quede un camino: renunciar a sus aspiraciones, resignándose a dejarse vivir . . . / . . . para el poeta anónimo el hombre nada debe esperar fuera de sí, ni en este ni en otro mundo posible." 'Tres poetas metafísicos', *loc. cit.*, 69-71.

world in order to keep faith with himself and to fulfil himself in his poetry in a way that was denied him in the world. This retirement into the hidden garden of his poetry is therefore a positive move, not evasion but self-affirmation, albeit in a manner that is essentially vicarious. Cernuda too, in solitude, jealously guards his integrity and uses his poetry as a means of attaining a free existence. Poetry, for him as for Góngora, was a salvation, but a salvation found within himself.

Cernuda was, however, well-aware of the exposed position in which the idea of poetry as a means of self-salvation placed him, a problem which is examined in "Noche del hombre y su demonio". The demonic *alter ego* in this dialogue is his personal devil's advocate who voices the fears and suspicions the man would prefer to forget.[30] Cernuda the man is awakened from the oblivion he had sought in sleep by the demonic inward monitor who invites him to see existence as "dolor puro" and reminds him mercilessly of his subjection to time. The demon torments him by declaring that his life as a poet has been futile, and mocks the claim that poetry can annul the effects of time by emphasising that whatever happens to his poetry Cernuda himself will disappear. Force is added to this argument by the suggestion that poetry has been, even more than an evasion, a waste of life; "Ha sido la palabra tu enemigo:/Por ella de estar vivo te olvidaste" (p. 223). Cernuda replies by admitting that poetry has been for him a vicarious existence, but he also reasserts his belief that his poetry will live on after his death:

> El amargo placer de transformar el gesto
> En són, sustituyendo el verbo al acto,
> Ha sido afán constante de mi vida.
> Y mi voz no escuchada, o apenas escuchada,
> Ha de sonar aún cuando yo muera.
> Sola, como el viento en los juncos sobre el agua. (p. 223)

The demon is quick to counter this challenge by playing on Cernuda's pained awareness of his lack of recognition, declaring that even if his work should survive no one would heed it, since only the "histrión elocuente" and "hierofante vano" receive public acclaim. This attack is then pushed home by the demon insinuating that even should this situation be redressed by recognition for him in the future this will be scant consolation since he can only hope for a minimal existence as "un són, un aire" in his poems. Cernuda cannot tolerate this assault on his hope that poetry may redeem his life and he is forced to attempt a defence of his commitment to poetry, although the despondent, self-deprecating manner in which this is done shows that the demon's systematic critique of his illusions has not been unsuccessful:

[30] This is a return of the demon of "La gloria del poeta". J. L. Cano, *Poesía española del siglo XX*, 379, has suggested an echo of the Devil's visitation to Ivan in *The Brothers Karamazov*. In J. Tello, 'Hablando a Luis Cernuda', *El Tiempo* (Bogotá), 7-X-45, Cernuda makes a passing reference to the "sueño del usurero en *Los Hermanos Karamazov*" and to the "soliloquio del inquisidor en *Torquemada en la hoguera*".

Me hieres en el centro más profundo,
Pues conoces que el hombre no tolera
Estar vivo sin más : como en un juego trágico
Necesita apostar su vida en algo,
Algo de que alza un ídolo, aunque con barro sea,
Y antes que confesar su engaño quiere muerte.
Mi engaño era inocente, y a nadie arruinaba
Excepto a mí, aunque a veces yo mismo lo veía. (p. 223)

The clarity and honesty of Cernuda's analysis of his motives in this stanza and in the poem as a whole are a product of the depth of the self-knowledge he acquires in and through the poems of his maturity. As the demon bursts the protective illusion that he will live on in his work, he is forced to admit that his poetic endeavours are a pretext for self-affirmation, and that even this may have been an illusion, yet he recognises that it is absolutely necessary to him. His poetry is something to justify his life, and this is why he must totally commit himself to his poetry. Moreover, since life and poetry for Cernuda are synonyms this commitment to poetry is a commitment to himself. "Noche del hombre y su demonio" makes clear that poetry provides a faith for Cernuda, or at least a substitute for the belief he has been unable to sustain in other things, and also demonstrates that the involvement with poetry is an act of faith in himself. Cernuda's poems are the last redoubt in his struggle to assert his identity, his personal truth, in a world he finds alien and hostile, so that, far from being a means of evasion, poetry is derived from and directed towards reality, his own reality.

This examination of Cernuda's attitudes towards poetry and the status of the poet has provided an illustration of the complexity of the thematic material in his mature work. The study of one theme has involved a discussion of its relationship to many others : time, beauty, the ancient gods, the daemonic power, society, homosexuality and personal integrity. This complexity is further intensified by the conflicting views Cernuda holds; the poet is both victim and redeemer, longing for recognition from society yet rejecting the values of society. But these are complementary attitudes not contradictions, the poet is rejected by society because he is a *vate* and his status as a prophet is the compensation for his rejection. Such conflicting, yet inter-related, views are the reflection of the central dilemma of Cernuda's existence, the schism between *realidad* and *deseo*. The analysis of Cernuda's concept of poetry has also revealed polar ideas about the function of the poet's occupation. On the one hand poetry is linked with the hidden garden syndrome, being a *huerto sellado* which offers the self-sufficient existence of the song-bird where time is nullified and the discovery of the mystic *rosa del mundo* brings that transcendent mode of existence for which Cernuda longs. The connection between poetry and the theory of the daemonic power and the invisible metaphysical reality of the world seems to make of poetry another manifestation of the evasive tendency in Cernuda's character, and yet this is balanced on the other hand by the idea that poetry is a vehicle for self-affirmation which enables him to seek for and come to understand the truth about himself. These two attitudes are also complementary; poetry is an instrument of both evasion and self-discovery because evasion and self-discovery are alternative ways of seeking redemption from the dilemma of Cernuda's existence. But whereas poetry as a means of communion with the transcendent dimension of the world provides redemption through escape from an alien social environment, poetry as a vehicle for the affirmation of Cernuda's personal truth presents him with an opportunity for self-redemption within the social reality. Both these ways of overcoming the alienated condition of his life are infected by wishful thinking, the mystic way by its very nature, and the way of salvation through poetry as a means of self-expression by Cernuda's diffidence which results from his awareness of the difficulties involved, yet the latter way is the more viable and, in fact, absorbs the several *caminos de evasión* which stand revealed as other attempts to assert his identity. Poetry is the testimony of Cernuda's life and of the integrity with which he tried to live that life, it is his personal story and his truth. His work seeks to integrate the conflicting elements of his *ser contradictorio* into that unity of spirit he found so praiseworthy in William Wordsworth. For Cernuda the exercise of his vocation as a poet becomes an act of auto-creation by which he redeems himself, not in a walled garden sheltered from the world, but in the world at large surrounded by his fellow men.

The evasive tendencies and Romantic attitudes that are a part of Cernuda's character are particularly in evidence in his ideas about poetry and the poet, yet I hope that this analysis has shown the dangers of placing too much emphasis on such aspects, which must be seen against Cernuda's existential involvement in his work. Poetry does seem to offer a haven from the problems of his life but it also provides him with a way of confronting and understanding these problems. The theme of the poet and poetry is a special centre of focus for Cernuda's examination of his relationship with society. The difficulties he experiences in the social environment have their primary cause in his homosexuality, as the poem "Aplauso humano" clearly demonstrates, but homosexuality is, in Cernuda's case, what might be called his subjective correlative for the mutual hostility he finds between the poet and society. The preoccupation with the status of the poet and the function of poetry as themes translates his personal problems into objective terms, so that the poet, whether himself or another writer, becomes a *Doppelgänger* for Cernuda the man. His private concern is thus given a universal dimension without sacrificing any of the dynamic or any of the validity which his personal experience provides. Cernuda's basic state of alienation is transmuted into aesthetic problems, and so he is able doubly to write himself into literature, leaving his work as the testimony of his struggle for self-affirmation.

V

LOVE AND DESIRE

Nunca han de comprender que si mi lengua
El mundo cantó un día, fue amor quien la inspiraba.
("A un poeta futuro", *Como quien espera el alba*, p. 201)

Cernuda's erotic aspirations and experience provide the most constant of all the themes in his work, being a major preoccupation of every one of his collections of poems from *Primeras poesías* to *Desolación de la Quimera.* But Cernuda's own statement, made in the lines from "A un poeta futuro" used as a rubric to this chapter, that love was the motivating force of his poetry is an over-simplification. The erotic concern of his poems is, in fact, just another vehicle for the analysis of his personality, albeit one of the most important vehicles for this purpose. This is, of course, the theme that should bring the reader into a direct confrontation with Cernuda's homosexuality, both because of the clarity and honesty with which the nature of his desires are expressed and also because it is physical desire rather than love that he deals with in his poems. Yet, despite the overt, and occasionally wilful exhibition of homosexual eroticism, the difficulties this might provoke with regard to the reader are skilfully avoided by the transference of the conflict between Cernuda and the values of heterosexual society to an aesthetic plane in the theme of the poet and poetry. Such possible difficulties are further minimised by the fact that it is the nature of love, rather than the object of that love, with which he is most preoccupied. Octavio Paz has asked whether it is even possible to talk of a loved one in Cernuda's poetry on account of the narcissism of homosexual passion and also because of Cernuda's belief in love as an impersonal force that possesses men.[1] His personal erotic experience is turned into an analysis of eroticism itself, and the examination of the nature of this experience becomes another avenue in the inquiry Cernuda conducts into his own character, until his search for love is finally revealed as part of his struggle for self-affirmation.

In the lucid pages he has dedicated to Cernuda's idea of love Octavio Paz distinguishes between the "amor activo" of the early poems and the "amor contemplativo" of the later work.[2] This is a most useful and perceptive distinction; while *Un río, un amor, Los placeres prohibidos,* and *Donde habite el*

[1] *Cuadrivio,* 192-3.
[2] *Ibid.,* 193.

olvido seem to be products of specific experiences of love, or the failure of love, the majority of the mature poems on erotic themes do not appear to be inspired by a particular love affair. The obvious exception to this characteristic of the later poems is the series "Poemas para un cuerpo", and there is also the possibility that the three song poems, "Canción de invierno", "Alegría de la soledad" and "El amor y el amante", included in *Las nubes,* and the "Cuatro poemas a una sombra", which begin the collection *Vivir sin estar viviendo,* may refer to a specific experience. But, in general, the mature poems on erotic themes have a detached, contemplative quality, and are frequently concerned with analysis of the experiences of youth as part of Cernuda's attempt to use his past to reach an understanding of his present self. Moreover, the detached, analytical attitude is strongly present even in poems which do treat new experiences of love, like the "Poemas para un cuerpo". The active search for love has already been studied in connection with the early poetry, and I want now to examine Cernuda's contemplation of love itself which begins in *Invocaciones* as a direct result of the crisis of *Donde habite el olvido.* In the reappraisal of beliefs undertaken after the disastrous experience of love recorded in his fifth book of poems Cernuda redefines his erotic desires in the light of the theory of the daemonic power. Still deeply scarred by the successive failures of his adolescent ideal of love, the dream of personal love is replaced by a concept of physical desire as a transcendent, suprapersonal force that is part of the daemonic power he now believes governs the world. Through the experience of this desire he seeks to commune with the superior hidden reality of which it is a reflection and so achieve that state of the *acorde,* the harmony of self and world, that he also pursues in a variety of other ways already examined in the theme of the hidden garden. During the time of his exile he is most concerned with elegiac memories of old loves and this sad contemplation of the past grows more intense when he reaches middle age and finds that the passing of time has alienated him from the youthful erotic ideal he had cherished. Running parallel to these two elements, desire as a means of access to the *acorde* and the preoccupation with memories and age, is the idea of love as a form of self-fulfillment, which links the erotic theme with Cernuda's existential concern. These three major threads of the theme are brought together in "Poemas para un cuerpo" when the tardy love affair in Mexico provides a climax to all his erotic aspirations and in so doing reveals that what he was seeking in love was in fact himself.

The Search for the "Acorde"

The traumatic shock that overcomes Cernuda as a result of the violent disillusionment in *Donde habite el olvido* of the erotic dream he had nurtured since his adolescence continues through to *Invocaciones* where he describes himself as a "momia de hastío sepulta en anónima yacija" (p. 115). However, the first attempt to break out of that condition of emotional numbness and to come to terms with the dream's failure is, in fact, made within *Donde habite el olvido* in that collection's final poem, "Los fantasmas del deseo", which in theme and style prefigures the pantheistic attitudes and hymnic mode of *Invocaciones.* The cynical, embittered view of the dream of love in this poem is balanced by a concept of desire as an omnipresent and eternal life-force resident in the earth. As with previous disillusioning experiences of love, love itself is declared to be a "lie", a travesty of the dream, while, by contrast, the force of desire contained in the elemental world of nature becomes the "truth", the uncorrupted ideal:

El amor no tiene esta o aquella forma,
No puede detenerse en criatura alguna;
Todas son por igual viles y soñadoras.
Placer que nunca muere,
Beso que nunca muere,
Sólo en ti misma encuentro, tierra mía.

. . . . .

Como la arena, tierra,
Como la arena misma,
La caricia es mentira, el amor es mentira, la amistad es mentira.
Tú sola quedas con el deseo,
Con este deseo que aparenta ser mío y ni siquiera es mío,
Sino el deseo de todos,
Malvados, inocentes,
Enamorados o canallas. (pp. 100-101)[3]

This is clearly a rationalization of love's failure, reminiscent of the attitude to love in *Los placeres prohibidos*, although Cernuda can no longer blame society since he has been forced to realize that the fault lies in the disparity between the dream of love and its experience. There is, however, a significant difference in this new pantheistic solution to his problem; in the earlier poems he had hoped to achieve harmony with the natural world through a personalised love, now he apparently seeks the same goal through a depersonalised desire. By making desire rather than love the supreme value of life he is protecting himself against the disastrous consequences of a further disillusioning experience while retaining an erotic ideal as a staff with which to sustain himself. The concept of desire as an elemental natural force for which man is a mere vehicle, the possessed, provides him with a sense of belonging to an external immutable reality, that same sense of belonging he had tried and failed to find in love. Following the collapse of one ideal Cernuda has again transposed it into different terms in the hope that it may be thus protected from further disillusionment. "Los fantasmas del deseo" was written before the theoretical essay 'Palabras antes de una lectura' but it clearly foreshadows the idea of the daemonic power, and the concept of desire postulated in this poem is easily absorbed into Cernuda's philosophy in the poems of *Invocaciones*.

The idea of desire as external to man, a force emanating from the natural world, is the subject of "El viento de septiembre entre los chopos", a delicate poem with Becquerian resonances, that avoids the inflated rhetoric marring

[3] There is a strong echo in this poem of the erotic dimension given to the Earth in Rimbaud's poem "Soleil et chair".

many of the compositions in *Invocaciones*.[4] The autumn breeze among the poplar trees on the Bay of Cadiz becomes the manifestation of this spirit of desire, bringing with it the echo of an "estelar melodía" (p. 109). Entranced by this reverberation from an extraterrestial harmony, he rejects the "frágiles amoríos" of man and even the beautiful youth of his dreams for the possibility of a communion with the landscape and the mysterious harmony that has been made manifest there. This concept of a suprapersonal desire as a means of access to a transcendental realm of harmony has a clear therapeutic function of redeeming Cernuda from disillusionment with his attempts to find the same harmony in a personal love, a function which is presented more explicitly in "*Dans ma péniche*". This poem begins with a line taken from a popular song, "quiero vivir cuando el amor muere", that is a categorical rejection of the despair of *Donde habite el olvido* where the loss of love was equated with death, although the attitude to love is still bitterly cynical.[5] The lover's affectation that the world dies with love is treated with heavy scorn; it is claimed that the end of love is rather a cause for rejoicing since the liberty lost in love is then regained. Love is compared to a beast of prey, to a Promethean vulture, and to a prison where lovers are chained to the apple trees of Eden. The loss of love, on the other hand, frees desire from an exclusive, restricting focus on a single person, and, in addition, brings a communion with the natural world from which desire emanates. Cernuda's attitude in this poem is one of total hedonism, typified by the appearance in the final stanza of the satyrs who rejoice at the death of love :

Pero tú y yo sabemos,
Río que bajo mi casa fugitiva deslizas tu vida experta,
Que cuando el hombre no tiene ligados sus miembros por las
 encantadoras mallas del amor,
Cuando el deseo es como una cálida azucena
Que se ofrece a todo cuerpo hermoso que fulja a nuestro lado,
Cuánto vale una noche como ésta, indecisa entre la primavera
 última y el estío primero,
Este instante en que oigo los leves chasquidos del bosque nocturno,
Conforme conmigo mismo y con la indiferencia de los otros,
Solo yo con mi vida,
Con mi parte en el mundo.

Jóvenes sátiros
Que vivís en la selva, labios risueños ante el exangüe dios cristiano,
A quien el comerciante adora para mejor cobrar su mercancía,
Pies de jóvenes sátiros,

[4] Cf. the fourth stanza of Cernuda's poem: "Oigo caricias leves, / Oigo besos más leves; / Por allá baten alas, / Por allá van secretos", and the line from Bécquer's *rima* X: "rumor de besos y batir de alas."

[5] Rosa Chacel, 'Respuesta a Ortega', *Sur*, no. 241 (1956), 115-17, has described how this poem was inspired by an old waltz entitled "Cuando el amor muere". I have been unable to trace the origin of the phrase "dans ma péniche".

Danzad más presto cuando el amante llora,
Mientras lanza su tierna endecha
De : 'Ah, cuando el amor muere'.
Porque oscura y cruel la libertad entonces ha nacido;
Vuestra descuidada alegría sabrá fortalecerla,
Y el deseo girará locamente en pos de los hermosos cuerpos
Que vivifican el mundo un solo instante. (p. 117)[6]

Here is a return to the defiant hedonism of *Los placeres prohibidos*, given an ethical value in contrast to the corruption of conventional society, although the tone is less exultant, being in part diminished by the loquacity of a style encumbered by repetition and enumeration. The exultancy is also subdued by Cernuda's implicit awareness that this is in essence a solution of despair, similar to the haven of solitude proposed in "Soliloquio del farero", to which the reference in the first stanza quoted above concerning the solitary communion with nature seems to provide a link. *"Dans ma péniche"* is another example of the wishful-thinking to which Cernuda is often susceptible; the exalted concept of desire is a means of evading the difficulties of love.

An elegiac tone is much more characteristic of the poems of *Invocaciones*, as in "A un muchacho andaluz" and "El joven marino", which are both laments for the impossibility of personal love. These two figures, successors to the young god of the "Oda", the "Corsario" of *Los placeres prohibidos*, and the "Arcángel" of *Donde habite el olvido*, represent those beautiful creatures who are declared in "*Dans ma péniche*" to bring a momentary flash of life into the world. The young sailor is a paragon of physical beauty, but he is merely an erotic object not an individual, a manifestation of the beauty that provokes desire free from any personalised attraction. The sailor is beyond the bounds of human love and the only possible consummation for him is with the elemental forces of nature as he drowns in the sea, a death which is presented in the terms of a sexual union :

Cambiantes sentimientos nos enlazan con este o aquel cuerpo,
Y todos ellos no son sino sombras que velan
La forma suprema del amor, que por sí mismo late,
Ciego ante las mudanzas de los cuerpos,
Iluminado por el ardor de su propia llama invencible.

. . . . .

Al amanecer es cuando debías ir hacia el mar, joven marino,
Desnudo como la flor;
Y entonces es cuando debías amarle, cuando el mar debía poseerte,
Cuerpo a cuerpo,
Hasta confundir su vida con la tuya
Y despertar en ti su inmenso amor

[6] A distinct echo exists here of "les temps de l'antique jeunesse, / Des satyres lascifs, des faunes animaux", from Rimbaud's "Soleil et chair". A similar scorn for love in favour of an elemental concept of desire is to be found in "Sacrilegio nocturno", *Ocnos,* 93-4.

El breve espasmo de tu placer sometido,
Deposados el uno con el otro,
Vida con vida, muerte con muerte. (pp. 120-121)

With desire given the proportions of an elemental force – the invincible flame that passes from one body to another, which merely provide a pretext for its existence – the only fulfillment can be with a power of similar dimensions, in this case the sea. The image of drowning in the sea appeared in *Los placeres prohibidos* and *Donde habite el olvido* but then it was Cernuda himself who had sought through love this union with the elemental world; the young sailor's cosmic fusion achieved by his suicide is a confession of love's impossibility. Desire is part of the daemonic power, a means of access to that hidden superior reality that lies behind the appearance of the world, but in "El joven marino" the price to be paid for entry into this higher realm is death.

The idea of desire as an external force which takes possession of man from time to time is also the subject of "A un muchacho andaluz", whose protagonist, like the young sailor, is another idealised physical beauty residing in an Andalusian terrestrial paradise where he enjoys a harmonious communion with the landscape and the sea. The boy is presented as a messenger from the natural world who brings to the melancholy poet the consolation of the "truth" of his beauty and the desire it provokes :

Eras tú una verdad,
Sola verdad que busco,
Más que verdad de amor, verdad de vida;

. . . . .

Creí en ti, muchachillo. (p. 106)

In the past tenses employed here, and in particular the preterite used in the last line above, which stands as an isolated line in the poem, Cernuda's elegiac mood reaches a stark intensity. The young boy, like the young sailor, is now absent from the world, leaving behind him in the poet's mind the empty longing for the erotic ideal he represented and the dream of what life might have been had that ideal been accessible. Nonetheless, the use of the image "verdad" in connection with the boy, and especially the phrase "verdad de vida", is a restatement of the equation between life and the erotic ideal that was made so vehemently in *Los placeres prohibidos*. Although the tone of exultancy has disappeared, this renewed statement of former faith marks a first step in the recovery from the despair of *Donde habite el olvido* and points to the attempt to reconstitute a system of values from the ruins of the failed dreams of the past, which is the major intention of *Invocaciones*.

The rehabilitation of the erotic ideal by shifting the emphasis from love to desire seen as an elemental life force and part of the daemonic power is carried further by the association of desire with the theme of the ancient gods. Such an association is implicit in the pagan sensuality of *"Dans ma péniche"* and the "muchacho andaluz", whom Cernuda makes into a divine being to replace sad, crucified gods. The young boy, together with the young sailor, recall the reference to Greek demi-gods in 'Palabras antes de una lectura'.[7] The link between desire and the world of the gods is made explicit in "A unos tulipanes amarillos" where Cernuda attributes the awakening of desire in his adolescence to a visit by a messenger from a god who brought to him the gift of desire symbolised in the yellow tulips of the poem's title. The transformation of the birth of sexual awareness into a meeting with a visitor from the realm of the gods turns desire into a means of access to this superior world. This poem is also an elegy, for the celestial visitor disappeared after he had awakened the adolescent's erotic aspirations, but the relationship between desire and that vision of a transcendent reality which the ancient gods represent is here firmly established. The association between the gods and desire is explored more fully in the poem "La fuente" from *Las nubes*, set in the Jardin du Luxembourg in Paris (*PL*, 259), which evokes inevitable echoes of the hidden garden of the Alcázar in Seville. It is the voice of the fountain which speaks in the poem :

Este brotar continuo viene de la remota
Cima donde cayeron dioses, de los siglos
Pasados, con un dejo de paz, hasta la vida
Que dora vagamente mi azul ímpetu helado.

Por mí yerran al viento apaciguados dejos
De las viejas pasiones, glorias, duelos de antaño,
Y son, bajo la sombra naciente de la tarde,
Misterios junto al vano rumor de los efímeros.

El hechizo del agua detiene los instantes :
Soy divino rescate a la pena del hombre,
Forma de lo que huye de la luz a la sombra,
Confusión de la muerte resuelta en melodía. (p. 144)

The fountain's jet, constantly rising and falling, is a symbol of the constant rebirth of desire, which never dies but merely changes its relationship to man; it is thus outside the normal flux of time and a direct link with the lost age of the gods. The experience of desire provides contact with the continuing spirit of the gods and an escape from subjection to time. "La fuente" reveals the intention of Cernuda's association of desire in *Invocaciones* with the concept of the daemonic power and the ancient gods; he wishes to reconstruct the erotic ideal so that it may become a means of attaining the longed-for state of the *acorde*.

This aspect of Cernuda's reassessment of the nature of desire in the light of the theory of the daemonic power is developed further in "Vereda del cuco", the final poem of *Como quien espera el alba*. Using the device of the self-contemplative monologue in the second person, he examines his relationship with desire since the time of his adolescence. The central image for desire is again associated with water, this time in the shape of a spring, to which he says he came as an adolescent to gaze at the reflection there, which was not himself

[7] *Loc. cit.*, 199.

but the object of desire, an idea that recalls, and illuminates, the narcissism of the early poems. The symbol of the spring stresses the concept of desire as an elemental life force and also demonstrates that desire is external to man, something of which he can partake but cannot control or possess. Once he had tasted these waters of life the adolescent's thirst was only increased and he found himself drawn ineluctably to follow again and again the "vereda del cuco" which led to the spring, although on each occasion the water held a different reflection. The change in the object of desire was of little importance since love itself remained constant. This idea, "que el amor es lo eterno y no lo amado" (p. 231), is a restatement of the lines from *Donde habite el olvido* : "No es el amor quien muere/Somos nosotros mismos", and the change from a subjective to an objective aspect in the expression neatly illustrates Octavio Paz's contrast between the "amor activo" of the early poems and the "amor contemplativo" of the later work. Cernuda is able to accept philosophically the transitoriness of an individual love affair and so redeem his attitude to love from the embittered cynicism with which it had been infected since the disastrous experience of *Donde habite el olvido*.

At this point in "Vereda del cuco", when the transitoriness of a particular love affair has been accepted because of the immortality of love itself, the mood of quiet contemplation which begins the poem acquires a subdued note of ecstasy, as love, despite its accompanying pain, is declared to be the fount of all life :

> Es el amor fuente de todo;
> Hay júbilo en la luz porque brilla esa fuente,
> Encierra al dios la espiga porque mana esa fuente,
> Voz pura es la palabra porque suena esa fuente,
> Y la muerte es de ella el fondo codiciable.
> Extático en su orilla,
> Oh tormento divino,
> Oh divino deleite,
> Bebías de tu sed y de la fuente a un tiempo,
> Sabiendo a eternidad tu sed y el agua. (p. 231)

The emphatic, parallelistic enumeration at the beginning of this passage, where love is exalted as the source of light, fertility and poetry, is reminiscent of the celebration of love as a life-force in some of the poems of *Los placeres prohibidos*. The reference to the desired death at the bottom of the spring could be read as a negative counterbalance to the preceding lines, evidence of the continuing shadow of disillusionment, but this idea also recalls the concept of death as a means of access to the hidden reality of the world, which first appears in *Invocaciones*. The exultancy in these lines is made complete by the incorporation of the poet's personal desire, his thirst, into the eternal spirit of desire in the spring, thus giving him a glimpse of eternity. In the following stanzas he declares that it is of no importance if he should never again walk the path to the spring, since once he has drunk from these waters of life, this experience can never be taken from him. Nor does it matter if love passes, leaving only the cold ashes of its fire, for these ashes are proof of the experience of love, of the contact with the life-force. The experience of love is, furthermore, capable of redeeming man from the negation of life threatened by death, because he has to accept the inevitable death of love in order to create life through love. Cernuda concludes the poem with a triumphant statement of the power of love to conquer death and time; while age may have robbed him of the desire of his youth, he, together with that desire, lives on in the new generation who have succeeded him along the path to the spring :

Aunque tu día haya pasado,
Eres tú, y son los idos,
Quienes por estos ojos nuevos buscan
En la haz de la fuente
La realidad profunda,
Intima y perdurable;
Eres tú, y son los idos,
Quienes por estos cuerpos nuevos vuelven
A la vereda oscura,
Y ante el tránsito ciego de la noche
Huyen hacia el oriente,
Dueños del sortilegio,
Conocedores del fuego originario,
La pira donde el fénix muere y nace. (p. 232)

The image of the phoenix here recalls the fountain of "La fuente", but this mythological allusion now makes clear that the link between the ancient gods and desire is a symbol of the relationship between desire and the hidden superior reality of the world. The image of the "fuego originario" is reminiscent of vocabulary used in connection with the daemonic power, while in the penultimate stanza of the poem love is described as the "razón del mundo que rige las estrellas". The most significant element of "Vereda del cuco" is that love, and not merely desire, is "la realidad profunda". The concept of love has been rehabilitated and has become again a means of attaining that mystic state of the *acorde* where the visible and invisible realities are fused. The escape from the flux of time, "el tránsito ciego de la noche", and the paradoxical rapture of love, "Oh tormento divino,/Oh divino deleite", which strongly recalls the language of mysticism, emphasise the transcendental nature of the experience Cernuda now claims love can offer.[8]

"Vereda del cuco" seeks to redeem the concept of love from disillusionment in a purely theoretical way; "Elegía anticipada", an earlier poem in *Como quien espera el alba*, is concerned with the reassessment of an actual love affair, as part of the investigation of past experience which Cernuda conducts in this collection. The poem is set in a cemetery, and attention is immediately attracted by the presentation of the cemetery as though it were a walled garden, a haven of quiet beauty where the birds come to nest, inevitably bringing to mind that

[8] Cf. the lines from San Juan de la Cruz's "Llama de amor viva": "¡Oh cauterio suave! / ¡Oh regalada llaga!"

hidden garden of adolescence. This idyllic place, with its symbolic overtones, was the setting for a love affair described as "el amor único", which, Cernuda claims, brought him to the peak of his existence, transferring him to the ecstatic state of "embeleso" :

Entre las hojas fuisteis, descuidados
De una presencia intrusa, y ciegamente
Un labio hallaba en otro ese embeleso
Hijo de la sonrisa y del suspiro.

. . . . .

No fue breve esa dicha. ¿Quién pretende
Que la dicha se mide por el tiempo?
Libres vosotros del espacio humano,
Del tiempo quebrantasteis las prisiones. (p. 216)[9]

In this accord with the natural world and this escape from the human dimension of time in a setting that is a paradigm of the garden in Seville where he had first experienced the possibility of harmony between self and world, the theoretical attitudes of "Vereda del cuco" are applied to a specific personal experience which acquires mystic proportions. "Elegía anticipada" redeems from disillusionment the idea of a personal love, which is the reason for the poem's title; looking to the past in fond memory rather than regret, it is an elegy for something not yet lost.

The attitude to love established in "Elegía anticipada" and "Vereda del cuco" is put to a practical test by what appears to have been a new experience of love, expressed in the series "Cuatro poemas a una sombra" which begins *Vivir sin estar viviendo.* This brief love. "destinado a vivir sólo un estío" (p. 240), seems to refer to the time Cernuda was in Cambridge; "La ventana", the opening poem of the series, begins with the evocation of another walled garden, "casi conventual", which is perhaps the garden he could see from the window of his room in Chapman's Garden, Emmanuel College.[10] The new love, which possibly existed only on Cernuda's part, has come as a surprise after long years of solitude, removing his sense of alienation by giving at last meaning and purpose to himself and to the world around him :

. . . y trae
El sentido consigo, la pasión, la conciencia,
Como recién creados admirables,
En su pureza y su vigor primeros
Que estando ya, no estaban,
Pues entre estar y estar hay diferencia.

. . . . .

[9] Cf. "Al amor no hay que pedirle sino unos instantes que en verdad equivalen a la eternidad, aquella eternidad profunda a que se refirió Nietsche" (*PL,* 279).

[10] I am indebted to Professor Edward M. Wilson for the information that Cernuda lived in Chapman's Garden during the time he was at Emmanuel College.

Miras la noche a la ventana, y piensas
Cuán bello es este día de tu vida,
Por el encanto mudo
Del cual ella recibe
Su valor; en los cuerpos
Con soledad heridos,
Las almas sosegando,
Que a una y otra cifra, dos mitades
Tributarias del odio,
A la unidad las restituye. (pp. 235-6)

Even when, in the second poem, "El amigo", autumn has come and the time of love has past, the feeling of gratitude does not give way to bitterness or recrimination. Although he is again conscious of his solitude, this is filled with the memories of love, and the presence of the friend is still as real as though he were there with him. The experience of love has become an integral part of Cernuda's existence, and he and the loved one are inseparably joined into a single being, just as it takes two wings to make a single bird. Similarly, in the final poem, "El fuego", where the season has moved on to winter, the mood of gratitude remains. The poplar tree with which he had identified his love has been cut down for fire-wood, but the *fuego originario* of love has merely been turned into another fire, offering him the warmth and comfort of memories. He has no sense of loss, for loss becomes a meaningless concept when love has acquired such an indestructible quality :

Cuanto el destino quita
Es luego recobrado en forma extraña;
Ganar, perder, son nombres sin sentido :
Mira como tu amor, tu árbol,
Con llama de otro impulso se corona. (p. 241)[11]

The detached, philosophical tone of the extensive contemplation of the nature of love in "Cuatro poemas a una sombra" shows the extent to which Cernuda has learnt from the rigorous self-analysis conducted in the years of his exile to dominate an experience which had, in his youth, completely overwhelmed him. But this series of poems is more than a demonstration of his ability to come to terms with the experience of love, for they form a detailed statement, with reference to a specific circumstance, of the mystic dimension contained in love. This new love has brought to Cernuda the feeling of integration with the true reality of the world outside time; in his own terms, it has fused the separated human and divine dimensions of life, and the "Cuatro

[11] It was beneath a poplar tree that love was consummated in "Elegía anticipada". Cf. these lines from section V of T. S. Eliot's "East Coker" :

There is only the fight to recover what has been lost
And found and lost again and again : and now, under conditions
That seem unpropitious. But perhaps neither gain nor loss.
For us, there is only the trying. The rest is not our business.

poemas a una sombra" are full of echoes of the ideas and the language of the mystic tradition, as the following two stanzas from "La ventana" show :

Recuerda la ventana
Sobre el jardín nocturno,
Casi conventual; aquel sonido humano,
Oscuro de las hojas, cuando el tiempo,
Lleno de la presencia y la figura amada,
Sobre la eternidad un ala inmóvil,
Hace ya de tu vida
Centro cordial del mundo,
De ti puesto en olvido,
Enajenado entre las cosas.

. . . . .

Un astro fijo iluminando el tiempo,
Aunque su luz al tiempo desconoce,
Es hoy tu amor, que quiere
Exaltar un destino
Adonde se conciertan fuerza y gracia;
Fijar una existencia
Con tregua eterna y breve, tal la rosa;
El dios y el hombre unirlos :
En obras de la tierra lo divino probado,
Lo terreno probado en el fuego celeste.

(pp. 235 and 237)

Cernuda is able to recover his belief in a personal love as a result of relating that personal love to his vision of a transcendental level of existence, and this aspect of the erotic theme in his work must therefore be associated with other attempts to reach the *acorde* between self and world already studied in the chapter on the theme of the hidden garden. The experience of a mystic order which he sees in love has evasive implications, offering him another private world to which he can escape. However, Cernuda's erotic aspirations continue to be deeply involved with his concern with personal identity, and this brings a wider significance to the erotic theme.

Memories and the Problem of Time

After the attempt made in *Invocaciones* to reconstruct the erotic ideal based on desire rather than love, the Civil War and the first shock of exile tend to push Cernuda's personal preoccupations into the background and only a small number of poems in *Las nubes* are concerned with the love theme. Nonetheless, the Spanish tragedy does not prevent the intrusion, in the poem "Tristeza del recuerdo", of the painful memory of past love, in what is apparently a reference to the love affair of *Donde habite el olvido*. The continuing memory of the lost love recreates that feeling of impotence associated with Cernuda's early poems as he sees with bitterness that his present solitude and hopelessness is the price he had to pay for those few moments of love :

¿Quién dice que se olvida? No hay olvido.
Mira a través de esta pared de hielo
Ir esa sombra hacia la lejanía
Sin el nimbo radiante del deseo.

Todo tiene su precio. Yo he pagado
El mío por aquella antigua gracia;
Y así despierto, hallando tras mi sueño
Un lecho solo, afuera yerta el alba. (p. 158)

These sentiments form a marked contrast to the mockery of grieving lovers in "*Dans ma péniche*", and show that, despite the rejection of love in favour of desire and despite the concept of love as a supra-personal force, Cernuda remains deeply preoccupied with his past disillusioning experience of love. The continuing concern with the past becomes more evident in the calmer, more analytical mood of *Como quien espera el alba* when he seeks to come to terms with the new situation exile has imposed on him.

The examination of the memories of past love in this latter collection acquires a more conciliatory tone, typified by the survey of his life made in "*Apologia pro vita sua*", although Cernuda can occasionally allow himself a cynical comment. The first concern in his apologia is to reconsider the loves of his life, which are all youthful loves for he admits that it is some years since he had any experience of love. The first memory is of the "Arcángel" from *Donde habite el olvido* from whom he seeks forgiveness; even though his attitude remains the equivocal one of *odi et amo*, he is now inclined to think that he did love him. The memory of the "Arcángel" gives way to that of those who came after him, but they are not addressed individually for they were only the product of the impetus of that major love affair, which they could not equal. This leads to the consideration that desire becomes a substitute for love when the ideal of love has been disillusioned :

A mí esos otros cuerpos me enseñaron
Que si amor palidece, cuando ya es imposible
Creer en la verdad de quien se ama,
Crece aún el deseo, y vence con un fuego
Presagio de aquéllos en infierno ya sin esperanza. (p. 205)

The contrast between the mixture of regret and resignation in these lines shows the way Cernuda's attitudes have developed since the exaltation of desire over love in *Invocaciones*, or perhaps even reveals the real motivation for the position he adopts in *Invocaciones*. The loss of love is viewed with sadness, and desire is no longer a protection against the disenchantment associated with love but a corollary of the disenchantment that makes love impossible. The key element here is the verb "enseñar"; the reflection on past experience is being used to produce self-understanding. Cernuda has now acquired sufficient detachment to comprehend and accept stoically the declension of his youthful ideal, although he allows himself a waspish comment in the final line quoted above.

Another poem which looks to the past in an attempt to come to terms with the present is "Otros tulipanes amarillos", whose title immediately links it with the poem about the birth of desire in *Invocaciones*. In the cold, grey, northern Spring of England the sight of some yellow tulips brings back the memory of another Spring in another country and those other yellow tulips that were the objective correlative for the awakening of desire in adolescence. The effect of this recall from the past is a dull pain and a meditation on the transitoriness of existence and the fragility of human aspiration. The tulips also bring a memory of an early love :

Así te vuelva hoy aquella sombra
Lejana, que por una lejana primavera,
También gris y amarilla, quiso amarte
Con capricho egoísta, como el hombre ama
En un mundo incompleto (y aun es mucho). (p. 220)

Despite the characteristic cynical sting in the final parenthesis, this seems a genuine expression of gratitude for a love that, although it may not have been ideal, was nonetheless still an experience of love. The acceptance of this in all its incompleteness because it was the most that could be expected is an admission that he is now willing to settle for less than the ideal, which, by implication, becomes an impossible ideal. Yet this attitude contains no real element of regret and the bitter conflict of youth between the dream and reality appears to have subsided with the passing of youth itself.

A similar philosophical attitude towards love appears earlier in "Canción de invierno", "Alegría de la soledad" and "El amor y el amante", three song poems, grouped together in *Las nubes*, that seem to refer to a new possibility of love. The first poem evokes the spirit of love as a winged and sacred impersonal force, the second describes the joyful life this love brings, while the third apostrophises the new love and questions its nature :

¿Eres amor? Pasa el fuego,
Cruza con alas el mar,
Despierta a la vida el sueño,
Da hermosura a lo real.

¿Eres tan sólo la sombra?
Cubre con su resplandor
Tu mentira. Haz que la sombra
Venza al fuerte, al puro amor. (p. 159)

The title, "El amor y el amante", expresses the distinction made between the ideal of love and its pale reflection in the figure of the loved one, yet Cernuda declares that the difference does not matter even while acknowledging that this shadow of love is only the "mentira" of his dream of love. A base reality is preferable to the pure ideal if the former is within his grasp and the latter beyond it. This adjustment to the gap between dream and reality is also reflected in Cernuda's willingness to make a more or less overt declaration of his homosexuality in "Aplauso humano" from *Como quien espera el alba* and "Amor oculto" from *Las nubes*. In this latter poem, using one of his favourite techniques, a series of similes with the expression of the subject of the comparison retarded, he compares love to the natural phenomena of the constant renewal of the waves in the sea, the return of Spring, the rebirth of the fire of human genius. This is the love condemned by the world, but to which he nevertheless commits himself :

Así siempre, como agua, flor o llama,
Vuelves entre la sombra, fuerza oculta
Del otro amor. El mundo bajo insulta.
Pero la vida es tuya : surge y ama. (p. 175)

The clearer understanding of the nature of love and the acceptance of its limitations have their effect in the tranquil, dispassionate treatment of the experience of love in "Cuatro poemas a una sombra". Although this love produces an ecstatic transcendence of normal existence, the shadow in the title of this series of poems has the same meaning as the shadow in "El amor y el amante". In the third poem of the series, "La escarcha", where the season has moved on to winter as love has passed, the hoar-frost is a mockery of Spring leaves on the trees; but the sadness implied by this lifeless landscape is rejected when Cernuda realises that the love that has gone was only the shadow of the ideal. There is no cause for sadness since the dream of desire has not been destroyed and he can continue to hope for its fulfillment in the future :

. . . Mas percibes en lo hondo,
Como presagio, siempre :
'No era en esos oídos
Adonde tu palabra
Debía resonar, ni era esos lugares
Donde debías hallar el centro de tu alma.

'Sigue por las regiones del aspirar oscuro,
No buscando sosiego a tu deseo,
Confiado en lo inestable,
Enamorado en lo enemigo'.
Contra el tiempo, en el tiempo
Así el presagio loco : 'espera, espera'. (pp. 239-40)

The end of love, which in Cernuda's youth had produced despair, is now calmly accepted, the fruit of the understanding derived from the analysis of past experience. However, the setting of this continuing desire against the background of passing time introduces the conflict with time which provides the dynamic for the erotic theme in the later poetry.

In *Las nubes* and *Como quien espera el alba* the sharpened consciousness of time, which is a characteristic of these collections, has only a minor effect on the love theme, since one of the principal qualities attributed to love is the ability to transcend time. But after "Cuatro poemas a una sombra" the consciousness of time presents a major problem confronting the decision to hope for a future fulfillment of desire. The problem posed by the passing of time is closely linked with the concern for lost youth that is a dominant preoccupation in *Vivir sin estar viviendo* and *Con las horas contadas*. The ideal of desire is intimately associated with youth; it is the youthful beauty of the "muchacho andaluz" and the "joven marino", and it is above all the dream Cernuda himself created when he was young. The poem immediately following "Cuatro poemas a una sombra" is entitled "El intruso"; the intruder is the poet's middle-aged self who interrupts a reverie on his past youth. In a painful variation of the narcissistic theme so often associated with poems about desire, the image he sees reflected in the mirror is not the figure of youth but the strange countenance of his own declining years. This produces a curious development in his sense of alienation. The dream of desire, inextricably linked with youth, comes into direct conflict with the alien reality of Cernuda's middle age. The face in the mirror is an obstacle to the realisation of the dream, and continuing desire is made painful by the consciousness of age :

Pero tu faz, en el alinde
  De algún espejo, vieja,
Hosca, abstraída, te interrumpe
  Tal la presencia ajena.

Hoy este intruso eres tú mismo,
  Tú, como el otro antes,
Y con el cual sin gusto inicias
  Costumbre a que se allane.

Para llegar al que no eres,
  Quien no eres te guía,
Cuando el amigo es el extraño
  Y la rosa es la espina. (p. 242)

This apparent incompatibility between the dream of desire and Cernuda's advancing years becomes a recurring preoccupation; in the poem "El árbol", for example, the sight of young students at Cambridge who are unaware of time's threat sharpens his awareness of the loss of his own youth. He feels again the painful sense of disassociation from his former self, as though the young man he was and the middle-aged man he is comprised two completely different people :

Ya su faz reflejada extraña le parece,
Más que su faz extraña su conciencia,
De donde huyó el fervor trocado por disgusto,
Tal pájaro extranjero en nido que otro hizo. (p. 244)

This is a reversal of the attitude of "Vereda del cuco" where he was able to console himself that his own desire could live on in the desire of the new generation of young people. Such an apparent recantation of "Vereda del cuco" is an indication of the acute self-consciousness now pressing on Cernuda and of the need he feels for the fulfillment of his erotic aspirations, a need which cannot be assuaged any more by substitutes or philosophical rationale.

The phrase "el fervor trocado por disgusto" contained in the lines from "El árbol" quoted above neatly states one of the problems age creates for desire: the incongruity of the ageing man pursuing a youthful erotic dream. An extreme case of the conflict between age and what youth represents is made the subject of examination in "El césar", the final poem of *Vivir sin estar viviendo*, where Cernuda uses the device of the *Doppelgänger* to construct a monologue by the Emperor Tiberius during the period of his retirement to the Isle of Capri.[12] The lasciviousness of the depraved Emperor is interpreted as the product of the old man's wish to humiliate youth and beauty in revenge for the way youth mocks his age. However, I do not believe that "El césar" reaches the same satisfying compatibility and interchange of character between the poet and the figure who becomes a projection of his experience that Cernuda is able to attain in the best of his poems which employ the *Doppelgänger* technique. It is as though he has overstretched himself in this poem, dealing with an area of experience of which he has little direct knowledge and thus failing to achieve the necessary empathy with the poem's protagonist. A more moderate effect of the consciousness of age is the suppression and impotence of desire, as in the curious poem "Las islas", which looks back with a sense of gratitude to a heterosexual erotic experience. But the recollection of this happy moment, which he declares is the only moment of his life he would be prepared to live again, is overshadowed by old age, and Cernuda comes to the tentative conclusion that desire is dead, its place taken by the vicarious desire of memories:

> Cuando el recuerdo así vuelve sobre sus huellas
> (¿No es el recuerdo la impotencia del deseo?),
> Es que a él, como a mí, la vejez vence;
> Y acaso ya no tengo lo único que tuve:
> Deseo, a quien rendida la ocasión le sigue. (p. 273)

The internal sense of alienation Cernuda now suffers, the disassociation of his ageing self from the youthful ideal of desire, is an obsessive theme in *Vivir sin estar viviendo* and *Con las horas contadas*, whose titles clearly express the feeling of living vicariously with the consciousness that time is running out, a feeling succinctly put in one poem by the line: "el tiempo te desvive" (p. 296). The poem "Después" from *Con las horas contadas* is an evocation of the eternal renewal of Spring and of love, but the poet is now separated from this process of rebirth by his age which has taken away desire and also the youthful body that befits desire. Punctuating the poem, set in tragic counterpoint, are two *estribillos*: "Pero tú sombra sin cuerpo"; "Mas tú sombra sin deseo" (p. 296). The oppressive consciousness of time and age encloses Cernuda in a situation of

[12] Silver "*Et in Arcadia ego*", 202, suggests that the Emperor in question is Hadrian, but the poem's opening reference to the "Isla, en su roca escarpada inaccesible" points conclusively to Tiberius.

anguished solitude similar to that of his early poems, and, as if to underline this return to past circumstances, there is a notable increase in the number of song-type poems reminiscent of his early collections. In "El viento y el alma", contained in *Vivir sin estar viviendo*, desire is symbolised in the wind from the sea, "llorando y llamando/Como perdido sin nadie", which comes to rattle the poet's window as he lies alone in bed at night. The strong resonance of "Como el viento" from *Un río, un amor* is reinforced in the poem's final stanza when the memories of lost youth overwhelm the insistent call of desire as the wind moves to the level of a directly personal image : "Fue viento libre, y recuerda" (p. 247). Even the dream of desire can bring no comfort to this oppressive consciousness of solitude; in "Versos para ti mismo", from *Con las horas contadas*, Cernuda dreams of the head of a friend resting upon his shoulder, only to be disturbed by the realisation that this is just a dream, a product of his loneliness and a reminder of the present impotence of desire :

> No. Eres tú quien sueña solo
> Aquel efecto noble compartido,
> Cuyos ecos despiertan por tu mente desierta
> Como en la concha los del mar que ya no existe. (p. 294)

Cernuda returns at this late stage in his life to that state of numbed indolence which was a characteristic of the periods of dejection in his youth, except that he is now dominated by a desperate awareness of time's flux. But as desire is suppressed by the vision of the ageing face in the mirror where once had appeared the face of youth, the object of Cernuda's concern tends not to be the dream of a hypothetical lover, as in "Versos para ti mismo", but his own youthful self. In poems like "Viendo volver" or "El perfume" there is a straightforward contrast between past youth and present age, but in other poems the youthful self is presented as an erotic object, replacing the conventional object of desire. The climax of the poem "El éxtasis", where death is seen as a reunion with lost youth, is presented as a sexual union in terms that strongly recall the closing lines of "Nocturno entre las musarañas" from *Un río, un amor* :

> E iremos por el prado a las aguas, donde olvido,
> Sin gesto el gozo, muda la palabra,
> Vendrá desde tu labio hasta mi labio,
> Fundirá en una sombra nuestra sombras. (pp. 253-4)

The intricate relationship Cernuda has with his youth is examined in more detail in "La sombra", a poem that demonstrates the masterful way Cernuda succeeds in adapting the discursive register of language preferred in his mature poems to the song-form he had used in his early work, enabling him to condense the analysis of his experience into a statement all the more effective for its concision. Because of the simple clarity of its expression and its significance for the development of the love theme, I shall quote "La sombra" in full :

> Al despertar de un sueño, buscas
> Tu juventud, como si fuera el cuerpo

Del camarada que durmiese
A tu lado y que al alba no encuentras.

Ausencia conocida, nueva siempre,
Con la cual no te hallas. Y aunque acaso
Hoy tú seas más de lo que era
El mozo ido, todavía

Sin voz le llamas, cuántas veces;
Olvidando que de su mocedad se alimentaba
Aquella pena aguda, la conciencia
De tu vivir de ayer. Ahora,

Ida también es sólo
Un vago malestar, una inconsciencia
Acallando el pasado, dejando indiferente
Al otro que tú eres, sin pena, sin alivio. (p. 260)

Here Cernuda's youthful self has quite openly replaced the usual object of desire in a poem of this nature, while desire itself has disappeared with the passing of youth. The erotic "pena aguda" was the motivating force of his youth and the absence now of the dynamic desire produced has left Cernuda in that numb state of emotional indolence so frequent in his early poetry.

"La sombra" clearly demonstrates how Cernuda's commitment to the youthful dream of desire leads him, in middle age, to an internal alienation between his young and old selves; he has become "el otro", a different personality from the youthful self with which life remains identified. Tragically, his future is now in the hands of this alien other self, which time and age have imposed on him, although without the aspirations youth inspired this other self is an empty, lifeless entity. The pressing problem facing Cernuda in the poems of *Vivir sin estar viviendo* and *Con las horas contadas* is how to reconcile the youthful self he no longer is, but on which his dreams are based, with his ageing reality that represents a denial of the erotic ideal to which he has committed his life. This problem is, in fact, solved by the love affair of "Poemas para un cuerpo", but the relationship between the concern for lost youth and the love theme in these mature poems points to an element in Cernuda's attitude to love and desire quite distinct from the association with the quasi-mystic *acorde*. The strong vein of narcissism present both in the figure of the *intruso* and in the substitution of his youthful self for the usual erotic object of his dreams clearly suggests that love and desire provide a vehicle for Cernuda's search for himself.

The Search for the True Self

The condition of indolence and the feeling of nullity which Cernuda experiences as a result of the waning of desire with age are negative indications that desire continues to be equated with life. In essence, the commitment to the erotic ideal Cernuda had made in his youth has not been diminished by the passing of time, only made more difficult. Given this continuing commitment, it is not surprising that the despairing attitude noted in his later poems should be balanced by attempts to keep hope for love alive, despite the depressing awareness that time is running out. The voice which had sounded within him in "Cuatro poemas a una sombra", repeating the "presagio loco : espera, espera", has not been stilled. Cernuda remains capable of promoting love and desire as supreme virtues even though the eyes that view the youthful body provoking desire are clouded with age. In "Escultura inacabada" from *Vivir sin estar viviendo* Michelangelo's statue of David Apollo is seen as the representation of ideal adolescent beauty on the threshold of desire but as yet without its disenchanting experience. The contemplation of the statue awakens a feeling of sadness inspired by the knowledge that this idyllic state is subject to the decay of time, yet the poem ends on a triumphant note since this ideal figure is the creation of love, the only force powerful enough to give it the breath of life :

Fue amor quien la trajera,
Amor, la sola fuerza humana,
Desde el no ser, al sueño
Donde latente asoma. (pp. 269-70)

In "Aguila y rosa ", the opening poem of *Con las horas contadas*, which treats the marriage of Philip II and Mary Tudor, the brief and inadequate experience of love given to Mary is regarded as at least some recompense for her unhappy life :

Pero su vida ha conocido,
Si no la flor, su sombra; entonces no fue estéril,
Y valía la pena de vivirse, con toda esa amargura. (p. 284)

Here is a restatement of the attitude of "Cuatro poemas a una sombra" : the shadow of love, the experience that is less than the ideal, has nonetheless, a positive value.

These two judgements on love, the one exultant, the other somewhat grudging, find an echo in poems devoted to Cernuda's contemplation of his personal relationship to the erotic ideal now that youth has given way to age. "Cara joven", from *Vivir sin estar viviendo*, contrasts another narcissistic contemplation of the youthful self with the disturbing reality of advancing years, but the wish to recapture youth is calmly put aside as an impossibility and the separation from youth wrought by age philosophically accepted. Although the face he sees in the mirror has changed, Cernuda finds that his delight in physical beauty has remained the same, providing a consolation for the loss of youth and a source of optimism for his dreams :

Sólo tu gozo
Es el de siempre si la miras.
Como lluvia clara, conforta;
Como sueño de amanecida,
Alienta; sugiere posibles
E imposibles, como la vida. (p. 261)

The continuing hope for love can exist even in moments of depression when the consciousness of time is strongest. "Pasatiempo", from *Con las horas contadas*, is dedicated to a brief examination of the sombre state his life has reached: alienation, exile, lack of recognition for his work. This is the poem that contains the phrase "el tiempo te desvive", and the title itself is a bitter pun on the threat posed by time. In this situation the possibility of a future love is presented as a salve for the apparent futility of his existence:

> De algún azar espera
> Que un cuerpo joven sea
> Pretexto en tu existencia.
>
> Acaso el amor puede
> Tener aquellos seres
> Que todo marco exceden. (pp. 296-7)

Love here represents a last despairing hope, almost parasitic in its exploitation of the youthful body of the loved one to give a vicarious life to the ageing poet. The idea of love as a mere pretext for Cernuda's existence is far removed from the emphatic declaration of love as the justification of life that was made in *Los placeres prohibidos*, yet even such a morose supposition still demonstrates the persistence of his commitment to the erotic ideal and the existential function of the ideal.

The sentiments expressed in a rather negative fashion in "Pasatiempo" are restated with greater force and positiveness in "Amor en música" where the idea that *el amor es lo eterno y no lo amado* is developed through the image of love as a musical theme that undergoes many different variations. Cernuda accepts that any particular love must end in disenchantment and admits that because of this inevitable pain he has at times sought to avoid love, but at the same time he declares that the force of love is too strong to be denied, just as music cannot be ignored by someone with a good ear. The pleasure or pain associated with love are purely circumstantial when love is, as this poem declares it to be, the supreme experience of life. "Amor en música" attempts to come to terms with the continuing involvement with the erotic ideal, through the recognition that the dream of love is an integral part of Cernuda's personality, so that the denial of love would be a denial of himself:

> Si éstos nacen para locos
> Y aquéllos para prudentes,
> De qué lado estás ya sabes:
> Canta tus aires fielmente.
>
> Y deja la melodía
> Llenarte todo el espíritu
> Ya qué más da gozo o pena
> Si en el amor se han fundido. (p. 301)

"Amor en música" provides a fittting introduction to "Poemas para un cuerpo". The meeting in Mexico with the mysterious "X" during the summer of

1951 was regarded by Cernuda as the climax of his life, a moment of great happiness that was all the more welcome coming after the long years of exile. While recognising the danger he ran of appearing a "viejo enamorado", he has stated that "ninguna otra vez estuve, si no tan enamorado, tan bien enamorado" (*PL*, 273-4); this was the experience of an order of love that demanded his total abandonment to it in the way he had described in "Amor en música".[13] The series of poems concerned with the love affair was begun in Mexico in 1951 and finished there after Cernuda had taken up permanent residence in that country in 1952 (*PL*, 273 and 279). Some of the poems refer to the period of the love affair itself but the majority look back after the end of the affair seeking to analyse the nature and effect of its experience. As a series of song-poems dealing almost exclusively with a single love affair, "Poemas para un cuerpo" evokes an immediate parallel with *Donde habite el olvido*, but while the earlier poems are the product of a violent passion that ends in equally violent disillusion, "Poemas para un cuerpo" has the benefit of many years' meditation on the nature of love. The ardent reaction of youth has given way to the calm understanding of age; there is no bitterness or resentment in these tardy love poems, only a feeling of gratitude for the happiness love has brought. Cernuda, in complete control of his emotions, is primarily concerned to investigate the relationship between himself and the experience of love, so much so in fact that the loved one has only a secondary importance in the poems compared with the central position occupied by Cernuda himself. José Olivio Jiménez has pointed out that the poems are free of any sensuousness, or indeed any sensuality, and has suggested that they are the expression of "una teoría intelectual del amor".[14] Elisabeth Müller has noted that although most of the poems are addressed to the loved one, the latter represents only a pretext for a monologue by Cernuda.[15] The cool detachment and self-analytial concern of "Poemas para un cuerpo" mean, in effect, that these poems are not really love lyrics but egocentric meditations which remove all doubt as to the fundamentally narcissistic nature of the love theme in Cernuda's work.

Donde habite el olvido was written to exorcise bitter memories, "Cuatro poemas a una sombra" to rationalise the transitoriness of love, but the intention of "Poemas para un cuerpo" is to fix and retain this supreme experience of love. The third poem of the series explains that memory is not sufficient to sustain in Cernuda's mind the living presence of the now absent lover, he needs a more tangible reminder, which he hopes to create in his poetry:

> Y aunque tú no has de verlas,
> Para hablar con tu ausencia
>
> Estas líneas escribo,
> Unicamente por estar contigo. (pp. 305-6)

[13] ". . . sabía . . . cómo hay momentos en la vida que requieren de nosotros la entrega al destino, total y sin reservas . . ." (*PL*, 273).

[14] 'Emoción y trascendencia del tiempo en la poesía de Luis Cernuda', *loc. cit.*, 77.

[15] *Die Dichtung Luis Cernudas*, 66.

This is a most significant statement; these poems are not written in order to recapture the presence of the loved one but as a result of the presence of the loved one within him. The lover has become a part of him. In the eleventh poem, musing on his attitude towards the love now ended, he proposes the idea that in Hell time is reversed so that the love affair would be unlived from its end through its beginning until the moment before the lovers' meeting. But this speculation is rejected since he cannot tolerate the idea of not knowing the loved one, whereas the "olvido" of him can be accepted because this means he is still part of Cernuda's life. The quiet, conceptual mode of expression taken by these ideas shows the control Cernuda now exercises over his experience, while the ideas themselves demonstrate the depth of his involvement in the tardy love affair :

Y yo no quiero
Vida en la cual ya tú no tengas parte :
Olvido de ti, sí, mas no ignorancia tuya.

El camino que sube
Y el camino que baja
Uno y el mismo son; y mi deseo
Es que al fin de uno y de otro,
Con odio o con amor, con olvido o memoria,
Tu existir esté allí, mi infierno y paraíso. (p. 312)[16]

The Mexican love affair gave to Cernuda's life a meaning which had been absent throughout the vicarious existence of exile. In poem XII, simply entitled "La vida", love is likened to the sun's rays bringing warmth and life to the earth. Poem X is, in effect, a reply to "Pasatiempo", that earlier poem in *Con las horas contadas* where he had hope for love as a solution to his feeling of alienation; love now becomes a substitute for the homeland he has lost and the sense of community which has been denied him. Poem IX declares that love has created the world anew, giving to nature a pristine quality as the eyes opened by love see the world as though for the first time. This idea of rebirth is developed in poem XIII which looks back from the standpoint of the end of the affair and sees that love has stripped Cernuda of all the circumstantial elements of his existence but has given him in return the new life created by love. He now lives in a dimension where only he and the loved one exist, having almost recaptured the state of lost innocence, except that he has the burden of solitude and a one-sided love :

Pero si deshiciste
Todo lo en mí prestado,
Me das así otra vida;
Y como ser primero
Inocente, estoy solo
Con mí mismo y contigo.

[16] There is an echo here of Heraclitus : "The way up and the way down is one and the same." K. Freeman, *Ancilla to the Pre-Socratic Philosophers* (Oxford, 1948), 29. T. S. Eliot also alludes to this Heraclitan fragment in "The Dry Salvages", line 129.

Aquel que da la vida,
La muerte da con ella.
Desasido del mundo
Por tu amor, me dejaste
Con mi vida y mi muerte.

Morir parece fácil,
La vida es lo difícil:
Ya no sé sino usarla
En ti, con este inútil
Trabajo de quererte,
Que tú no necesitas. (p. 313)

Although the end of love is likened to death this is not the same as the spiritual death associated with the loss of love in the poems of youth; the death brought by the end of love is accepted as a concomitant of the life love creates. Even when the affair is over Cernuda is not the empty shell he had become after the youthful failures of love, since the experience of love remains with him and continues to be the dynamic in his life.

"Poemas para un cuerpo" establish, through actual experience, that equation between love and life Cernuda had made in his youth and had then later tried to reassert intellectually in such poems as "Vereda del cuco". This final crowning affirmation of the identity of love and life helps Cernuda to reconcile the conflict between age and the youthful erotic ideal. Poem VII examines the tardiness of his love and rejects this as an irrelevant matter. By comparing his love to an autumn rose or the last grapes on a vine he emphasises its naturalness; for those things that represent life it is never too late. In any case, love, by creating for itself a moment of eternity, is outside time: "el tiempo de amor nos vale toda una eternidad" (p. 315). Love is, in effect, a rejuvenating experience, as Cernuda has declared: "jamás en mi juventud me sentí tan joven como en aquellos días en México" (*PL*, 274). The resolution of the problem of age through the fulfillment of the erotic ideal, and the coincidence of this with the discovery of Mexico, make "Poemas para un cuerpo" the climax of Cernuda's poetic autobiography. As he himself clearly saw, the Mexican love affair swept away his sense of alienation: ". . . el afán constante de partir, de irme a otras tierras . . . Y sólo el amor alivió este afán, dándome la seguridad de pertenecer a una tierra, de no ser en ella un extranjero, un intruso" (*PL*, 278). For once it might appear that through the experience of love in a land to which he felt he belonged Cernuda genuinely attained the quasi-mystic state of the *acorde*. Yet, strangely, "Poemas para un cuerpo" lack any sense of triumph; the dominant mood of these poems is the feeling of gratitude, which, one suspects, is almost relief that all his dreams should not have been in vain. This, of course, does not militate against the love affair representing an attainment of the *acorde*, but, when other factors are taken into consideration, it does appear that this element of love's experience is of only secondary importance.

Rather than the sense of loss of self in a transcendent experience, the Mexican love affair brings a heightened awareness of self, as is illustrated by the way

"Poemas para un cuerpo" focus on Cernuda and not the loved one. The egocentricity of these poems is clearly evident in the repeated declaration that the loved one was entirely created by Cernuda's love for him.[17] Poem IX expresses surprise that the loved one should have parents when it seems to Cernuda that he was brought into existence by their first meeting. Poem XI proposes the idea that love was concentrated in Cernuda and that the object of his love was merely its instigator :

. . . esta historia nuestra, mía y tuya
(Mejor será decir nada más mía,
Aunque a tu parte queden la ocasión y el motivo,
Que no es poco) . . . (p. 311)

A similar passive rôle is ascribed to the loved one in poem XIV, who is here presented as simply an example of physical beauty which engages the poet with an irresistible attraction. Again the loved one is no more than a stimulus, a projection of the lover's desire, given substance by the lover so that he becomes an extension of the lover's own personality :

. . . un ser que llenamos
Con nuestro pensamiento,
Vivo de nuestra vida.

El da el motivo,
Lo diste tú; porque tú existes
Afuera como sombra de algo,
Una sombra perfecta
De aquel afán, que es del amante, mío. (p. 314)

Here the idea that *el amor es lo eterno y no lo amado* has been joined with the element of narcissism always present in Cernuda's concept of love. The same attitude is expressed more fully in poem IV, which, with the title "Sombra de mí", is a meditation on the relationship between the lover and the beloved. The loved one is again the visible image of the lover's desire, but nonetheless necessary for without him love could not have been exteriorised. He is only an excuse for love, and yet the poem ends with a statement of profound gratitude for the life this love brought :

Bien sé yo que esta imagen
Fija siempre en la mente
No eres tú, sino sombra
Del amor que en mí existe
Antes que el tiempo acabe.

. . . . .

[17] The idea that the beloved is created by love is also found in Salinas's *La voz a ti debida;* "Poemas para un cuerpo" are often reminiscent of Salinas's love poetry, although they also owe something to the English "Metaphysical" poets.

Y aunque conozco eso, luego pienso
Que sin tí, sin el raro
Pretexto que me diste,
Mi amor, que afuera está con su ternura,
Allá dentro de mí hoy seguiría
Dormido todavía y a la espera
De alguien que, a su llamada,
Le hiciera al fin latir gozosamente.

Entonces te doy gracias y te digo :
Para esto vine al mundo, y a esperarte;
Para vivir por ti, como tú vives
Por mí, aunque no lo sepas,
Por este amor tan hondo que te tengo. (p. 306)

Love is here not so much the object of life as the life-force itself, although it needs to be projected onto someone before it can become fully operative. The dream of love within the lover is, however, the active element of the life-force, and the subject of love merely the "motivo" or "pretexto" that awakens the dream to reality.

"Poemas para un cuerpo" are, thus, the fulfillment of that hope expressed in "Pasatiempo" : "Que un cuerpo joven sea/ Pretexto en tu existencia" (p. 296). The loved one is just a pretext for the erotic ideal's realisation, playing the rôle of an objective correlative for love's dream. The loved one's function as an excuse for love explains the complete lack of any physical description in the poems and the use of the word "cuerpo" in the title of the series. It may be recalled here that "cuerpo" is a common term of reference for previous lovers whose physical description was also not considered worthy of mention. The view of the loved one as a mere *pretexto* is the most striking element of "Poemas para un cuerpo", and even though this can be regarded as a development of the attitude associated with the contrast between the eternity of love and the transitoriness of the lover, it is surprising to find such detachment on Cernuda's part. This detachment can be explained by a significant statement in the final poem of the series :

Tú y mi amor, mientras miro
Dormir tu cuerpo cuando
Amanece. Así mira
Un dios lo que ha creado.

Mas mi amor nada puede
Sin que tu cuerpo acceda :
El sólo informa un mito
En tu hermosa materia. (p. 316)

Again the loved one is created by the lover as an image of physical beauty, but this body is now described as giving substance to a myth. Here is another repetition of the distinction between the shadow of love and its ideal, yet the use of the term "mito" adds a broader dimension to this idea, recalling the concept of the *mito personal* discussed in the opening chapter of this study. Philip Silver suggests that "Poemas para un cuerpo" represent a confrontation with Cernuda's other, youthful self in the shape of the loved one, making Cernuda himself the spiritual side of the erotic ideal which has been his life's concern, while the object of his love provides the physical aspect of the ideal he has lost with age.[18] In Silver's view the myth referred to in the lines quoted above is that which he believes Cernuda has made out of his youth, a youth now regained through the experience of love. This is a perfectly viable explication, the experience of love does resolve the conflict between age and the youthful erotic ideal, but this is, perhaps, too narrow a view of the significance of this series of poems as the climactic moment in Cernuda's poetic autobiography.

A notable characteristic of "Poemas para un cuerpo" is the reversal of the tendency to objectivise experience which is a principal stylistic trait of the poetry from *Invocaciones* onwards. Only four of the poems in the series employ the distancing technique of the poet speaking of himself in the second person, which is so common in the mature poetry, the other twelve poems utilise a direct, first person mode of address. The change from the technique of *dédoublement* to direct personal statement is indicative of a change in Cernuda's attitude towards himself. The second person form of address is a product of the intense solitude and alienation he experiences in exile, which cause him to create a second self, the "tú" who turns his poetry into an interior dialogue investigating his character and circumstances. The sense of disassociation from himself reflected by this technique, which becomes more extreme when, as in "El intruso", he feels alienated from his youthful self, is absent from the great majority of the compositions in "Poemas para un cuerpo". The place of the other self is taken by the loved one, although he too, as we have seen, is only a creation of Cernuda's desire. Not only does he change in these poems the mode of address from "tú" to "yo", but he inserts in poem III the quite extraordinary and unique personal reference : "Y yo, este Luis Cernuda/Incógnito." Mentioning his predilection for this series of poems, Cernuda has suggested that he might be reproached here for not having maintained the necessary distance between the man who suffers and the artist who creates (*PL*, 279). From this statement by the poet himself and from the internal evidence of the change in mode of address, it would appear that in these poems the literary mask has been withdrawn, at least to a certain extent. Clearly something of importance has happened in "Poemas para un cuerpo" which can, I believe, be explained if the identification of love and life is considered together with the change to the first person in the poems. The Mexican love affair, coinciding with the discovery of Mexico as a substitute for Cernuda's native Andalusia, and with the successful resolution of his fears that age was stifling the erotic ideal, is in the manner of a resuscitation from the empty, vicarious existence of exile. This love does not merely provide a justification for the travails of the preceding years; it is an affirmation of Cernuda's existence after the nebulous life spent in the alien environment of England and the United States. The love in Mexico is the

[18] *"Et in Arcadia ego"*, 120 ff.

experience "que da valor al hombre/Para el hombre en el mundo" (p. 313). Cernuda has recovered from his oppressive sense of alienation and he can therefore speak of himself as "yo" rather than "tú". Love has reintegrated his personality which had been divided between the dream of youth and the reality of age. This is more than a recapture of lost innocence, for he has found the life that had been denied him by the failure of love in his youth and by the years of exile. In "Poemas para un cuerpo" he found himself.

This last climatic experience of love shows that Cernuda's constant commitment to the erotic ideal is more than the result of an identification of love with life; he goes beyond this common trope to equate love with his personality. He *is* the dream of love he had carried with him since his adolescence. The dream is his identity, that *verdad de sí mismo* he had proclaimed it to be in *Los placeres prohibidos*; the search for love is thus an existential imperative, already prefigured in that youthful declaration of *Primeras poesías* :

Vivo un solo deseo,
Un afán claro, unánime;
Afán de amor y olvido. (p. 15)

In the mature poems the recognition of the link between his personality and the dream of love becomes clearer. The analysis of his relationship with his family made in "La familia" contains the realisation that all he received from his family was accidental to his character, while the very essence of his being was what they did not give him, his desire :

Pero algo más había, agazapado
Dentro de ti, como alimaña en cueva oscura,
Que no te dieron ellos, y eso eres . . . (p. 197)

This assertion is repeated in substance in "Vereda del cuco", where, after having declared love to be the fount of life, Cernuda goes on to say that the experience of love will always remain with him, "Lo que el amor te ha dado/ Contigo ha de quedar, y es tu destino" (p. 231), thus proclaiming love as both an integral part of his identity and as the very force that moulds that identity.

The clearest and most significant statement of the link between Cernuda's pursuit of love and his character is contained in "Nocturno yanqui", that excellent example of the meditative, self-analytical vein of his mature work, where he examines and tries to evaluate his life from the standpoint of his solitary situation in exile. Although he finds little to console him in the empty existence his middle age has become, the result of this meditation is to make him realise that the life-long search for love has been, in effect, a struggle for self-affirmation :

Lo mejor que has sido, diste,
Lo mejor de tu existencia,
A una sombra :
Al afán de hacerte digno,
Al deseo de excederte,

Esperando
Siempre mañana otro día
Que, aunque tarde, justifique
Tu pretexto.

Cierto que tú te esforzaste
Por sino y amor de una
Criatura,
Mito moceril, buscando
Desde siempre, y al servirla,
Ser quien eres. (p. 287)

The dream of love is here again described as a myth, but this myth is itself the pretext for affirming his existence. These lines from "Nocturno yanqui" point, I believe, conclusively to the existential rôle played by the love theme in Cernuda's poetry. Love and desire are vehicles in the search for a complete, integrated existence, which may be attained through the experience of the *acorde* love can provide, but mostly this is because, having identified himself with love, it is only in love that he can fully exist. Without love Cernuda is overwhelmed by a sense of lifelessness or else finds himself torn between the youthful dream of desire and the reality of his advancing years. However, when in "Poemas para un cuerpo" the dream at last comes true, he not only creates the loved one out of his dreams of desire but also, by the realisation of the dream, creates himself. Such a view of the love theme's function can explain both the strong narcissistic element in the erotic ideal and the process of *dédoublement* in the mature poems. The evasive facet of his concept of love, the possibility of gaining through love access to a transcendent reality is thus more than balanced by the emphasis on love as a means of self-affirmation. Love for Cernuda means a realisation of his truth, and a profession of his identity.

VI

THE TRUTH OF ONE'S SELF

Hablan en el poeta voces varias :
Escuchemos su coro concertado,
Adonde la creída dominante
Es tan sólo una voz entre las otras.
("Díptico español", *Desolación de la Quimera*, p. 329)

The examination of the themes of love and of poetry in Cernuda's work has shown that beneath the longing for a transcendent reality and the evasive attitudes this entails there is an inquiry into the nature of his personal identity. The word *verdad* recurs again and again as he seeks to discover and affirm the truth about himself. The early poems recount the discovery of this truth while the mature poems refine his knowledge of it as the accumulation of lived experience is used to deepen self-understanding. In this final chapter I shall study this process in the mature poems by examining the development of Cernuda's view of life and of himself, with the intention of uncovering that truth of the *hombre interior* of whom *La Realidad y el Deseo* is a portrait. This chapter will also include an analysis of the last collection of poems, *Desolación de la Quimera*, which until now has been deliberately left aside. Coming after the climatic experience of "Poemas para un cuerpo", these final poems form an epilogue to all the preceding poetry and provide concluding evidence of the fundamentally ethical quality of that poetry.

In his early poems Cernuda makes the discovery that his aspirations, in particular his erotic aspirations, are his identity, a discovery later reflected in the conclusion of 'Palabras antes de una lectura' that the tangible world is a mirage and the only real thing his desire to possess it. The attempt made in *Invocaciones* to reconstruct his shattered ideals is, in effect, an endeavour to recover the sense of identity lost with the loss of love in *Donde habite el olvido.* A concern with identity at this time turns Cernuda's poetry into a survey of his personal values and leads to the meditative, self-analytical manner of his maturity. The change in his poetry from a simple recording function in the early work to a defining one in *Invocaciones* is then confirmed by the upheaval in his life brought by the Civil War and exile, which creates a further crisis of identity and sharpens the focus of his self-contemplative gaze. Cernuda has commented on the spur to poetic activity that exile was for Unamuno, adducing from this a general rule that a disturbance in a poet's life is a fillip to his work.[1] This is certainly so in his own case since during the time of the war and the first years of exile he produced some of his finest poems, in *Las nubes* and *Como quien espera el alba,* as well as many of the prose poems of *Ocnos.* He himself has remarked on the fecundity of inspiration he felt particularly in the period 1941-1942 (*PL,* 263).

The opening elegies of *Las nubes,* inspired directly by the war, provide clear examples of the new meditative reaction to experience, even to experience as disturbing as that brought by the war. The detachment which the mood of meditation requires becomes more marked in the poems written in exile when Cernuda begins to develop the *Doppelgänger* technique by which he can distance himself from his experience. The despairing feeling of lifelessness and the sense of alienation which exile brings tend to be viewed with a laconic coolness, typified by the attitude of the reluctantly resurrected Lazarus, who would have preferred to remain in the oblivion of death rather than face the pain of life once more. The risen man's disenchantment with the world is a form of detachment that enables him to see himself and his life with a curious impartiality, just as the device of the *Doppelgänger* enables Cernuda to see himself objectively in Lazarus. "Lázaro" is in large part a meditation on the nature of man's life. The release from the grave is presented as having occurred at some fairly distant time in the past; Lazarus's own memory is unsure of the event and he has to rely in part on eye witness accounts as he tells his story. The purpose of this recounting of past experience is to try to come to terms with a life that Lazarus finds essentially meaningless, and this poem is a paradigm of the dominant intention of the poetry of Cernuda's exile. Cernuda, like Lazarus, wants to understand his apparently empty existence, and he too becomes engrossed in self-contemplation.

The immediate direction taken by the search for a sense of purpose to combat the alienation of exile is the attempt by Cernuda to seek consolation in Christianity. While the appeal for help to religion is desperate and short-lived, the tenor of a poem like "La visita de Dios", with its emphasis on disillusionment, loss of youth, and the difficulties of life in exile, demonstrates that the effect of Cernuda's changed circumstances is to make him look for something to give meaning to his life. A more lasting consequence of exile is the increased self-awareness brought about by the sharpened sense of alienation. The combined effect of passing the *mezzo del cammin di nostra vita* and the violent imposition of a foreign environment create in Cernuda a willingness to reassess himself with a new measure of objectivity. The effect on his self-awareness is most visible, somewhat paradoxically, in "Lázaro" and "La adoración de los Magos", the two poems of *Las nubes* that use the device of the *Doppelgänger.* The precision with which he creates the world-weary character of Lazarus, dragged unwillingly back to a life he considers futile, reveals both a technical maturity and a well-developed analytical capability. Lazarus is in part a portrait of Cernuda himself, reflecting his own attitude to life at that time, but the coherence and credibility he is able to give to Lazarus as a separate individual is an indication of the way Cernuda is now able to view himself with an element of

[1] *Estudios sobre poesía española contemporánea,* 97.

dispassion. This deeper insight into himself is even more evident in the tripartite division of character in "La adoración de los Magos", where the three different personalities of the Kings, reflecting three facets of Cernuda's own character, show a remarkable degree of self-knowledge on his part.

The meditative vein in Cernuda's mature poems has been linked by José Angel Valente with a tradition of meditative poetry that Valente finds in Jorge Manrique, Aldana, San Juan de la Cruz, and the English "metaphysical" poets. Valente believes that Cernuda was brought into contact with this tradition by his exile in England which greatly increased his acquaintanceship with English poetry, and in particular with the "metaphysical" poets, the Romantics who had continued the meditative manner, and the Moderns such as Eliot and Yeats who had themselves been influenced by the "metaphysicals". From this knowledge of English meditative poetry, Valente suggests, Cernuda was then led to rediscover the Spanish tradition of meditative poetry.[2] Support for this idea can be found in Cernuda's sympathetic and illuminating comments on San Juan de la Cruz in the article 'Tres poetas clásicos', which dates from 1941, and in his excellent article 'Tres poetas metafísicos', written in 1946 and concerned with Manrique, Aldana, and the "Epístola moral a Fabio".[3] Moreover, if "Lázaro" is taken as an example of Cernuda's meditative poetry, it is perhaps not accidental that this poem contains a very strong echo of Browning.[4]

While many of the poems of *Las nubes* are directly concerned with Spain or the immediate effects of exile, there are a number of compositions in which Cernuda muses in a simple, unforced way on the nature of life without the intervention of a projected self like Lazarus. In "Violetas", a poem Valente has mentioned as an outstanding example of his meditative poetry,[5] the contrast between the beauty and the transitoriness of the unprepossessing flower leads to a pensive reflection on the fragility of life and the ability of beauty to escape corruption by time. The next poem, "Pájaro muerto", is in a similar manner but expresses more clearly the underlying reason for this contemplative mood. The poet has found a dead bird in the early days of spring and this sad discovery of a creature once ecstatically alive causes him to ponder on the apparent futility of life and his own unhappy experience :

> Inútil ya todo parece, tal parece
> La pena del amor cuando se ha ido,
> El sufrir por lo bello que envejece,
> El afán de la luz que anegan sombras. (p. 178)

The same sense of an empty, futile existence is given voice, with greater force, in "Cementerio en la ciudad", an evocation of an urban cemetery, most probably in Glasgow, set amidst the din of a railway and the depressing ugliness of a working-class district. The dead have been abandoned in this grim place, ignored by the life that goes on around them and denied the tranquility that

[2] 'Luis Cernuda y la poesía de la meditación', *La caña gris,* nos. 6-8 (1962), 29-37.
[3] *Poesía y literatura,* 37-53 and 57-74 respectively.
[4] See Chapter Three, note 25.
[5] 'Luis Cernuda y la poesía de la meditación', *loc. cit.,* 35-6.

death should bring. The clatter of a passing train is likened to the "bronce iracundo" that will herald the Day of Judgement, but Cernuda calms the fears of the dead with a desolate and cynical supposition :

> No es el juicio aún, muertos anónimos.
> Sosegaos, dormid; dormid si es que podéis.
> Acaso Dios también se olvida de vosotros. (p. 166)[6]

This dismal impression of the cemetery is really another meditation on the purpose of life, in which Cernuda, weighed down by the difficulties of exile, asks himself what meaning can there be in an existence that ends in such a place. The pessimism of this poem hides a desperate need to find some justification for life in general and his own life in particular, a need which will come to preoccupy him more and more, and which, as it is clarified, will lead him to a deeper understanding of himself. The need to find a meaning in life is the dynamic the experience of exile creates for the mature poetry, so that the poems of exile become that *criticism of life* recommended by Mathew Arnold and which Cernuda himself has accepted as the aim of poetry.[7]

A clearer insight into his own personality and the concern to discover some justifying purpose in life are the first fruits of Cernuda's new contemplative manner. But in *Las nubes* he is still numb from the shock of the events that have so drastically changed his circumstances, and he thus lacks the tranquility necessary to exploit fully his increased powers of self-analysis. The required calm is attained in *Como quien espera el alba* when the immediate painful effects of exile are subdued, leaving him in that empty existence in which he can only contemplate himself. The majority of the compositions in this book can be classed as meditative poetry in which he makes a concentrated effort to appraise his life up to that time and to establish a set of values on which his existence may rest. This attitude of intensive meditation is set against an acute consciousness of time; scarcely a single poem is without this sense of temporality, and for some, like "Mutabilidad", "Los espinos" and "Amando en el tiempo", it is the sole preoccupation. The pathetic contrast between man's ephemerality and the permanence of the world about him or the things he can create is a constant theme. The hawthorn trees of "Los espinos", blossoming in spring, are proof of the continuation of the rhythm of the seasons, and a reminder that he has no such hope of a continuing existence. Sooner or later, one spring, he will not be there to see the hawthorns in flower. This is the substance of the reproach made to God in "Las ruinas" : that man is made to die while endowed with the gift to conceive of eternity. Such musings on the temporal world are expressed with great clarity and simplicity in the poem "Jardín". The garden is a haven from the weary existence of exile; seated in a corner, the poet lapses into an indolent reverie, gratefully absorbing the tranquil scene of birdsong, light, trees,

[6] Juan Ferraté, *La operación de leer* (Barcelona, 1962) 224-32, sees a parallel between this poem and Thomas Hardy's "Channel Firing", although the similarity is not perhaps as close as he suggests. "Cementerio en la ciudad" also awakens distant echoes of Unamuno's "En un cementerio de lugar castellano".

[7] *Estudios sobre poesía española contemporánea,* 32.

and the lilies on the still surface of the pool of water. This is another version of the *jardín escondido* of Cernuda's adolescence, but he is now unhappily conscious of the rarity of the tranquil experience the garden offers and acutely aware of the destructive presence of time in the garden. The stillness of the water in the pool is contrasted with the sun-dial measuring out the changing hours, and the poem concludes with the recognition that the poet, the garden, and the moment of peace discovered there will all succumb to time. The meditative mood of this poem is given simple point by the strategic placing of the injunction "mira" at the beginning of the first and fifth stanzas of this eight stanza composition. The meaning of "look and take heed" in this imperative reveals that understanding is the aim behind the contemplative gaze.

Beset as he is by an intense consciousness of time and with the vacuous life of exile offering no clear prospect for the future, Cernuda's meditations tend to be directed towards his past experience, since only the events of the past seem to have any firm reality; as he says in "Otros tulipanes amarillos", a poem almost entirely concerned with the pressure of memories, "ya en tu vida las sombras pesan más que los cuerpos" (p. 220). The mulling over of the past produces some of the best poems of *Como quien espera el alba*, such as "La familia" and "*Apologia pro vita sua*", and is one of the major ways by which he tries to come to an understanding of himself. The state of mind leading to this introverted examination of the self is clearly portrayed in the poem "Tarde oscura", where mist and the fading light of evening create a strange, unreal, lifeless world that parallels the emptiness and unreality of Cernuda's existence. He wanders aimlessly through streets of slums, forced to seek solace within himself by the unremitting enmity of the world around him :

La vida, y tú solo,
No muerto, no vivo,
En el pecho sientes
Débil su latido.

Por estos suburbios
Sórdidos, sin norte
Vas, como el destino
Inútil del hombre.

Y en el pensamiento
Luz o fe ahora
Buscas, mientras vence
Afuera la sombra. (p. 199)

Here is a precise statement that it is the sense of futility, the feeling of suspended animation, the "destino inútil" created by exile, that turn Cernuda in on himself even more than usual in order to establish values and beliefs which can give to his existence the support and justification he so desperately needs.

The rôle of poetry and of love in this context have already been examined, and we must now look at Cernuda's general concept of life as he conducts his inquiry into it. "La familia", where the memory of his childhood relationship with his family provokes an analysis of the meaning of life, can serve as a good introduction to this aspect of *Como quien espera el alba.* The poem begins with an evocation of the family seated at the dinner table, but this domestic scene is presented with little sympathy, composed as it is of "el padre adusto, la madre caprichosa, la hermana mayor imposible y desdichada, y la menor . . . quizá no menos dichosa". The child's sense of awe is expressed by a deliberate confusion of the family meal with the Mass, the table-cloth becomes an altar cloth, the bread the host, and those grouped around the table a "concilio familiar". Cernuda obviously finds this picture of unbending bourgeois respectability distasteful, and he claims that even as a child he was conscious that the apparent security and stability in the family group was a hollow sham :

. . . en ellos presentiste,
Tras la carne vestida, el doliente fantasma
Que al rezo de los otros nunca calma
La amargura de haber vivido inútilmente. (p. 196)[8]

The perception of the futility of life within the basic social unit of the family extends the personal feeling of aimlessness found in the poem "Tarde oscura" to encompass the general human condition. This totally jaundiced attitude leads Cernuda to mock man's efforts to seek his own good and to counteract the corrosive effect of time, when nothing ever really belongs to him and the flux of time cannot be detained. Cernuda's survey of his debt to his family concludes that even the gift of life itself, created by his parents in a moment of "olvido indiferente", was unwanted, and in any case nullified by its limitation by death :

Te dieron todo, sí : vida que no pedías,
Y con ella la muerte de dura compañera. (p. 197)

The bitter view of life that Cernuda draws from what is a seemingly ungrateful and unfeeling attitude to his family has aroused some unfavourable critical comment and has undoubtedly added to his legend as a disdainful person with a diminished capacity for normal emotional responses.[9] But quite a different conclusion can be drawn from his attempt to calculate his debt to his family; Francisco Brines has declared that "La familia" is "uno de los [poemas] más sinceros y estremecedores de nuestra poesía; todo él es un acto de amor, de perdón a sí mismo y a los demás".[10] While it is true that the poem ends with a plea for forgiveness and the pious wish that his parents may rest in peace, there is an even more positive intention in the wish by Cernuda to understand himself and be understood. The replacement of the sentimentalism, which might be expected in a poem on the subject of the family, by an almost brutal frankness, is a clear indication that the primary function of "La familia" is self-analysis.

[8] A remark in Cernuda's short story "En la costa de Santiniebla" helps to illuminate his attitude in "La familia" : ". . . esa nauseabunda atracción que tienen en nuestra memoria determinadas escenas familiares que misteriosamente se graban para siempre en el recuerdo infantil." *Hora de España,* no. X (1937), 42.

[9] Gullón, 'La poesía de Luis Cernuda', *Asomante,* no. 3 (1950), 62-3.

[10] 'Ante unas poesías completas', *La caña gris,* nos. 6-8 (1962), 138.

The search for some meaning in the life thrust upon him without his consent, and for some way of dispelling "la amargura de haber vivido inútilmente" is the basic preoccupation of *Como quien espera el alba.* Cernuda is seeking to come to terms with the contrast between the expectations he had of life and the reality of his experience of what life has been, a contrast made with quiet pathos as he contemplates his lost youth in the poem "Primavera vieja", and concludes that the promise of youth was all in vain: "cuán bella fue la vida y cuán inútil" (p. 208). The muted questioning of life's purpose, which stimulates the analysis of the past and the musings on temporality, is occasionally formulated more openly, as in "Otros tulipanes amarillos":

> ¿Qué empresa nuestra es ésta, abandonada
> Inútilmente un día? ¿Qué afectos imperiosos
> Estos, con cuyos nombres se alimenta el olvido? (p. 220)

The same query is put more incisively, and even half-answered, in "A un poeta futuro":

> Los elementos libres que aprisiona mi cuerpo
> ¿Fueron sobre la tierra convocados
> Por esto sólo? ¿Hay más? Y si lo hay ¿adónde
> Hallarlo? No conozco otro mundo si no es éste. (p. 202)

This recognition that the answer to the inquiry into the purpose of life can only be found in this world points to the direction the inquiry is leading Cernuda. By this time, one by one, the various avenues of evasion he had pursued had been closed to him, and in particular, the dream of a transcendent reality, which had been a source of hope in *Invocaciones*, had been dimmed. In "Las ruinas", at the beginning of *Como quien espera el alba*, the religious faith with which he had tried to fill the emptiness of exile is cast aside, deliberately and in full consciousness of the consequences:

> Yo no te envidio, Dios; déjame a solas
> Con mis obras humanas que no duran. (p. 188)

By an act of his own will he annuls the existence of God, and is thus forced to seek his own redemption through his own actions. "Las ruinas" is a statement of Cernuda's acceptance of the human condition, and especially of the limitations of existence in a temporal world, an acceptance that becomes clearer and firmer in the course of *Como quien espera el alba* and the subsequent poetry. This acceptance is a further stimulus to the mood of self-analysis, since, having made the decision to rely on his own inner strength to support him, he must know himself in order to do this.

The idea that a man must seek his salvation within himself becomes a recurring theme; the poem "Góngora", for example, is partly an exemplary study of the effects of self-reliance. Góngora is not a *Doppelgänger* for Cernuda but a symbol of the poet whose values are opposed to those of the society in which he lives. Cernuda sees Góngora as prizing the things of the spirit more than mundane power and wealth, yet being humiliated by his poverty and the need to depend on the favours of rich, ignorant patrons. He further sees Góngora's retirement to his native Cordoba as a renunciation of the pursuit of fame and fortune, and of the shallow world of the Court. But Góngora had the consolation of his poetry which provided him with a fullness of life he could not obtain in the world. Cernuda's admiration for what he interprets as Góngora's motives is obvious; the withdrawal into himself and into his poetry was not an escape but a strategic retreat into a prepared position of strength. He abandoned any external source of hope and sought sustenance only from within himself :

> Ya restituye el alma a soledad sin esperar de nadie
> Si no es de su conciencia. (p. 193)

An almost exactly similar attitude is expressed in "A un poeta futuro", where Cernuda tells of his own feeling of alienation from his fellow men and of the misunderstanding which his poetry has encountered. The concluding hope that his poems may be read and understood by a young poet of the future makes of his work more than just a means of self-perpetuation since it also acts as a vehicle for self-justification. In the vicarious existence of exile poetry offers Cernuda a way of life, but a way of life he must create entirely by his own efforts, like Góngora, in solitude and with only his conscience to guide him. As he says in "La familia", from the lessons learnt from the analysis of his experience he must seek his truth :

> Fuerza de soledad, en ti pensarte vivo,
> Ganando tu verdad con tus errores. (p. 197)

There is a recurring injunction in these poems to recognise the fact of man's solitude and to come to terms with it. In "Las ruinas" the stanza that follows the declaration of intent to stand alone, rejecting God, begins with the words : "Esto es el hombre. Aprende pues . . ." In "Amando en el tiempo" the painful awareness of the way time destroys physical beauty evokes the comment :

> Pero la vida solos la aprendemos,
> Y placer y dolor se ofrecen siempre
> Tal mundo virgen para cada hombre. (p. 225)

The lessons of life can only be learnt from the actual process of living, and this is why Cernuda's poetry now becomes almost totally preoccupied with the examination of past experience.

Having been forced by the failure of his youthful dreams and by the alien environment of exile into a position where he must seek his own salvation within himself, Cernuda comes to place great emphasis on the value of personal integrity. Mention has been made in an earlier chapter of the poem "Aplauso humano" where he refuses to compromise with the conventions of society by hiding his homosexuality in exchange for acceptance in society. In "A un poeta futuro" he makes it clear that his declared indifference to the lack of recognition given to his work in the present, and the hope of understanding in the future, are based on the need for his poetry to be accepted in its entirety, so that he may then attain the fullness of life in his work. The maintenance of his integrity, in the context of his poetry above all, is an act of self-preservation, a process of being true to his truth. Once again it is the attempt to explain and understand his relationship with his family background made in "La familia" that offers a concise statement of this attitude :

Al menos has tenido la fuerza de ser franco
Para con ellos y contigo mismo. (p. 196)

Honesty with one's self and fidelity to one's self become clear ethical imperatives for Cernuda. In the poem "Quetzalcóatl" Hernán Cortés's loss of the power and position he had won for himself is attributed to his abandonment of his true rôle as conqueror to play the courtier. Failure to keep faith with one's self can lead to destruction, but, by implication, success in this endeavour can be a means of salvation. What Cernuda particularly admires in his portrait of Góngora is Góngora's refusal to compromise his poetry with the mean values of society :

Mas él no transigió en la vida ni en la muerte
Y a salvo puso su alma irreductible
Como demonio arisco que ríe entre negruras. (p. 194)

By his steadfast intransigence Góngora preserved his own integrity and that of his poetry, which are, in any case, almost the same thing. It will be recalled that in the much later poem "Silla del rey", Philip II refers to his creation of the Escorial as "alma, fuego inextinguible", closely echoing Góngora's "alma irreductible". Cernuda's aim in life and the purpose of his poetry are much the same as those that he ascribes to Góngora : the creation and preservation of his own truth in a form that is incorruptible.

Cernuda's recognition that his personal integrity and the exercise of that integrity in his poetry are all that he possesses to give meaning to his life gives rise to one of his greatest poems, "Noche del hombre y su demonio". The inquisitorial interrogation to which he is subjected here by his familiar demon is a probing in depth of his beliefs and values, as the demon who had appeared in "La gloria del poeta" now returns not just to mock him but to tempt him and undermine his hopes. The poem begins with the demon awakening the man and inciting him not to waste the limited span of his life in sleep. He is urged to confront the suffering of existence and examine its implications in a way which strongly recalls the first of Jorge Manrique's "Coplas que fizo por la muerte de su padre". The man aroused from sleep to examine the meaning and purpose of life has the same petulant reaction as the resurrected Lazarus; he wants to be left in peace to forget the life he calls a "carnaval de sombras". But the demon, harking back to the erotic symbol he had been in "La gloria del poeta", reminds the man that he has lost his youth, just as he, the demon, is no longer the "cuerpo de ángel" he once was. This sharpening of the consciousness of time is the beginning of the man's torment, and the poem now moves on to the critical assessment of the function of poetry in his life. The demon's reproach that he, the man, had used poetry as a substitute for life, and the ridicule of his belief that he will live on in his poems, prompt a reply already quoted in an earlier chapter, but it is of such importance it should be repeated here :

> Me hieres en el centro más profundo,
> Pues conoces que el hombre no tolera
> Estar vivo sin más : como en un juego trágico
> Necesita apostar su vida en algo,
> Algo de que alza un ídolo, aunque con barro sea,
> Y antes que confesar su engaño quiere muerte.
> Mi engaño era inocente, y a nadie arruinaba
> Excepto a mí, aunque a veces yo mismo lo veía. (p. 223)

As I commented when examining these lines before, this is an admission by Cernuda that he has staked everything on his poetry, and therefore on himself. His poetry is an act of faith in himself. This, moreover, is an admission he is forced to make to counter the demon's destruction of his pretensions, and it may therefore be assumed that it represents a statement of his relationship with his craft that is stripped bare of all illusion. He is even able to recognise the element of self-deception in this most basic, existential involvement with his poetry, and, in addition, to see the tragic debility this reveals; yet, notwithstanding the awareness of the probable futility of his attitude, he still declares that he cannot relinquish this last article of faith, this last staff of life, his poetry. He is, in effect, declaring that when there is nothing left to believe in he will cling, against all odds, to his belief in himself. The worldly-wise melancholy of this stanza from "Noche del hombre y su demonio" reveals an extraordinary degree of self-knowledge and understanding, brought into view by the demon's systematic destruction of cherished illusions.

Cernuda's refusal to yield the truth of himself, which his poetry contains, forces the demon to change his attack to another front. He tempts the man with the prospect of a comfortable life governed by middle-class conventions : money, marriage, the public observance of religion. The man regards this as a sick joke, but the demon again tempts him with material well-being in exchange for the abandonment of his personal beliefs. His reaction is an unequivocal refusal :

> Dos veces no se nace, amigo. Vivo al gusto
> De Dios. ¿Quién evadió jamás a su destino?
> El mío fue explorar esta extraña comarca,
> Contigo siempre a zaga, subrayando
> Con tu sarcasmo mi dolor. Ahora silencio,
> Por si alguno pretende que me quejo : es más digno
> Sentirse vivo en medio de la angustia
> Que ignorar con los grandes de este mundo,
> Cerrados en su limbo tras las puertas de oro. (p. 224)

The man's firm acceptance of his destiny, despite the pain it entails, forms a bold contrast with the indolent withdrawal from reality that is Cernuda's standard reaction to the difficulties of life in his earlier poems. Now in the guise of the man in "Noche del hombre y su demonio" he sees suffering as an affirmation of existence, and prefers to confront reality rather than evade it. Moreover, what he is accepting in this poem is his own reality, which has been revealed to him by the demon's criticism and mockery. Having been made to recognise with an almost searing clarity that the real purpose of his poetry is self-affirmation, when the demon tempts him with a solution to his difficulties that would compromise his values, he rejects this with a simple dignity.

Cernuda has come to embrace his own integrity both as a support and a justification for his existence, and this moral strength by which he defeats the demon's temptations, together with the very device of demonic temptation itself, firmly indicate the ethical standpoint from which he now views himself, his life and his work. "Noche del hombre y su demonio" can, in fact, be seen as a summary of the endeavours in *Como quien espera el alba* to find a meaning and purpose in life. It is, moreover, no accident that the two essays in which Cernuda outlines his theory of the interrelationship of ethics and aesthetics, 'Tres poetas clásicos' of 1941 and 'Tres poetas metafísicos' of 1946, should be contemporaneous with the poems of this collection, written between 1941 and 1944. The later essay, in particular, could almost be taken as a theoretical statement of the attitudes expressed in *Como quien espera el alba*. Echoes of these three "metaphysical" poets, Manrique, Aldana, and the anonymous author of the "Epístola moral a Fabio", appear in a number of poems. The resemblance between the opening of "Noche del hombre y su demonio" and the first of Manrique's "Coplas que fizo por la muerte de su padre" has already been noted, and the meditative attitude of many of the poems represents a conversation with his own *hombre interior* after the manner of Aldana, but the strongest echoes are those from the "Epístola moral a Fabio". Cernuda's view of Góngora's retirement to Cordoba recalls the anonymous Sevillian poet's decision to withdraw from the search for fame and fortune in the world. Other poems contain more direct references. "Río vespertino" laments the disappearance of the possibility of retreat from the world which the seventeenth-century author of the epistle had accepted :

> Alguno en tiempos idos se acogía
> Al muro propio, al libro y al amigo,
> Mas ahora vería roto el muro,
> Vacío el libro y el amigo inútil. (pp. 226-7)[11]

The final lines of the "Epístola moral",

> ven y sabrás al grande fin que aspiro,
> antes que el tiempo muera en nuestros brazos.

[11] Cf. Un ángulo me basta entre mis lares,
un libro y un amigo, un sueño breve
que no perturben deudas ni pesares.
"Epistola moral a Fabio", *The Oxford Book of Spanish Verse* (Oxford, 1953), 166.

can be heard in the closing lines of "Otros tulipanes amarillos" :

> Ya en tu vida las sombras pesan más que los cuerpos;
> Llámales hoy, si hay alguno que escuche
> Entre la hierba sola de esta primavera,
> Y aprende ese silencio antes que el tiempo llegue. (p. 220)

and in the final stanza of "Los espinos" :

> Antes que la sombra caiga,
> Aprende cómo es la dicha
> Ante los espinos blancos
> Y rojos en flor. Vé. Mira. (p. 212)

This is not just the case of a simple echo of a phrase from the "Epístola moral", for "Otros tulipanes amarillos" and "Los espinos" are both expressions of the stoic resignation to life's limitations that Cernuda's anonymous predecessor had attained.

The very distinct presence of the "Epístola moral" in *Como quien espera el alba* can be explained further by some of the opinions in the essay 'Tres poetas metafísicos'. Cernuda begins his comments on the "Epístola moral" with a characterisation of its author that could well apply to himself : "hay en el poeta anónimo . . . un cansancio vital evidente, evidente aun descontando cierta afectada languidez hedonista . . ."[12] The gloss he puts on this indolence is of great significance for his own poetry :

> Gastado el impulso heroico, agotado el amoroso, para un alma desmedida, si quiere ser sincera consigo mismo, acaso sólo quede un camino : renunciar a sus aspiraciones, resignándose a dejarse vivir.[13]

The "impulso heroico" can have little meaning for Cernuda, although in "Quetzalcóatl" he does express a strong regret for the passing of the time when it was still possible, but the exhaustion of the "impulso amoroso" is certainly something he has experienced, and he does suffer from a similar "cansancio vital". What is particularly interesting, however, is that the solution that life's limitations be accepted is proposed as the only way in which a man can be honest with himself. This is precisely the attitude Cernuda adopts in "Noche del hombre y su demonio" when he renounces the illusion of survival through his poetry and determines to sustain himself by the exercise of his integrity. The final lines of that poem offer as a consolation a view of life very similar to that held by the author of the "Epístola moral" :

> Pues el mundo no aprueba al desdichado,
> Recuerda la sonrisa y, como aquel que aguarda,
> Alzate y vé, aunque aquí nada esperes. (p. 225)[14]

[12] *Poesía y literatura,* 69.

[13] *Ibid.*

[14] There is an echo here of the line "I said to my soul, be still, and wait without hope", from the third section of T. S. Eliot's "East Coker".

Although apparently a statement of renunciation, this is a positive, not a negative response, the product of a decision to make the best of life as it is and not chase after elusive dreams.

Through the analysis of his experience in *Como quien espera el alba* Cernuda reaches a degree of self-knowledge that enables him to come tentatively to terms with life, based on the conclusion that he can have no hope in anything outside himself. The ethical nature of this view of life can be illuminated by further comments from the essay 'Tres poetas metafísicos'; Manrique is praised for the way in which he asserts "la responsabilidad ética del hombre para con su propia vida, según una finalidad terrena", while Aldana's concept of the *hombre interior* is variously described as "ese yo profundo", the "proyección interior del compuesto espiritual que llamamos personalidad", and as "la verdad íntima".[15] It is precisely Cernuda's intention to accept responsibility for his own destiny, and, in order to achieve this, to discover and sustain the essential truth of his personality. But he has less in common with Manrique's heroic confrontation with time and Aldana's mystic aspirations than he has with the attitude of resigned acceptance of life in the "Epístola moral a Fabio". The coincidence between the ethic propounded in *Como quien espera el alba* and that set out in the anonymous seventeenth-century poem is made quite clear in a commentary by Cernuda already quoted in part in the first chapter of this study :

> Su realidad sólo puede hallarla el hombre, relativamente, en la aprobación y satisfacción de la conciencia; aprobación y satisfacción nacidas del equilibrio entre esa porción espiritual y esa material que componen la existencia, guiadas por el distante estímulo de una virtud en parte ética y en parte estética. Así acompasará y medirá el hombre su naturaleza propia y las acciones 'que han de ser compañeras de la vida'. Ello parece resultar menos de una creencia religiosa determinada que de su escepticismo, sometida por estética a normas éticas. Es decir, que si en Manrique hallamos el arquetipo del héroe y en Aldana el del santo, en el poeta anónimo sevillano hallamos, pura y simplemente, el del hombre.[16]

The ethic of integrity is here related specifically to the existential concern of self-affirmation and to that concurrence of ethical and aesthetic values which is one of the bases of Cernuda's poetic theory. The idea that by the exercise of his integrity a man may come to know himself directly coincides with the aim of the self-analysis in the poems of his maturity. This comment on the Sevillian poet who had preceded him by three centuries is a statement of Cernuda's own attitude to life, reflected as so often happens with his criticism, in another's work. The distinction made between Manrique, Aldana and the author of the "Epístola moral" points directly at the reason for Cernuda's affinity with his fellow-Sevillian, he is neither saint like Aldana, nor hero like Manrique, but, like the seventeenth-century poet he has tried to discover and come to terms with his human condition.

[15] *Loc. cit.*, 63-5.
[16] *Ibid.* 70-1.

In *Como quien espera el alba*, with the attainment of the ability to dominate experience, seeing it in a clear and objective light, Cernuda reaches maturity, the sort of maturity that he has defined in some detail in his essay on Gide :

> . . . ese relativo dominio sobre la vida que el hombre semeja adquirir precisamente cuando gran parte de la suya propia es ya pasada; una clarificación y objetividad de sus experiencias, que van dibujándose entonces en la memoria, a la manera de esas escrituras invisibles que sólo un reactivo revela, y en tal sentido, ¿no se diría que el reactivo de nuestra vida es el tiempo? A medida que el futuro se reduce y estrecha ante nuestro paso, el pasado adquiere importancia, y vuelve entonces, descubriendo su significado antes desapercibido, como algo que no ha muerto, como una especie de futuro visto de espaldas.[17]

These remarks written in 1946, the same year as 'Tres poetas metafísicos', provide a succinct description of Cernuda's own experience; his acute consciousness of time has led him to take a critical look at his life, and as exile dimmed the future his gaze became even more firmly directed towards the past. The comment on Gide also indicates that the purpose of this analysis of the past is to discover its "significado antes desapercibido", the meaning which can only be seen when time has supplied a perspective. Cernuda's own contemplation of his past has the aim of understanding what that past has made him, and it is precisely this spirit of objective inquiry into himself, prompted above all by the experience of exile, that turns his poetry definitively into the account of a journey of self-discovery.

The decision Cernuda makes in *Como quien espera el alba* to accept an ethic responsibility for his own existence, relying on the inner strength of his integrity to give significance to his life, is a major step in his development, and in the poetry which follows, up to the time of "Poemas para un cuerpo", he reaffirms this decision and continues the investigation of himself. But having arrived at this deeper self-understanding, his ever-increasing consciousness of time and the vicariousness of his existence in exile present him with a new problem as they tend to diminish the personal reality he has struggled so hard to establish. In addition, this existential difficulty is accentuated by the conflict between age and the youthful erotic ideal. The affirmative mood of *Como quien espera el alba* tends to be subdued by the melancholy which the awareness of age provokes, but this, in its turn, sharpens Cernuda's sense of alienation and acts as a new stimulus for his self-analysis. The poem "El intruso", where he confronts his ageing self in the mirror, begins in a way that almost exactly reproduces the sentiments of "Tarde oscura";

Lejos de ti, de la conciencia
Desacordada, el centro
Buscas afuera, entre las cosas
Presentes un momento. (p. 241)

[17] 'André Gide', *Poesía y literatura*, 152.

Despite the internal disassociation he now experiences, in the poems of *Vivir sin estar viviendo* Cernuda sustains his determination to come to terms with himself, accepting what life has to offer without recrimination for what might have been and without striving after impossible ideals. In the course of a contemplation of his life against the background of the inexorable passing of time contained in the poem "Para estar contigo" he is able to come to an explicit acceptance of the gap between the two dimensions of *realidad* and *deseo*, although this acknowledgement is not proffered without regret :

Pues el fuego no la anima
Sino en lumbre pasajera,
Entiende la paradoja
De tu existencia incompleta.

. . . . .

No digas que no esperabas
Todo ello en el principio,
Y acepta, como si iguales,
Lo esperado y lo vivido. (p. 270)

Here is again the injunction to understand himself that is a recurring feature of *Como quien espera el alba*, as well as the decision to accept the reality of experience even when it is not in accord with the ideal, which is the response to love in "Cuatro poemas a una sombra". This attitude of acceptance is also strongly present in the poem "La fecha", written on the occasion of his 43rd birthday,[18] and clearly the result of a meditation on his life prompted by its completion of another year :

Allá están los caminos,
A esta luz todavía
Vacíos, y entre ellos
Uno aguarda tu ida.

No preguntes si vale
La pena haber venido. (p. 246)

Although there is a hint of a begrudging aquiescence with regard to the present, the equanimity with which he feels able to face the future is a measure of the composure Cernuda has acquired. At the time of his move from England to the United States this equanimity even turns to cautious optimism. The poem "Otros aires", which evokes the American countryside as a world of promise where Cernuda at last feels he can belong, contains a direct injunction to live for the future not the past :

No mires atrás y sigue
Hasta cuando permita el sino . . . (p. 262)

Even though the optimism prompted by America was short-lived, this apparent

[18] C. P. Otero, *Letras I* (London, 1966), 191.

reversal of his concern with the past is an indication of the extent to which Cernuda has managed to come to terms with that past.

The degree of self-knowledge which makes such an attitude possible is vividly expressed in that verbal portrait of himself given in "Un contemporáneo" by a fictional acquaintance. The middle-aged man scraping a precarious living in a junior teaching post is undoubtedly Cernuda. The reference to his move to a place in the south where he felt more at ease after a difficult time in the north is a clear allusion to Cernuda's move from Glasgow to Cambridge. After a description of this person as a shy, retiring character who evoked little sympathy in those who knew him and who seemed to hold his fellow men in scorn, the acquaintance admits that he had little real knowledge of him and then comes to a most significant conclusion :

> Nuestro vivir, de muchedumbre
> A solas con un dios, un demonio o una nada,
> Supongo que era el suyo también. ¿Por qué no habría de serlo?
>
> (p. 256)

This admission that the man, for all his curious character, was fundamentally no different from anyone else, is an oblique demand by Cernuda for the unconditional acceptance of himself. Now that he has accepted himself he wants to know why he should not be accepted by other people. The technique of "Un contemporáneo" is particularly interesting in this respect; in essence it is a development of the *Doppelgänger* technique, but instead of Cernuda's experience being projected onto another person, another person is allowed in the poem to describe Cernuda himself. Moreover, the picture presented of Cernuda as a misanthropic recluse is reminiscent of that distorted public image that he came to call his *leyenda*; he was already conscious by this time that he had acquired such a personality in the eyes of the public and was beginning to react against those who were fostering such impressions of him.[19] The presentation of himself as he believed others saw him, as what might be called the *hombre exterior* in contrast to the truth of the *hombre interior*, acts like a confidence trick on the reader of the poem. The reader is led to a point in the poem where he should by rights give an affirmative answer to the question about the common humanity of the rather odd person the poem describes, and if he can admit the common humanity of such a character then he must do the same for the more complex, real Cernuda. "Un contemporáneo" is a remarkable example of the control over himself that Cernuda acquires in his maturity; his ability in this poem to stand back from himself and produce a self-portrait that is a gross distortion of the true picture he has laboured to construct in his work, argues for a very great degree of confidence in the strength of that truth. Having found himself, he is now quite sure of himself.

The mood of stoic acceptance, and the occasional glimmer of optimism, continue in *Con las horas contadas* until the Mexican love affair, which, as an affirmation of Cernuda's personal truth, finally justifies the integrity with which

[19] See Chapter One, note 20.

he has preserved that truth. "Nocturno yanqui", one of the major poems in *Con las horas contadas,* provides a further example of the acute powers of self-analysis Cernuda has now developed and also a very clear statement of his existential preoccupations. The critical objectivity and uncompromising self-searching of this poem may be compared to "Noche del hombre y su demonio", except that he now has no need to invent an interlocutor to examine his motives and attitudes, since he knows himself well enough by this time to commune directly with himself in a monologue. The poem begins with a laconic evocation of his solitary, empty existence and the mocking suggestion that he substitute dreams for the reality his life is lacking. This leads to an examination of his acute consciousness of time and of his regret for the passing of youth; the concern with time is reinforced by the poem's use of the octosyllabic metre with a *pie quebrado*, which is inevitably reminiscent of Jorge Manrique. Cernuda then turns his attention to his work as a teacher, by which he has earned his living in exile, viewing it with sarcasm and distaste, and finally dismissing it as a futile occupation :

Nadie enseña lo que importa,
Que eso ha de aprenderlo el hombre
Por sí solo. (p. 287)

Here, expressed as a direct statement, is the lesson Cernuda has learnt from the concentrated effort of self-analysis in the poems of his maturity. Immediately after this axiom comes the declaration that the dream of love, the "mito moceril", was a pretext for self-affirmation and a vehicle for self-discovery. This is what matters to Cernuda, this is what he has had to learn for himself from the experience of his life. The poem concludes with his acceptance of himself and his situation :

Y al que eras le has hallado.
¿Mas es la verdad del hombre
Para él solo,
Como un inútil secreto?
¿Por qué no poner la vida
A otra cosa?

Quien eres, tu vida era;
Uno sin otro no sois,
Tú lo sabes.
Y es fuerza seguir, entonces,
Aun el miraje perdido,
Hasta el día
Que la historia se termine,
Para ti al menos.

Y piensas
Que así vuelves
Donde estabas al comienzo

Del soliloquio; contigo
Y sin nadie.

Mata la luz, y a la cama. (pp. 287-8)

Cernuda's recognition here that he is, at least in part, what his life has made him helps him to come to terms with his internal sense of alienation, the disparity between his ageing reality and the youthful erotic dream, but beyond this, "Nocturno yanqui" offers a clear statement that the aim of his introspection is the discovery of his personal truth, "la verdad del hombre". Having found this truth, he resists the temptation to withdraw from the struggle to realise his dreams; he knows he cannot escape this truth and must therefore live it out as faithfully as possible. The poem's melancholy ending is of little consequence beside the determination to be true to himself which will justify and authenticate his life despite its apparent emptiness. The almost casual, conversational tone gives a moving sincerity to this fine poem, which, as José Olivio Jímenez has noted, provides an unequivocal expression of the ethical basis of Cernuda's poetry.[20] The sense of personal dignity, the search for the truth of himself, and the careful preservation of his integrity, which are the main elements of "Nocturno yanqui", are the primary features of his system of moral values.

In the poems of his maturity Cernuda discovers himself and by accepting what he finds he regains the control over his destiny he had lost as a result of the painful experiences of his youth and the early years of his exile. The love affair of "Poemas para un cuerpo" then brings its own justification for this decision to come to terms with himself. The poems of *Desolación de la Quimera*, coming after the climactic experience of the Mexican love affair and written in what were to prove to be the closing years of his life, form an attempt to summarise the lessons he has learnt from the long investigation of himself. This final collection of poems is his own conclusion to his life, produced under the shadow of a presentiment that he was soon to die, a presentiment that turns this book into a poetic last will and testament designed to leave behind him an accurate self-portrait and a duly notarised statement of his account with life.

Carlos Otero has revealed a certain amount of the background to *Desolación de la Quimera*.[21] Cernuda wrote no poetry from 1956 until the summer of 1960 when the new environment of California, where he had taken a teaching post, reawakened the need for self-expression. An additional cause for the return to poetry was the profound effect on him of the death in that same year of his two sisters, who were the last members of his immediate family. Los Angeles delighted him but his return to Mexico produced a mood of depression for which poetry offered a form of therapy; he comments in a letter to Otero : "en verdad sueño a veces con que escribo versos, y comprendo que *I must write some lines for peace sake's* [*sic*]."[22] By February of 1961 he had written nineteen

[20] 'Emoción y trascendencia del tiempo en la poesía de Luis Cernuda', *loc. cit.*, 59.
[21] 'Cernuda en California', *Letras I*, 190-7.
[22] *Ibid.* 191. Letter dated 29-IX-60.

poems to add to the eight which had appeared in the section *Sin título, inacabada* of the third edition of *La Realidad y el Deseo*. In September 1961 he took up a post as Visiting Professor at San Francisco State College where he experienced an acute sense of solitude for which poetry again provided a possible antidote, although this depression seems later to have been tempered by the material well-being he enjoyed in America. *Desolación de la Quimera* was completed in February 1962, and in a letter to Carlos Otero written in the following June he tried to sum up the experience of his stay in San Francisco :

> Creo que la preocupación constante con los cursos me apartó de ese estado libre y gratuito del poeta mirando a la vida. Es cierto, además, que la edad me hace tener más en cuenta cosas que nunca tuve en cuenta cuando era más joven : he caído en el mundo, sus recelos, preocupaciones, opiniones, y todo eso entra en mi mente, que siempre estuvo libre de tales consideraciones.[23]

This admission of a loss of detachment, and in particular the phrase "he caído en el mundo", reveal one of the outstanding characteristics of Cernuda's last book of poems where on a number of occasions the mask of the literary *persona* employed in earlier collections is set aside for him to write slight, circumstantial poems and even polemical verses. Some compositions, such as "Bagatela", "Málibu", and "Hablando a Manona", are little more than *divertissements*. Two poems, "Amigos : Enrique Asúnsolo" and "Amigos : Víctor Cortezo", are simple expressions of gratitude for friendship, while in others Cernuda gives free rein to the waspish side of his character in virulent attacks on people who have displeased him. "Otra vez con sentimiento" is an abusive, although oblique, attack on Dámaso Alonso;[24] "Supervivencias tribales en el medio literario" is a sharp-tongued defence of Manuel Altolaguirre against critics who have misrepresented him; and "Respuesta" is an unpleasant and totally unnecessary attack against some unidentified person.

The underlying reason for such poems on trivial themes or private squabbles, which are marginal to Cernuda's main preoccupations, is the same as that for the major poems of this collection : the fall into the world, the loss of detachment, which was prompted above all by his conviction that he was approaching the time of his death. The death of his two elder sisters had strengthened a belief that it was a characteristic of his family to die at about the age of sixty; now he too was approaching that age. A direct statement of this belief appears in the poems "Antes de irse" and "Despedida", where death is calmly accepted.[25] His attitude to death is the same as that he ascribes to Titian in "*Ninfa y*

[23] *Ibid.* 195. Letter dated 3-VI-62.

[24] This is a resurgence of the strained relationship with Dámaso Alonso. See 'Carta abierta a Dámaso Alonso', *Insula,* no. 35 (1948). "Otra vez con sentimiento" alludes to Dámaso Alonso's reference to Lorca as "Federico, mi príncipe muerto", in *Poetas españoles contemporáneos* (Madrid, 1952), 167.

[25] See Otero, *Letras* I, 191. The belief that death was near appears before 1960. See "La casa", *Ocnos,* 181-3. The typescript of this prose poem amongst Cernuda's papers in Seville is dated "Mexico 29-XI-3 XII 1957". On the back of this typescript is a typed copy of "Antes de irse".

pastor, por Ticiano" : "Acaso cerca de dejar la vida,/De nada arrepentido y siempre enamorado" (p. 326), but although he shows neither fear nor regret for the ending of his life he is deeply concerned with making preparations for it. In *Desolación de la Quimera* Cernuda tries to settle his affairs, endeavouring to make a last assessment of his experience and his beliefs, and because he has lost to a certain extent his former detachment he speaks in these poems more directly and openly than before. The task of self-appraisal, which would be given sufficient spur by the thought of death, is stimulated further by the preoccupation with that unsympathetic public image which he calls his *leyenda*. The nearness of death causes him to take issue directly with the false personality, projected onto him by friend and critic alike, which was a distortion of the truth he had sought to express in his poetry. What troubles Cernuda most is that, once he is dead, his work will be at the mercy of critics and readers who will impose on it their false idea of its character and finally condemn it to oblivion. This concern is at the centre of the poem "A sus paisanos", the last poem he wrote,[26] where he bitterly attacks the Spanish reading public for what he believes is their hostility to his work :

Contra vosotros y esa vuestra ignorancia voluntaria,
Vivo aún, sé y puedo, si así quiero, defenderme.
Pero aguardáis al día cuando ya no me encuentre
Aquí. Y entonces la ignorancia,
La indiferencia y el olvido, vuestras armas
De siempre, sobre mí caerán, como la piedra,
Cubriéndome por fin, lo mismo que cubristeis
A otros que, superiores a mi, esa ignorancia vuestra
Precipitó en la nada, como al gran Aldana. (p. 366)

An even more specific confrontation with the *leyenda* is made in the poem "*Malentendu*" where he attacks Pedro Salinas, who had helped him so much at the beginning of his career, for having described him as a *licenciado Vidriera* : "Hizo de ti un fantoche a su medida : /Raro, turbio, inútilmente complicado" (p. 348). The acidity of this personalised attack on Salinas is a symptom of the very real fear Cernuda now feels for the future of his work, a fear that its truth may be distorted.[27]

This is not the only fear Cernuda has for his work after his death; he is also preoccupied with the possibility of an even worse form of distortion, the threat of appropriation and acceptance by society that he had foreseen many years before in "La gloria del poeta". In *Desolación de la Quimera* Cernuda does not approach this problem from the point of view of his own poetry but examines society's attitudes to other poets. "Supervivencias tribales en el medio literario" depicts the way Manuel Altolaguirre's achievement as a poet has been pushed into oblivion by people who, indifferent to his poetry, continued to see in him

[26] Otero, *op. cit.*, 193. "A sus paisanos" dates from February 1962.

[27] The title "*Malentendu*" is a malicious allusion to Salinas's use of this term in his "Poética" in Gerardo Diego's anthology *Poesía española contemporánea*, third edition (Madrid, 1966), 303-4.

the facile characterization of the sympathetic "Manolito" which he had acquired as a young man. "*Birds in the night*" is a mordant attack on the society that had hounded Rimbaud and Verlaine while they lived and then praised their poetry when they were dead. This posthumous acceptance by society is a betrayal of these poets' work through an accommodation of it into established social values, thereby negating the truth of its defiance of those values :

> ¿Verlaine? Vaya, amigo mío, un sátiro, un verdadero sátiro
> Cuando de la mujer se trata; bien normal era el hombre,
> Igual que usted y que yo. ¿Rimbaud? Católico sincero como está
> demostrado. (p. 325)

The violently aggressive sarcasm of these two poems is a sign of Cernuda's deep involvement in their theme; he too, like Altolaguirre, had suffered from a facile and uncomprehending characterization, his *leyenda*, that had been formed in his youth and had been unthinkingly applied to him ever since, and he had also, like Rimbaud and Verlaine, defied the conventions of society. Cernuda is clearly concerned with the possibility that after his death the truth of his poetry, his personal truth, may suffer either oblivion, or, what is perhaps worse, deformation, and it is this fear that makes of *Desolación de la Quimera* a summary of his beliefs.

On a superficial level many of these last poems are a statement of Cernuda's admiration for a wide range of writers and artists, like Mozart, Dostoievski, Goethe, Keats, Galdós, and a number of others. This has led one critic to see Art itself as the central preoccupation of the book,[28] but Cernuda is really using such poems about other writers to make a profession of his belief in the values he sees enshrined in them. The examination of what other writers have meant to him is one of the ways he tries to put on record his own attitude to life. Other poems are directly self-analytical, dealing with his relationship to Spain, his childhood and his family, or offering a final examination of his concept of love and poetry. All the poems have the intention of establishing his character and beliefs with a view to the time when only his poetry will remain as a testimony to his existence.

The concerted effort to make a concluding statement to the major preoccupations and problems of his life is typified by the appearance of two extensive poems on the theme of Spain, gathered together under the title "Díptico español". As Cernuda himself has noted, the passing of time had blurred and almost severed his sense of involvement with his native land; the previous poem to have dealt with this theme was the acerbic, Machado-like caricature of Spain in "Ser de Sansueña" from *Vivir sin estar viviendo*. The first half of "Díptico español" is a savage attack on Spain since the Civil War, which is seen as a spiritual waste-land, the second half is a meditation on the Spain that appears in the novels of Galdós, which is accepted as a poetic truth compensating for the sad contemporary reality. The Spain of Galdós is turned into another version of

[28] E. Müller, 'Die Bedeutung der Kunst in Luis Cernudas *Desolación de la Quimera*', *Romanische Forschungen*, nos. 1-2 (1964), 202-8.

Sansueña, now a symbol of human freedom and dignity, in contrast to the grotesque deformation of Franco's Spain. These are not entirely happy poems – the moralising element is made too overt – but this last statement of Cernuda's ambivalent emotions concerning Spain is also a very clear symptom of the urgent need he feels to establish his identity. The first part of the diptych is very much involved with his situation as a poet in exile, a Spanish poet writing inevitably for a Spanish audience, whether he likes it or not, and the rejection of the reality of Spain for the idealised vision is a means of reflecting and affirming his personal values. In essence, rather than being about Spain, "Díptico español" is a definition of Cernuda's character.

A similar defining function is carried out by the poems dealing with his family and his childhood. "Dos de noviembre" is a short meditation on the death of his two sisters, and apart from "La familia" this is the only poem in the whole of *La Realidad y el Deseo* containing a direct reference to his family. The concern with his background is pursued further in a number of poems that look back to his childhood seeking to understand its rôle in his life and his present relationship to that most influential period of his existence. "Niño tras un cristal" is an evocation of the adolescent world of *Primeras poesías*, a picture of the child alone in his room gazing out of the window at the evening twilight, which leads to the conclusion that this was the moment of genesis of his personality; "En su sombra ya se forma la perla" (p. 222). "*Animula, vagula, blandula*" and "Luna llena en Semana Santa" are both expressions of regret for the lost innocence of childhood. The first of these poems, which is concerned with Manuel Altolaguirre's second grandson, sees with pity the child's incoherent attempts to formulate questions about the nature and purpose of life, questions which have no answer.[29] This provokes the pious wish from Cernuda that the child may not have to suffer the bitterness of his own adolescence. "Luna llena en Semana Santa" is in the same manner as the earlier poems "Viendo volver" and "Lo más frágil es lo que dura", a meditation on the memory of childhood which is now a mocking reminder of age and of the loss of the child's blissful sense of belonging in the world. The memory of Holy Week in Seville takes him back to the childhood beginning of his life and the poem concludes with the line "*Et in Arcadia ego*". Philip Silver appears to see this poem as expressing the quasi-mystic recovery of the youthful self which he claims is one of Cernuda's central concerns; that final line gives the title to his study and he uses the poem's closing stanzas as an epigraph. However, the phrase "et in Arcadia ego" is not of a Virgilian nature as Silver tacitly assumes but is first recorded in the late Renaissance and has specific associations that are totally incompatible with Silver's interpretation. The most probable immediate source for the quotation is a painting by Poussin where two youths and a maiden in a pastoral setting gaze at a tombstone bearing that phrase as an inscription. The general significance of Poussin's picture is clear: either death also exists in Arcady (or Arcady is death), or, with an even greater degree of *desengaño*, it is

[29] See Otero, *op. cit.*, 193. The phrase "animula, vagula, blandula" is taken from Hadrian's dying address to his soul. It is also found in Valle-Inclan's poem "¡Aleluya!" from *La pipa de Kif*, and "Animula" is the title of one of T. S. Eliot's Ariel poems.

saying that the dead person once thought that he too dwelt in Arcady.[30] Childhood was Cernuda's Arcady, the time when the *acorde* between self and world was sustained by his innocence, and the use of the phrase "et in Arcadia ego" in connection with the memories of childhood is intensely sardonic, a recognition of the irretrievable loss of that paradise. "Luna llena en Semana Santa" is another expression of the theme of *nessun maggior dolore* which occurs so frequently throughout Cernuda's poetry, yet it is not a true elegy but part of the attempt to come to terms with experience and define his identity.

Cernuda's concern to make an accurate statement of his attitude towards life and of what he believes himself to be is most clearly visible in the poems of *Desolación de la Quimera* concerned with the major themes of love and poetry. The thought of death reawakens the awareness of age which had been suppressed by the love affair of "Poemas para un cuerpo". Two poems, "Pregunta vieja, vieja respuesta" and "Despedida", bring a return of the conflict between age and the youthful erotic ideal; the former poem is an elegy for the capacity to love that time has destroyed, the latter a stoic farewell to the beautiful youths who inspire desire but are beyond the reach of the old man near to death whom Cernuda has become. The problem of the ageing man still attracted by the beauty of youth finds a possible solution in "*Ninfa y pastor*, por Ticiano" where Cernuda expresses his admiration for the sensuality of a painting done when Titian was nearly a hundred years old. This poem is, in effect, an elaboration of the idea that the delight in physical beauty is unaffected by time, first expressed in "Cara joven" from *Vivir sin estar viviendo.* The attitude he admires in Titian may perhaps have born fruit, for towards the end of *Desolación de la Quimera* the possibility of a new love seems to be referred to in two song poems, "El amor todavía" and "Lo que al amor le basta", which are very reminiscent of the style and mood of "Poemas para un cuerpo". Most of the poems concerned with the love theme, however, deal with eroticism in general, taking a retrospective view of the part love has played in his life, like the "Epílogo" where he gives thanks for the Mexican love affair. His attitude to love and desire remains ambivalent to the last. In "Antes de irse" he reaffirms the old declaration that love was the sole purpose of his existence :

A otros la ambición
De fortuna y poder;
Yo sólo quise ser
Con mi luz y mi amor. (p. 324)

In contrast, "Las sirenas" likens desire to the song of sea-sirens entrancing man but leading him to frustration and despair : "El que una vez las oye viudo y desolado queda para siempre" (p. 323). These polar attitudes are neatly summed up in "Música cautiva", despite the slightness of this poem which is little more than a casual jotting :

[30] See Silver, *op. cit.,* chapters III, IV and V, *passim.* For the origin and use of the phrase "et in Arcadia ego" see *King's Classical Quotations,* third edition (London, 1904), 400-401, and also E. Panofsky, *'Et in Arcadia ego* : Poussin and the Elegiac Tradition', *Meaning in the Visual Arts* (New York, 1955).

'Tus ojos son los ojos de un hombre enamorado;
Tus labios son los labios de un hombre que no cree
En el amor.' 'Entonces dime el remedio, amigo,
Si están en desacuerdo realidad y deseo.' (p. 326)[31]

From "Música cautiva" it might appear that Cernuda has progressed little beyond the simple confrontation with the tragic disparity between *realidad* and *deseo,* but "Ludwig de Baviera escucha *Lohengrin*", a major poem equal to the finest compositions of *Como quien espera el alba,* which examines the ambivalence of homosexual desire, reveals the striking extent of his understanding of the nature of his erotic experience. A mention of the mad Ludwig II of Bavaria occurs in an article Cernuda had written some thirty years before this poem, indicating perhaps the length of gestation of some of his compositions and also the way in which he is now turning over in his mind the material of the past.[32] The poem begins with a description of the king at a performance of the opera arranged for him alone. Lohengrin, on the stage, becomes the physical representation of Ludwig's erotic dreams, fusing dream and reality together in a moment of ecstasy that frees the king from the mundane existence of the Court. He achieves that transcendent, mystical state of the *acorde,* turned into an elf running free through the woods, an image that recalls the much earlier poem "*Scherzo* para un elfo". The world of his dreams is declared to be the only dimension in which he can truly exist as himself, and the poem then proceeds to examine the nature of this erotic fantasy, which is revealed as a kind of narcissism :

El rey no puede, ni aun pudiendo quiere dividirse a sí del otro
Sobre la música inclinado, como extraño contempla
Con emoción gemela su imagen desdoblada
Y en éxtasis de amor y melodía queda suspenso. (p. 340)

Ludwig is the protagonist in the last of a long series of poems on the narcissistic character of the erotic ideal which begins in *Primeras poesías* and includes such compositions as "Veía sentado" and "Vereda del cuco". Now, Cernuda is able to see quite distinctly in this new *Doppelgänger,* who even shares his Christian name, that the erotic ideal is really a vehicle for self-affirmation :

En el vivir del otro el suyo certidumbre encuentra.
Sólo el amor depara al rey razón para estar vivo.

. . . . .

Fundido con el mito al contemplarlo, forma ya de ese mito
De pureza rebelde que tierra apenas toca,

[31] There is an echo here of the line "Your eyes are the eyes of a woman in love" from the song "A Woman in Love" in the musical show "Guys and Dolls".

[32] See 'El espíritu lírico', *Heraldo de Madrid,* 21-I-32, 12. In *"Birds in the Night"* the reference to the unveiling of a plaque on the house in London where Rimbaud and Verlaine lived together is echoed by a similar mention in the essay 'Epistolario de Rimbaud', *Heraldo de Madrid,* 15-X-31, 12.

Del éter, huésped desterrado. La melodía le ayuda a conocerse,
A enamorarse de lo que él mismo es. Y para siempre en la música vive.
(pp. 341-2)

This is, in substance, a repetition of the assertion made in "Nocturno yanqui" that Cernuda's search for the *mito moceril* was a search for himself. However, the price Ludwig has to pay for his self-discovery in the erotic object is madness and isolation, which are a grotesque travesty of that ideal self-sufficient existence in the hidden garden where dream and reality combine. In this poem Cernuda is trying to look in two directions at once; desire is both the elixir of life and the siren's song which lures man to his doom. He is now perfectly conscious of the dangers inherent in the mode of life Ludwig represents and for which he himself has felt a persistent attraction. "Ludwig de Baviera escucha *Lohengrin*" is a final statement of the existential imperative of the erotic ideal and also a criticism of the hidden garden syndrome, the wish to live in a private world, which may be compared to the criticism of isolationist existence in "El césar". Cernuda regarded his poem about Ludwig II as one of the best poems of *Desolación de la Quimera* and certainly the depth of self-knowledge revealed in this poem makes it a fine example of his mature work.[33]

A high proportion of the poems of *Desolación de la Quimera* are concerned with poetry itself or with the status of the artist in society, forming a compendium of the contradictory attitudes Cernuda takes towards his vocation as a poet. "Mozart", a homage to Cernuda's favourite composer on the second centenary of his birth, sees in him the supreme example of the artist as a communicant with the invisible world of the gods. Mozart is the creator of eternal beauty and his music is the incarnation of an "armonía impalpable e invisible", which brings an echo of the concept of the daemonic power. Such music offers a vision of another, more noble world which gives solace to an ugly, empty life.[34] Mozart is proclaimed as another redeemer, like Philip II in "Silla del rey", who brings virtue and order to the chaos and misery of man's life:

Si de manos de Dios informe salió el mundo,
Trastornado su orden, su injusticia terrible;
Si la vida es abyecta y ruin el hombre,
Da esta música al mundo forma, orden, justicia,
Nobleza y hermosura. Su salvador entonces,
¿Quién es? Su redentor, ¿quién es entonces?
Ningún pecado en él, ni martirio, ni sangre. (pp. 320-1)

This is a restatement of Cernuda's distaste for sad, crucified gods and of his preference for the hellenistic cult of beauty rather than the Christian cult of

[33] Cernuda himself regarded "Luis de Baviera escucha *Lohengrin*" as one of the best poems of *Desolación de la Quimera*. See letter from Cernuda to Carlos Otero dated 21-XI-60, *apud* Otero, *op. cit.*, 192.

[34] Cf. ". . . en ciertas melodías de Mozart el bien y el mal quedan aceptados con divina serenidad, siendo ambos elementos de una realidad superior a la normal comprensión humana". 'Cervantes', *Poesía y literatura II*, 41. See also 'Historial de un libro', *PL*, 265.

death. Art is a means of access to a transcendent reality, and "Mozart" is thus another poem dealing with the relationship between the artist and the ideal existence of the *acorde.* In complete contrast to this, Rimbaud and Verlaine in "*Birds in the night*" are presented as *poètes maudits,* outlawed when alive by the society whose conventions they defied, then having to suffer after their death the appropriation by that society which denies the truth of their work. "Mozart" and "*Birds in the night*" contain the polar extremes of Cernuda's view of the artist : the redeemer of the world and the victim of a hostile society. But in "A propósito de flores" he seeks to come to terms with the tragic disparity in the artist's status. This poem is a meditation on the dying statement of a poet, who is seemingly Keats, that the only happiness he had had in life was to watch flowers grow.[35] Cernuda ponders whether this remark was a symptom of bitterness or of purity, and comes to the following conclusion :

> ¿Amargura? ¿Pureza? ¿O, por qué no, ambas a un tiempo?
> El lirio se corrompe como la hierba mala,
> Y el poeta no es puro o amargo únicamente :
> Devuelve sólo al mundo lo que el mundo le ha dado
> Aunque su genio amargo o puro algo más le regale. (pp. 347-8)

Despite the touch of Cernuda's own bitterness in the penultimate line he is attempting here to reconcile the extremes of the poet as both redeemer and outcast, neither superhuman nor completely subjugated by his environment. This acceptance of a middle way between the two extremes is indicative of the intention in *Desolación de la Quimera* as a whole to come to terms with himself.

The general mood of willingness to seek an accommodation with what in "Díptico español" is referred to as "la paradoja de estar vivo" is dominant in these last poems, although Cernuda can still express an extreme point of view, as in the poem of unrelieved pessimism which gives its title to the collection. The poem "Peregrino" makes an unequivocal statement of a determination to accept the reality of his life with all its limitations. The temptation of a return to the past, to familiar places and old friends, perhaps even to Spain, is examined and rejected; such a pleasant retirement from life is only possible for those who have a home and family to greet their return. Cernuda has nothing to gain from turning back and so he resolves to press on with his life as it is :

> Mas ¿tú? ¿Volver? Regresar no piensas,
> Sino seguir libre adelante,
> Disponible por siempre, mozo o viejo,
> Sin hijo que te busque, como a Ulises,
> Sin Itaca que aguarde y sin Penélope.
>
> Sigue, sigue adelante y no regreses,
> Fiel hasta el fin del camino y la vida,
> No eches de menos un destino más fácil,

[35] I have been unable to trace the source of the dying words to which Cernuda refers. The title "A propósito de flores" seems to be an echo of Rimbaud's "Ce qu'on dit au poète à propos de fleurs".

Tus pies sobre la tierra antes no hollada,
Tus ojos frente a lo antes nunca visto. (p. 353)

This is a restatement of the attitude to life expressed in "Noche del hombre y su demonio", an attitude of positive although resigned acceptance, but the image employed here of the journey of experience is of great significance, all the more so because of the recognition that there is no Ithaca for Cernuda at the journey's end. It is Cernuda's view that the poet's task is to unite experience with understanding, and here he is declaring his refusal to withdraw from this responsibility despite the knowledge that no tangible reward is to be gained from such an action. Since life's odyssey has no final goal to sustain it, the only help the pilgrim has to keep him on his journey is his own integrity, the will to be true to himself. The journey itself is an act of self-realisation, and so "Peregrino" is a statement of the spirit that has sustained Cernuda throughout *La Realidad y el Deseo.*

A very similar acceptance of the reality of life is made in the opening stanza of the poem about Goethe, "El poeta y la bestia" :

Hay en la vida quienes dejan que la vida les viva
Y quienes imponen a la vida dirección y sentido,
Mas son excepcionales los unos y los otros :
El hombre medio, si no acepta
Enteramente que la vida se le imponga,
Tampoco acepta el imponerse a ella,
Esto se aprende, si se aprende, tarde,
Cuando de nada sirve y, aun sabido,
Poco puede servirnos solo :
Conocimiento sin poder resulta inútil. (p. 343)

Cernuda is here acknowledging his own status as a "hombre medio", who, like the poet in "A propósito de flores", neither dominates life nor is dominated by it. The acquisition of this awareness of the nature of life is part of life's paradox, yet merely to recognise this can be of value. The understanding that most people, who are not geniuses like Goethe, cannot mould the world to suit their aspirations and must accept from life something less than the ideal is the major lesson Cernuda has learnt from the pilgrimage of his existence, but one which could not have been learnt without the experience of the journey. These sentiments are a development of the suggestion made much earlier, in "Un contemporáneo", that he is no different from any other man. The recognition that he is a common man and that there is no haven from the pressures of life shows the extent to which he has turned aside from seeking a transcendent dimension in his life and is prepared to justify himself within the limitations of an everyday existence. Strangely enough for the Cernuda who has so often been accused of cynicism, he is able in "Díptico español" to make a direct statement of his faith in man :

He aprendido
El oficio de hombre duramente,
Por eso en él puse mi fe. (pp. 330-1)

This simple declaration of faith contains the whole evolution of Cernuda's ethics : one by one his escapist dreams have been disillusioned and he has been left to find support in the inner strength of his integrity, this assumption of faith in himself has then been broadened to embrace mankind as a whole.

Some of the ethical values Cernuda prizes in himself and in man may be seen in the poem "1936", inspired by a chance meeting with an American who had fought in the International Brigade during the Spanish Civil War. Cernuda is impressed that this man should have chosen to offer his life for a country that was not his because he believed that the issues at stake in the war were worthy of such a sacrifice. This is not essentially a political poem, as Cernuda has pointed out;[36] what is praised is the man's act of faith in his ideals, which he made when he decided to risk his life on behalf of his beliefs. It is of no consequence that the cause for which he fought now seems lost or that many people have since betrayed it; the sustained faith of this one old soldier in the Lincoln Brigade is sufficient proof to Cernuda of the nobility of man. The integrity, the personal fidelity, he finds in this chance acquaintance is an example of his own attitude to life. His own passionate concern with his integrity is the primary motivating force of his poetry, which is the means he employs to reveal and assert that integrity. As he declares in "Díptico español", in a definitive statement of his moral principles, the poet must above all be true to himself, and the maintenance of this truth, in its turn, sustains the truth of his poetry :

Poeta alguno
Su tradición escoge, ni su tierra,
Ni tampoco su lengua, él las sirve,
Fielmente si es posible.
Mas la fidelidad más alta
Es para su conciencia; y yo a ésa sirvo
Pues sirviéndola, así a la poesía
Al mismo tiempo sirvo. (p. 330)

Desolación de la Quimera contains poems of very uneven quality; some, like "Luis de Baviera escucha *Lohengrin*" can stand comparison with the best of Cernuda's poetry, others, such as the polemical poems, could be discarded without injury to the book. Those poems in which he has turned so furiously on friends, acquaintances and the public in general provide more evidence for those critics who wish to see in Cernuda a waspish, embittered personality, yet, paradoxically, it is the preoccupation with his public image, which so strongly motivates these last poems, that makes of *Desolación de la Quimera*, in intention, if not always in poetic quality, a work of consolidation comparable to *Como quien espera el alba*. Moreover, the attempt to confront and refute the distorted image of himself which he calls his *leyenda* results in more than a summary of his beliefs and values; it is the final testimony that self-affirmation is the primary function of Cernuda's poetry.

[36] Letter from Cernuda to Carlos Otero dated 10-XII-61, *apud* Otero, *op. cit.*, 194-5.

CONCLUSION

> La desdichada historia humana que
> rescata la palabra pura del poeta.
> ("El poeta", *Ocnos*, p. 58)

The existential problem of disassociation between self and world, which Cernuda formulates as the conflict between *realidad* and *deseo*, inevitably provokes a dual reaction : the tendency to withdraw from an inimical reality into the hidden garden of dreams and the tendency towards self-assertion within that unfriendly reality. Both of these tendencies are firmly established in the early poetry, although the first is dominant and leads to the theories of 'Palabras antes de una lectura'. The conviction that the tangible world is an illusion hiding an invisible, superior realm of harmony is the philosophical justification for Cernuda's sense of alienation. His longing for a transcendental mode of existence where the division between self and world is healed, is, in fact, a search for an environment where his personality can be fully realised, and therefore a complement to the pursuit of his *verdad del hombre*. The search for the state of bliss he calls the *acorde* is Cernuda's primary motivating force, yet, while he never completely abandons the desire to live in a private world tailored to his own aspirations, what becomes increasingly significant is his developing relationship with this ideal as he comes to understand its impossibility. Something of the nature of this relationship can be seen reflected in a comment by Cernuda on Fray Luis de León :

> Pertenece Fray Luis de León a una clase de espíritus heroicos dividos entre un ideal inasequible y una urgente realidad. Creen tales espíritus que alcanzarían la paz al alcanzar la posesión de su ideal; pero nosotros sabemos, y acaso ellos también lo reconozcan sin confesarlo, en el fondo de su alma, que no es el ideal mismo sino su dramático contraste con la realidad lo que da precio a su vida.[1]

The conflict between dream and reality provides the dynamic for existence and becomes the means by which the existence of the individual in the grip of the conflict is affirmed. Cernuda's poetry is the record of the process by which he

[1] 'Tres poetas clásicos', *Poesía y literatura*, 47.

comes to understand that what validates his life is not his ideal but the conflict the ideal provokes. The search for the *acorde* leads him to the discovery of himself and then involves him in a struggle to preserve the personal truth he has found. The exercise of integrity, being true to himself, becomes for him an existential necessity.

In 'Historial de un libro' Cernuda illustrates his attitude to life by quoting Heraclitus's axiom "carácter es destino" (*PL*, 280). The discovery that a man is what he is does not offer a profound insight into the human condition, but what is significant in Cernuda's poetry is the way in which he faces up to this discovery. In the last analysis the exact nature of a man's truth is of little import compared to the integrity with which it is pursued and preserved, as Cernuda declares in the closing lines of one of the prose poems of *Ocnos* :

> La importancia o fortuna de una existencia individual no resulta de las circunstancias trascendentales o felices que en ella concurran, sino, aun cuando anónima o desdichada, de la fidelidad con que haya sido vivida.[2]

On the level of his search for a transcendent reality Cernuda is, in his own terms, a metaphysical poet, on the level of the struggle to affirm and sustain his identity he is an ethical poet. What he is not is the effete *licenciado Vidriera* or the astringent pessimist that so many critics have tried to make of him.

La Realidad y el Deseo is the result of Cernuda's experience of life, the account of the growth of his personality as the experience of life is absorbed and understood. As he says in 'Historial de un libro' : "Yo no me hice, y sólo he tratado, como todo hombre, de hallar mi verdad, la mía, que no será mejor ni peor que la de los otros, sino sólo diferente" (*PL*, 278-9). A concern with identity is a common feature of a large part of twentieth-century literature, but unlike authors influenced by existentialist ideas Cernuda knows only too well who and what he is. His problem is that of coming to terms with himself and his situation. Yet while he is seeking to affirm his personal truth, the honesty with which he examines his experience is able to produce a deep insight into the human condition in general. Octavio Paz, looking at the idea of the "verdad diferente" in the light of Cernuda's homosexuality, comes to the following conclusion : "sus tendencias eróticas no explican a su poesía pero sin ellas su obra sería distinta. Su 'verdad diferente' lo separa del mundo y esa misma verdad, en un segundo movimiento, lo lleva a descubrir otra verdad, suya y de todos."[3] Through the discovery of his private truth Cernuda throws into relief the common human truth of his situation; his own sense of estrangement in the world is thus turned into a metaphor for the struggle of any individual for self-affirmation. The contrast between what Cernuda calls his *leyenda* and his idea of the *mito personal* illustrates the existential concern of his poetry and the attempt to produce a universalised statement from his individual experience of life. He uses the term 'myth' in the sense of the embodiment of a truth, which in this case is his own truth pieced together from the analysis of the circumstantial details of his life. His poetry is an act of self-creation and self-redemption, as he himself

[2] "Las campanas", *Ocnos,* 171.
[3] *Cuadrivio,* 187.

admits when he says that he wrote the autobiographical essay 'Historial de un libro': "para ver, no tanto cómo hice mis poemas, sino, como decía Goethe, cómo me hicieron ellos a mí" (*PL*, 279). His unswerving commitment to his vocation as a poet was precisely the same as he observed in Baudelaire, and his comment on the French poet can illuminate his own attitude to his work:

> Baudelaire tuvo como poeta una conciencia insobornable, la cual le movía, pero que fue también agente principal de su grandeza como poeta. A su conflicto interior, a la lucha dentro de él de fuerzas contradictorias, su obra propuso una solución. De ahí su autenticidad y su inevitabilidad.[4]

For Cernuda poetry was also a means of resolving the contradictions of his character and of producing a solution to the problems of life. *La Realidad y el Deseo* has the qualities of authenticity and compulsive necessity, the ring of truth. The passionate concern to find and preserve this truth gives to his poetry its ethical character and also a dimension of common human significance, as Cernuda has said of Gide: "por haber sido Gide fiel a sí mismo, ha sido a la larga fiel al hombre."[5] The struggle for self-affirmation makes him into an exemplary figure, in the sense of being an example of an ethical attitude to life.

Cernuda's personal integrity is matched by an equal literary integrity, immediately apparent in the way in which he handles the various influences on his work. From his earliest poems he has a strong tendency to respond only to those influences with which he has an affinity, shunning literary fashion. Yet this careful selection of influences does not lead to an insular attitude avoiding new ideas or new sources of inspiration. The progressive discovery of himself is paralleled by a discovery of that part of the Spanish poetic tradition to which he feels he belongs and also of that part of the corpus of European poetry with which he finds himself in sympathy. Beginning with his reading of Hölderlin before the Civil War and continuing through his concentrated study of English poetry during his exile he discovered and absorbed a tradition of meditative poetry that had had little impact in Spain. As a result Cernuda broke out of the restricted environment of French literary ideas, which have provided the basic influence on Spanish poetry for more than two hundred years, and set an example for the young poets of Spain today, who show interest and awareness for a wide area of foreign literature. Cernuda is now an active influence on a new generation of Spanish poets, and although it is still too early to assess the ultimate effect of this influence, I believe it can only be a salutary one. Cernuda is not a poet who can be imitated, but he is a poet from whom other poets can learn by example, and there is a further dimension to his exemplarity.[6]

The complexity and contradiction of Cernuda's character are reflected faith-

[4] 'Baudelaire en el centenario de *Las flores del mal*', *Poesía y literatura II*, 147.

[5] 'André Gide', *Poesía y literatura*, 161.

[6] Cf. "Quizá porque ahora es tan necesaria, la presencia de Cernuda empieza a sentirse en poesía española con una intensidad, con una profundidad como no se había sentido antes, y de la mejor manera: no influye, enseña. Cernuda es hoy por hoy, al menos para mí, el más vivo, el más contemporáneo entre todos los grandes poetas del 27, precisamente porque nos ayuda a librarnos de los grandes poetas del 27". Jaime Gil de Biedma, 'El ejemplo de Luis Cernuda', *La caña gris*, nos. 6-8 (1962), 116.

fully in his poetry, but the poetry itself absorbs these contradictions into an organic unity, just as the figure of Cernuda the man is transfigured by the literary form given to his life. The search for self-knowledge embraces all the multiple facets of his personality, as Octavio Paz has noted so acutely :

> Canto y examen, soliloquio y plegaria, delirio e ironía, confesión y reserva, blasfemia y alabanza, pero todo presidido por una conciencia que desea transformar la experiencia vivida en saber espiritual.[7]

In *La Realidad y el Deseo* the reader is given the opportunity to watch Cernuda's emotional and spiritual development, to watch a man grow in moral stature and self-awareness under conditions of almost constant stress. We are presented with Cernuda's experience, with the effect on him of that experience, and with what the accumulated experience of a lifetime makes of him. In a situation where life, as Cernuda comes to realise, is an odyssey without an Ithaca, he provides an example of how that life can be lived with integrity, and the dignity that comes from integrity. His poetry stands before us like a mirror that reflects his truth and invites us to measure ourselves against that reflection.

[7] 'Luis Cernuda', *Nivel,* no. 32 (1961), 5.

Appendix:

A Chronology of Cernuda's Early Poems

The source for this chronology of Cernuda's early poems is Cernuda's own copy of the first edition of *La Realidad y el Deseo* (Madrid, 1936), preserved amongst his books in Seville, in which he had entered the place and date of composition of every poem. I have not included the dates of composition for *Primeras poesías*, since these poems are emended versions of the original *Perfil del aire*. For the chronology of *Perfil del aire* and also of the uncollected poems from the period 1924-1928 the reader is referred to *Luis Cernuda: "Perfil del aire". Edición y estudio de Derek Harris* (London, 1971). I have not been able to include the dates of composition of the prose poems incorporated into *Los placeres prohibidos* in the third edition of *La Realidad y el Deseo* (Mexico, 1958).

Egloga, elegía, oda

All poems dated Seville.

"Homenaje"	1 - I - 28
"Egloga"	27 - VII - 27
"Elegía"	15 - XII - 27
"Oda"	23 - VII - 28

Un río, un amor

The first eight poems are dated Toulouse, the remainder Madrid.

"Remordimiento en traje de noche"	15 - IV - 29
"Quisiera estar solo en el sur"	20 - IV - 29
"Sombras blancas"	21 - IV - 29
"Cuerpo en pena"	29 - IV - 29
"Destierro"	2 - V - 29
"Nevada"	8 - V - 29
"Como el viento"	10 - V - 29
"Decidme anoche"	19 - V - 29
"Oscuridad completa"	2 - VII - 29
"Habitación de al lado"	15 - VII - 29
"Estoy cansado"	6 - VII - 29
"El caso del pájaro asesinado"	7 - VII - 29
"Durango"	9 - VII - 29
"Daytona"	11 - VII - 29
"Desdicha"	19 - VII - 29
"No intentemos el amor nunca"	19 - VII - 29
"Linterna roja"	27 - VII - 29
"Mares escarlata"	31 - VII - 29
"Razón de las lágrimas"	6 - VIII - 29

"Todo esto por amor"	6 - VIII - 29
"No sé qué nombre darle en mis sueños"	8 - VIII - 29
"Duerme, muchacho"	9 - VIII - 29
"Drama o puerta cerrada"	16 - VIII - 29
"Dejadme solo"	16 - VIII - 29
"Carne de mar"	18 - VIII - 29
"Vieja ribera"	22 - VIII - 29
"La canción del oeste"	28 - VIII - 29
"¿Son todos felices?"	28 - VIII - 29
"Nocturno entre las musarañas"	29 - VIII - 29
"Como la piel"	31 - VIII - 29

Los placeres prohibidos

All poems are dated Madrid.

"Diré como nacisteis"	20 - IV - 31
"Telarañas cuelgan de la razón"	abril 1931
"Adónde fueron despeñadas"	13 - IV - 31
"Qué ruido tan triste"	13 - IV - 31
"No decía palabras"	13 - IV - 31
"Si el hombre pudiera decir"	13 - IV - 31
"Unos cuerpos son como flores"	14 - IV - 31
"Los marineros son las alas del amor"	15 - IV - 31
"Quisiera saber por qué esta muerte"	17 - IV - 31
"Déjame esta voz"	29 - IV - 31
"De qué país"	30 - IV - 31
"Tu pequeña figura"	22 - V - 31
"Qué más da"	15 - VI - 31
"El mirlo, la gaviota"	23 - IV - 31
"Como leve sonido"	23 - IV - 31
"Te quiero"	23 - IV - 31
"Veía sentado"	abril 1931
"He venido para ver"	29 - IV - 31

Donde habite el olvido

All poems dated Madrid. The prose introduction bears the date, "enero? 1933".

I	"Donde habite el olvido"	5 - V - 32
II	"Como una vela sobre el mar"	10 - V - 32
III	"Esperé en mis días"	10 - V - 32
IV	"Yo fui"	11 - V - 32
V	"Quiero, con afán soñoliento"	7 - VI - 32
VI	"El mar es un olvido"	3 - VIII - 32
VII	"Adolescente fui en días idénticos a nubes"	13 - VIII - 32
VIII	"Nocturno, esgrimes horas"	17 - VIII - 32
IX	"Era un sueño, aire"	19 - IX - 32
X	"Bajo el anochecer inmenso"	26 - IX - 32
XI	"No quiero, triste espíritu, volver"	28 - IX - 32
XII	"No es el amor quien muere"	27 - XI - 32
XIII	"Mi arcángel"	19 - II - 33
XIV	"Eras tierno deseo, nube insinuante"	17 - III - 33
XV	"El invisible muro"	24 - III - 33

XVI	"No hace al muerto la herida"		28 - III - 33
	"Los fantasmas del deseo"		10 - V - 33
Invocaciones			
	"A un muchacho andaluz"	Huelva	22 - VIII - 34
	"Soliloquio del farero"	Olvera (Cádiz)	24 - IX - 34
	"El viento de septiembre entre los chopos"	Olvera (Cádiz)	25 - IX - 34
	"No es nada, es un suspiro"	Madrid	2 - X - 34
	"Por unos tulipanes amarillos"	Madrid	22 - III - 35
	"La gloria del poeta"	Madrid	25 - III - 35
	"*Dans ma péniche*"	Madrid	23 - VI - 35
	"El joven marino"	Madrid	27 - VI - 35
	"Himno a la tristeza"	Madrid	28 - X - 35
	"A las estatuas de los dioses"	Madrid	8 - XI - 35

Bibliography

I list here only those works cited in this study. For a more detailed listing of works relating to Cernuda the reader is referred to E. Müller, *Die Dichtung Luis Cernudas* (Geneva, 1962), and to the bibliography by Carlos Otero in *La caña gris*, nos. 6-8 (1962).

WORKS BY CERNUDA

Perfil del aire. Málaga. 1927.
La invitación a la poesía. Madrid. 1933.
Donde habite el olvido. Madrid. 1934.
La Realidad y el Deseo. Madrid. 1936. 2nd. ed. Mexico. 1940. 3rd. ed. Mexico. 1958. 4th. ed. Mexico. 1964.
Como quien espera el alba. Buenos Aires. 1947.
Desolación de la Quimera. Mexico. 1962.
Ocnos, London. 1942. 2nd. ed. Madrid. 1949. 3rd. ed. Xalapa. 1963.
Variaciones sobre tema mexicano. Mexico. 1952.
Tres narraciones. Buenos Aires. 1948.
Estudios sobre poesía española contemporánea. Madrid. 1957.
Pensamiento poético en la lírica inglesa (siglo XIX). Mexico. 1958.
Poesía y literatura. Barcelona. 1961.
Poesía y literatura II. Barcelona. 1964.
Crítica, ensayos y evocaciones. Barcelona. 1970.

'Poesía'. ["Sólo escollos de sombra débilmente".] *Litoral*, nos. 5-7. October 1927. [Reprinted in *Luis Cernuda: Perfil del aire*. Ed. Derek Harris. London. 1971.]
'A Little River, A Little Love'. *Nueva Revista*, no. 6. May 1930. ["Drama o puerta cerrada" and "Duerme muchacho" from *Un río, un amor*.]
'En la costa de Santiniebla'. *Hora de España*, no. X. October 1937.
'Sombras en el salón'. *Hora de España*, no. XIV. February 1938.
'Pedro Salinas y su poesía'. *Revista de Occidente*, no. LXXIII. July 1929.
'José Moreno Villa o los andaluces en España'. *El Sol*. 18-1-31.
'Poesía y verdad. Carta a Lafcadio Wluiki'. *Heraldo de Madrid*. 10-IX-31. [In *Poesía y literatura II*.]
'Epistolario de Rimbaud'. *Heraldo de Madrid*. 15-X-31. [In *Crítica, ensayos y evocaciones*.]
'La escuela de los adolescentes'. *Heraldo de Madrid*. 5-XI-31.
'El espíritu lírico'. *Heraldo de Madrid*. 21-I-32. [In *Crítica, ensayos y evocaciones*.]

'Los que se incorporan'. *Octubre*, nos. 4-5. 1933. [In a censored form in *Crítica, ensayos y evocaciones.*]
'Bécquer y el romanticismo español'. *Cruz y raya*, no. 26. May 1935. [In *Crítica, ensayos y evocaciones.*]
'Hölderlin'. *Cruz y raya*, no. 32. November 1935. Reprinted as Hölderlin. *Poemas*. Mexico. 1942. [The introductory essay to the translations is reprinted in *Crítica, ensayos y evocaciones.*]
'Divagación sobre la Andalucía romántica'. *Cruz y raya*, no. 37. April 1936. [In *Crítica, ensayos y evocaciones.*]
'Antonio Machado y la actual generación de poetas'. *Bulletin of Spanish Studies*, vol. XVII, no. 67. July 1940. [In *Crítica, ensayos y evocaciones.*]
'Poesía popular'. *Bulletin of Spanish Studies*, vol. XVIII, no. 72. October 1941. [In *Poesía y literatura.*]
'Juan Ramón Jiménez'. *Bulletin of Spanish Studies*, vol. XIX, no. 76. October 1942. [In *Crítica, ensayos y evocaciones.*]
'Cervantes'. *Bulletin of Spanish Studies*, vol. XX, no. 80. October 1943. [In *Poesía y literatura II.*]
'Tres poetas metafísicos'. *Bulletin of Spanish Studies*, vol. XXV, no. 98. April 1948. Also published in *Insula*, no. 36. December 1948. [In *Poesía y literatura.*]
'Carta abierta a Dámaso Alonso'. *Insula*, no. 35. November 1948. [In *Crítica, ensayos y evocaciones.*]
'André Gide'. *Asomante*, no. 1. 1951. [In *Poesía y literatura.*]
'Historial de un libro'. *Papeles de Son Armadans*, vol. XII, no. XXXV. February 1959. [In *Poesía y literatura.*]
'Souvenir de Pierre Reverdy'. *Mercure de France*, no. 1181. 1962. Published in a Spanish version in *Insula*, no. 207. February 1964. [In *Poesía y literatura II.*]

WORKS ON CERNUDA

Aleixandre, V. 'Luis Cernuda deja Sevilla'. *Cántico*, nos. 9-10. 1955. Reprinted in *Mito*, no. 7. 1956, and in *Los encuentros*. Madrid. 1958.
———, 'Luis Cernuda en la ciudad'. *La caña gris*, nos. 6-8. 1962.
Anon. 'Libros recientes'. *La Nación*, sección tercera. 21-V-59.
Aub, M. *La poesía española contemporánea.* Mexico, 1954. pp. 175-8.
Azcoaga, E. 'Sereno llanto'. *Ardor*. Primavera 1936.
Brines, F. 'Antes unas poesías completas'. *La caña gris*, nos. 6-8. 1962.
Cano, J. L. 'La poesía de Luis Cernuda'. In *Poesía española del siglo XX*. Madrid. 1960. pp. 313-80.
———, 'En la muerte de Luis Cernuda'. *Revista de Occidente*, vol. IV, no. 12. 1964.
Coleman, J. A. 'The meditative poetry of Luis Cernuda'. Ph.D. dissertation, Columbia University, 1964.
———, *Other Voices: A Study of the Late Poetry of Luis Cernuda.* Chapel Hill. 1969.
Debicki, A. P. 'Luis Cernuda : la naturaleza y la poesía en su obra lírica'. In *Estudios sobre poesía española contemporánea.* Madrid. 1968.
Ferraté, J. 'Luis Cernuda y el poder de las palabras'. In *La operación de leer*. Barcelona. 1962.

Florit, E. 'Como quien espera el alba'. *Revista hispánica moderna*, vol. XVI, nos. 1-4. 1950.
García Lorca, F. 'Homenaje a Luis Cernuda'. In *Obras completas*. Madrid. 1957.
Gil de Biedma, J. 'El ejemplo de Luis Cernuda'. *La caña gris*, nos. 6-8. 1962.
Gullón, R. 'La poesía de Luis Cernuda'. *Asomante*, vol. VI, nos. 2 and 3. 1950.
Harris, D. *Luis Cernuda: Perfil del aire*. London. 1971.
Jiménez, J. R. 'Héroe español : Luis Cernuda'. *Héroe*, no. 4. 1934. Reprinted in *Españoles de tres mundos*. Buenos Aires. 1942, and in *Cuadernos de Juan Ramón Jiménez*. Madrid. 1960.
———: 'Con la inmensa minoría : Crítica'. *El Sol*. 26-IV-36.
López Estrada, F. 'Estudios y cartas de Cernuda'. *Insula*, no. 207. 1964.
Méndez, C. 'Luis Cernuda'. *Insula*, no. 207. 1964.
Muller, E. *Die Dichtung Luis Cernudas*. Geneva. 1962.
———. 'Die Bedeutung der Kunst in Luis Cernudas *Desolación de la Quimera*'. *Romanische Forschungen*, vol. LXXVI, nos. 1-2. 1964.
Olivio Jiménez, J. 'Emoción y trascendencia del tiempo en la poesía de Luis Cernuda'. *La caña gris*, nos. 6-8. 1962. Reprinted in *Cinco poetas del tiempo*. Madrid. 1964.
Otero, C. P. 'Cernuda en California'. *Insula*, no. 207. 1964. Reprinted in *Letras I*. London. 1966.
Paz. O. 'Luis Cernuda'. *Nivel*, no. 32. 1961.
———. 'La palabra edificante'. *Papeles de Son Armadans*, vol. XXXV, no. CIII. 1964. Reprinted in *Cuadrivio*. Mexico. 1965.
Salinas, P. 'Nueve o diez poetas'. In Turnbull, E. L. *Contemporary Spanish Poetry*. Baltimore. 1945. Reprinted in *Ensayos de literatura hispánica*. Madrid. 1958.
———. 'Luis Cernuda, poeta'. In *Literatura española siglo XX*. Mexico. 1949.
Serrano Plaja, A. 'Notas a la poesía de Luis Cernuda'. *El Sol*. 17-V-36 and 4-VI-36.
Silver, P. *'Et in Arcadia ego': A Study of the Poetry of Luis Cernuda*. London. 1965.
Tello, J. 'Hablando a Luis Cernuda'. *El Tiempo*. Bogotá, 7-X-45.
Tovar, A. 'El paso del tiempo y un libro sobre la poesía española'. *Papeles de Son Armadans*, vol. VIII, no. XXIV. 1958.
Valente, J. A. 'Luis Cernuda y la poesía de la meditación'. *La caña gris*, nos. 6-8. 1962.
Vivanco. L. F. 'Luis Cernuda en su palabra vegetal indolente'. In *Introducción a la poesía española contemporánea*. Madrid. 1957.

OTHER WORKS CITED

Alonso, D. 'Una generación poética (1920-1936)'. In *Poetas españolas contemporáneos*. Madrid. 1952.
Aranguren, J. L. *Crítica y meditación*. Madrid, 1955.
Altolaguirre, M. *Poesías completas*. Mexico. 1960.
Castellet, J. M. *Veinte años de poesía española 1939-1959*. Barcelona. 1962.
Ciplijauskaite, B. *La soledad y la poesía española contemporánea*, Madrid. 1962.
Diego, G. *Poesía española contemporánea*. 3rd. ed., Madrid. 1966.

Eliot, T. S. *Selected Essays.* 2nd. ed., London 1953.
Eluard, P. *Choix de poèmes.* Paris. 1946.
Freeman, K. *Ancilla to the Pre-Socratic Philosophers.* Oxford. 1948.
Gide, A. *Oeuvres Complètes.* Vol. 2. Paris. 1933.
Guillén J. *Cántico.* Buenos Aires. 1950.
———, 'Carta a Fernando Vela sobre la poesía pura'. *Verso y prosa,* no. 2. February 1927.
Hamburger, M. *Poems of Hölderlin.* London. 1943.
Ilie, P. *Documents of the Spanish Vanguard.* Chapel Hill. 1969.
King's Classical Quotations. 3rd ed. London. 1904.
Ley, C. D. *Spanish Poetry since 1939.* Washington. 1962.
Llobera, Fr. José, (Ed.). Fray Luis de León. *Obras poéticas.* Cuenca. 1931.
Matthiessen, F. O. *The Achievement of T. S. Eliot.* 2nd ed., New York. 1947.
Moreno Villa, J. *Vida en claro.* Mexico. 1944.
Morla Lynch, C. *En España con Federico García Lorca.* Madrid. 1958.
Morris, C. B. *A Generation of Spanish Poets.* Cambridge. 1969.
Panofsky, E. "*Et in Arcadia ego:* Poussin and the Elegiac Tradition", *Meaning in the Visual Arts.* New York. 1955.
Reverdy, P. *Les Epaves du Ciel.* Paris. 1924.
Risco, V. "O poema do mar". *Alfar,* no. 26. 1923.
Salzberger, L. S. *Hölderlin.* Cambridge. 1952.
Torre, Guillermo de. "Ultra-manifiestos", *Cosmópolis,* no. 29. 1921.
Weinberg, H. G. 'The Legion of Lost Films'. *Sight and Sound.* Autumn. 1962.